PUBLICATION NUMBER 13
Duke University Commonwealth-Studies Center

Tradition, Values, and
Socio-Economic Development

Duke University Commonwealth-Studies Center Publications

Tradition, Values, and Socio-Economic Development

Joseph J. Spengler, Wilbert E. Moore, Bert F. Hoselitz, Melville J. Herskovits, Ralph Braibanti, Ishtiaq Husain Qureshi, John D. Montgomery, Mason Wade

Edited by

Ralph Braibanti and Joseph J. Spengler

PUBLISHED FOR THE

Duke University Commonwealth-Studies Center

DUKE UNIVERSITY PRESS, DURHAM, N. C.

1961

PRINTED IN THE UNITED STATES OF AMERICA

BY THE SEEMAN PRINTERY, INC., DURHAM, N. C.

INTRODUCTORY STATEMENT

In this series of nine analytical essays a group of scholars in anthropology, economics, history, political science, and sociology explores the effect of tradition and values in socio-economic development. The editors and five of the contributors were participants in the Duke University Joint Seminar on the Commonwealth in the Spring of 1959. The papers were presented and discussed at the Seminar, except those of Professors Braibanti and Montgomery which were written early in 1960. Professor Montgomery's essay was presented before the graduate seminar of the department of political science at Duke early in 1960 at a session held under auspices of the Commonwealth-Studies Center.

Each of the essays is an independent contribution presenting points of view not necessarily in agreement with the others. All are based on the common effort to understand the process of socio-economic development using the apparatus of particular social science disciplines and experience in various cultural contexts. The range of experience from which the authors can draw their empirical data is extensive and includes study or teaching in India, Pakistan, the Union of South Africa, Israel, Singapore, Japan, Cuba, Malaya, Vietnam, Taiwan, Thailand, Okinawa, Canada. Joseph J. Spengler, James B. Duke Professor of Economics at Duke University and Director of Graduate Studies in Economics, distinguishing among theory, ideology, and non-economic values, suggests that the rate and direction of development depend on the emotional and intellectual predispositions of the elites and the masses. Ralph Braibanti, Professor of Political Science at Duke University and on leave for 1960-62 as Professor and Chief Advisor, Civil Service Academy of Pakistan, surveys the role of political science in analyzing underdeveloped areas and explores six questions to which subsequent political science research may be directed. Wilbert E. Moore, Professor of Sociology and Faculty Associate of the Center of International Studies at Princeton University, explores types of relationships among relevant variables found in the social framework of economic development. Bert Hoselitz, Professor of Social Sciences and Director of the Research Center in Economic Development and Cultural Change at the University of Chicago, analyzes the components of tradition, suggests four forms of tradition-oriented behavior, and argues that tradition is not always adverse to economic development. Melville J. Herskovits, Professor of Anthropology and Director of the Program of African Studies at Northwestern University, surveys the role of anthropology in determining the weight of cultural influences in enhancing or deterring social innovation.

The remaining four essays are somewhat more empirically oriented in the respect that they deal with development problems in particular cultural contexts. In two related essays, I. H. Qureshi, Director of the Institute of Islamic Culture of Pakistan, traces the development of Islamic political thought which provides a background to understanding ideological forces at work in modern Pakistan. John D. Montgomery, Resident Director, International Cooperation Administration Personnel Training for Africa, African Research and Studies Program, Boston University, analyzes the impact of technical assistance on the internal policies of Taiwan, Vietnam, Burma, and Thailand. A pragmatic account of social change in French Canada is given by Mason Wade, Associate Professor of History and Director of the Canadian Studies Program at the University of Rochester.

Since the Commonwealth-Studies Center is concerned exclusively with the encouragement of research, specific theories or interpretations of Commonwealth affairs appearing in these publications do not constitute an expression of the view of the Center nor of the Carnegie Corporation, which has furnished financial support to the Center. The respective authors of the several essays are responsible for the conclusions expressed in them.

THE EDITORS

CONTENTS

CONTENTS

Tradition, Values, and
Socio-Economic Development

1

Theory, Ideology, Non-Economic Values, and Politico-Economic Development*

Joseph J. Spengler

> All perceptions, as well of the sense as of the mind, are according to the measure of the individual and not according to the measure of the universe. And the human understanding is like a false mirror, which, receiving rays irregularly, distorts and discolors the nature of things by mingling its own nature with it.
>
> FRANCIS BACON, in *Novum Organum*, Bk. I, xli

> We start with given notions, preconceptions, and prejudices about knowledge, evidence, method, and science which it is mere folly to pretend to ignore.
>
> MAX BLACK, in "The Definition of Scientific Method"

> In the development of scientific thought the anthropomorphic element is progressively forced into the background until it entirely disappears in the ideal structure of physics.
>
> ERNST CASSIRER, in *An Essay on Man*, p. 241

The papers composing this volume center upon the role of ideology, broadly defined, in politico-economic development. In this essay ideology is quite narrowly defined and the values underlying it are distinguished from both elements constituting theory and development-affecting values not included under ideology. Most of this essay has to do with the separate roles played in politico-

* I am indebted to the Rockefeller Foundation for making possible the completion of this paper.

economic development by theory, by ideology, and by relevant non-economic values not included under theory or ideology.   My point of departure is described in Section I, which is followed by two sections dealing with development, developmental policy, and the role of theory.   The significance of the nature of the social universe for developmental inquiry and policy is examined in Section IV.   Section V has to do with ideological and other non-rational elements, and Section VI, with the genesis of development-oriented mental phenomena.   The concluding section treats of the manipulation of such phenomena.

I. Point of Departure

My point of departure in this essay is what may loosely be called the content of men's minds.   I have deliberately chosen this somewhat ambiguous term rather than alternative psychological terms (e.g., habits of thought), since I wish to avoid involvement in psychological controversy relating to "mental" phenomena and their description.   This point of departure has been chosen in order both to focus attention upon the role of non-physical phenomena in politico-economic development and to emphasize the potentially dynamic and strategic character of what is called the content of men's minds.   Hereunder are included phenomena pertaining to analytical theory as such, phenomena pertaining to ideology (narrowly defined) which runs counter to analytical theory, and finally relevant residuary mental phenomena.   Within this last, vast residuum are to be found the values, and value-orientations, which largely determine the degree to which a people is effectively interested in politico-economic development; these phenomena relate to ends.   The first two types of phenomena, on the contrary, bear upon the construction and selection of means to ends—in the present discussion, of instruments for political or economic development.

It is my thesis that the state of a people's politico-economic development, together with its rate and direction, depends largely upon what is in the minds of its members, and above all upon the content of the minds of its elites, which reflects in part, as do civilizations, the conceptions men form of the universe.[1] The content of men's minds is looked upon as the potentially dynamic element, as the source whence issue change and novelty, in a world or universe that is otherwise essentially passive. Accordingly, transformation of an underdeveloped society into a developed one entails transformation of the contents of the minds of the elite who direct and of the men who man such underdeveloped society. Above all it entails transformation of the contents of the minds of individuals who are interacting in ways significant for politico-economic development.[2]

The degree to which a people's politico-economic development may be said to depend upon the content of the minds of its members is a function of time; its magnitude is positively associated with the length of the period of time under consideration. In the short run what can be done is subject to many constraints; for then, in the world of mental phenomena as in that of the physical, it is constants rather than variables that rule. Thus, at any moment, how fast a society can progress economically depends upon the state of mental phenomena relating to science in that society, upon its level of technology, upon the rate at which it forms capital, upon the manner in which it disposes of newly formed and hence mobile capital, upon the plenitude of the fertile land and resources it has at its disposal, upon the position of its economy in the network of international commerce and communication, and so on. Furthermore, the decisions, even when rational, of such a society's decision-makers, be they simple housewives allocating weekly consumption allowances or top executives determining the amounts and the purposes of gigantic corporate capital budgets, are restricted by the alternatives physically present in the environment of decision confronting them. Yet, many if not most of these constraints are outgrowths of the contents of men's minds in earlier periods, even as the policies of today often are the progeny of the ideas of yester-

[1] See F.S.C. Northrop, *The Taming of the Nations* (New York, 1952), pp. 113-114; also K. Jaspers, *The Origin and Goal of History* (London, 1953), Part I, and Chiang Monlin, *Tides from the West* (New Haven, 1947).

[2] Cf. K. R. Popper, *The Open Society and Its Enemies*, II (London, 1949), pp. 205-208; A. M. Rose, "The Comparative Study of Institutions," in *The Institutions of Advanced Societies* (Minneapolis, 1958), pp. 30-32. On circumstances that shape the outlooks of men, see W. Stark, *The Sociology of Knowledge* (Glencoe, 1958).

day.[3] Because these constraints have been so largely conditioned by mental phenomena of earlier periods, they may be looked upon as readily modifiable through appropriate modification of the contemporary content of men's minds. For in the longer run these contents may change and much of that which was constant may become temporarily variable and hence subject to human regulation.[4]

The manner in which men respond to what is for them largely an environment of constraints is affected both directly and indirectly by the contents of their minds. It is upon the contents of a decision-maker's mind that depend both his manner of sizing up his environment and his subsequent response thereto. He does not respond to an environment as such. Instead he responds to his image of that environment, to an image that is conditioned by his map of the somewhat larger and more inclusive but seemingly relevant world. This image depends upon the content of the responder's mind, since that mind is neither an empty organ (as psychologists have at times supposed), nor largely impervious to external influences; it resembles rather an apparatus that reflects, refracts, assembles, selects, classifies, and interprets decision-conditioning information and other stimuli that flow from a decision-

---

[3] "The ideas of economists and political philosophers, both when they are right and when they are wrong, are more powerful than is commonly understood. Indeed the world is ruled by little else. Practical men . . . are usually the slaves of some defunct economist. Madmen in authority" distill their frenzy from academic scribblers "of a few years back." See J. M. Keynes, *The General Theory of Employment, Interest and Money* (New York, 1936), p. 383. See also J. L. Talmon, *The Origins of Totalitarian Democracy* (London, 1955). It has sometimes been suggested (e.g., by exponents of the cycle-of-generations theory) that a comparatively definite time interval, or sequence of time intervals, separates the period when an idea is initially formulated and the period when its impact upon policy is felt. There is no warrant in the history of the development and impact of ideas, however, to support this view in respect of relatively large societies. It is only within the framework of a very small group, especially the family, that the replacement of generations and the consequent replacement of ideas and goals may be quite significant; in large societies this sort of replacement is swamped by year-to-year changes in the composition of the labor force. See P. A. Sorokin, *Social and Cultural Dynamics* (New York, 1937, 1941), *passim*, on the various theories. The role of generations has been stressed by K. Mannheim, in *Essays on the Sociology of Knowledge* (London, 1952), pp. 193 ff., 276 ff.

[4] What takes place may resemble what takes place in a determinate system whose current state is characterized more and more "by the experiences that have come to it than by its state initially." See W. R. Ashby, "The Effect of Experience on a Determinate Dynamic System," *Behavioral Science*, I (1956), 40, 42.

maker's external environment.[5]　The image, furthermore, may also condition its own future form in that it may suggest the questions which our responder asks of nature (the objective world) and thus give shape to the impression he forms of nature and of "reality" in general.[6]

There exist, in the world of history as in the world of fiction, many illustrations of the great importance of the role played by the content of men's minds. We may turn, for example, to the response of Lisbon's inhabitants to the massive earthquake of 1775, a catastrophe immortalized by Voltaire, whose impact has recently been quite fully described by Sir Thomas D. Kendrick. He re-

[5] See F. A. Hayek's account of the manner in which past experience creates a "semi-permanent map" of the world in the brain, in his *The Sensory Order* (London, 1952), pp. 2 ff., 112 ff.; this is discussed in Section VI below. See also K. E. Boulding's discussion of the "image" or "knowledge structure" in his account of "eiconics," in *The Image* (Ann Arbor, 1956), pp. 6-7; also Ernst Cassirer's account, in *An Essay on Man* (Garden City, 1953), p. 43, of the role of language, myth, art, and religion in producing a "symbolic universe" in which man lives, or weaving a "symbolic net" or "medium" through which the impact of his external world must pass. According to A. D. Weisman, "perception, conception, symbolization, and logical systems" structure and differentiate experience and render its meaning susceptible of rational definition, whereas "reality sense," the source of man's belief in experience, "intuitively appreciates the nature, direction, and purpose of events, in accordance with their libidinal claims." See "Reality Sense and Reality Testing," *Behavioral Science*, III (1958), 228, 236-237, 259-260. See also Egon Brunswik's "The Conceptual Framework of Psychology," *International Encyclopedia of Unified Science*, Vol. I, No. 10 (Chicago, 1952), pp. 50 ff.; also K. R. Popper, *op. cit.*, II, 201-202. On the environment of decision referred to in this and the preceding paragraphs, see H. A. Simon, *Models of Man* (New York, 1957), chaps. xiv-xv; also G. Karlsson, *Social Mechanisms* (Glencoe, 1958). For summary accounts of the determinants of economic development see B. Higgins, *Economic Development* (New York, 1959); also Joseph J. Spengler, "Economic Factors in the Development of Densely Populated Areas," *Proceedings* of the American Philosophical Society, XCV (1951), 21-24, and a brief review of relevant literature in "Economic Factors in Economic Development," *American Economic Review*, Vol. XLVII, No. 2 (1957), pp. 42-56.

[6] See V. F. Weisskopf's review of Werner Heisenberg's *Physics and Philosophy: The Revolution in Modern Science*, in the *Scientific American*, CXCIX (September, 1958), 215-216. Here Weisskopf, following Heisenberg, argues that application only of concepts already developed and in use may tend to restrict extension of our knowledge of nature, since the laws by which nature is governed include some (of which we are not yet aware) whose discovery might entail use of new concepts. At times exclusive adherence to certain concepts has blocked the development of science. See R. H. Shryock, "The Interplay of Social and Internal Factors in the History of Modern Medicine," *Scientific Monthly*, LXXVI (1953), 224; also J. Needham, *Science and Civilisation in China*, II (Cambridge, 1956), 286, for criticism of L. Levy-Bruhl's application to China of the principle that premature crystallization of concepts checks scientific progress. On the genesis of ideas of "reality," see A. D. Weisman, *op. cit.*

ports that the king's able minister, the future Marques de Pombal, proceeded energetically to salvage and rebuild, and that various scientists sought natural explanations of the convulsion. Meanwhile, however, many of the clergy, describing it as a divinely inspired but ominous visitation upon a wicked city, sought to hinder Pombal's efforts at reconstruction and to frighten out of their remaining wits masses of men long suckled on superstition.[7]

Members of these groups thus interpreted the event differently, each governed in part by his private image of the world. Again, we may turn to Mark Twain's description of the difficulties encountered by a practical Yankee who sought to bring education, modern technology, and a greatly heightened material standard of life to the miserable inhabitants of a mythical King Arthur's realm, to a people "in the world for one object, and one only; to grovel before king and Church and noble." In the end, despite his initial successes, the efforts of the Yankee, along with those of the small number of youths the content of whose minds he was able to transform, were swamped by deep-rutted habits, by a roused superstition, and by development-preventing values, all inculcated by a despotic church and supported as much by servile victim as by noble beneficiary. He could not change the outlook of enough of King Arthur's subjects.[8]

II. POLITICO-ECONOMIC DEVELOPMENT AND POLICY

Development in general takes place when an index of that which is deemed desirable and relatively preferable increases in magnitude. Augmentation of this index may be looked upon (for the purposes of the present discussion) as a tentatively ultimate end,

[7] *The Lisbon Earthquake* (New York, 1957); also a review by J. R. Newman (*Scientific American*, CXCVII [July, 1957], 164-169), whose phrasing is partially reflected in my wording. Giovanni Villani in 1333 noted similar rational and irrational responses to a great flood in Florence. See F. Schevill, *History of Florence* (New York, 1936), p. 235.

[8] See Mark Twain, *A Connecticut Yankee in King Arthur's Court* (Modern Library edition; New York, 1917), esp. chaps. viii-x, xxii-xxvi, xl-xliii; also R. J. Lampman, "Point IV in Literary Perspective," *Current Economic Comment*, XIX (1957), 23-29. That the problem with which Twain dealt is still unsolved is well illustrated in Norbert Wiener's account of the absurdity of treating information as effectively subject to control for mercantile or other purposes. See his *The Human Use of Human Beings* (New York, 1954), chap. vii.

even though it immediately entails various non-economic costs of the sort associated with "modernization."[9] Such augmentation is accomplished through the transformation of more elementary and less valuable entities (e.g., materials, human effort) into that entity which is represented by the index in question. The relatively elementary entities, together with whatever enters into the transformation process as such, may be looked upon as means to the achievement of the kind of developmental objective under consideration. Logicality consists in selecting relatively elementary entities, together with transformation processes, suited to give rise to the kind of development sought. Rationality or efficiency consists in selecting that set of entities and processes which minimizes the cost, appropriately defined, of achieving a given amount of the specified kind of development. Development thus proceeds along logical and efficient lines when, its objective having been carefully assessed and chosen from among the set of objectives attainable, this objective is sought through recourse to the most economical means available. It should be noted, of course, that while political or economic development is here treated as an end or objective, it is really but a means to higher purposes or even to ultimate ends.

Economic development entails the diversion of a nation's scarce resources and productive powers to the augmentation of its stock of productive wealth and to the progressive enlargement of its gross and net national product of goods and services. The objective may be stated in aggregate or in per capita terms. If, with McKean, we assume that economizing decision-makers are trying "to make

[9] Modernization entails the replacement of sacred revelation and revealed codes by secular enlightenment in respect of guidance in human affairs, enlightenment which "each man must get for himself." It involves tensions—"village *versus* town, land *versus* cash, illiteracy *versus* enlightenment, resignation *versus* ambition, piety *versus* excitement." See Daniel Lerner *et al.*, *The Passing of Traditional Society* (Glencoe, 1958), pp. 43-44. Modernization is a "systemic" process, involving complementary changes in the "demographic, economic, political, communication, and cultural 'sectors'" of a society (*ibid.*, p. 401); it is carried through primarily by those who are relatively urban, literate, industrially oriented, capable of appreciating the situations of others, disposed to have opinions on public matters, and inclined to share with others interest in matters of common concern. See *ibid.*, pp. 49-50, 70-71. Furthermore, individuals suited to carry through modernization apparently do not experience much unhappiness despite the tensions and choices involved, unless their efforts at modernization are greatly checked by traditional institutions, in which event they tend to resort to political action. See *ibid.*, pp. 398-399, 401-403.

the 'most,' as they conceive of the 'most,' of whatever resources they have,"[10] then decision-makers interested in economic development will stress such factors as capital formation, growth-oriented education, and the accumulation and effective application of scientific knowledge.   Above all they will emphasize improvement in the contents of men's minds, since thereon depend both the disposition and the capacity of men to put forth effort, extend their time horizons, and subordinate wants of the moment to the requirements of tomorrow; and they will seek to internalize in a society's members motivational and value orientations that make for economic growth and for political organization favorable to such growth.[11] Political development may be treated analogously to economic development when the components of political development are carefully specified, but this is seldom done.

Development-fostering policy may be private, public, or mixed in character.   Policy is here conceived to embrace three distinguishable elements: a sought objective, institutional and related instruments suited to realize this objective, and arrangements for the administration of these instruments.   A policy is public rather than private whenever the mechanisms employed to select and realize policy objectives are operated by agencies of the state, or by the state as such.   In the present case the policy objective is economic or political development as manifested by increases in the values of designated indicators (such as per capita income).   The institutional instruments consist in sufficiently stable systems of interacting individuals who co-operate to realize specific elements or components in the overriding growth objective.[12]   Arrangements for the administration of these instruments consist in the structure, the rules, and the distribution of the decision-making responsibility incorporated in such a system of interacting individuals.   The contents of men's minds accordingly are reflected at all three levels—policy-objective, institution, and administration, but especially at the policy-objective level, since such an objective manifests values

[10] See R. N. McKean, *Efficiency in Government through Systems Analysis* (New York, 1958), pp. 3-4.
[11] On motivational orientation and value-orientation, see T. Parsons and E. A. Shils, eds., *Toward a General Theory of Action* (Cambridge, Mass., 1951) pp. 56-60; also Parson's earlier work, *The Structure of Social Action* (New York, 1937).
[12] On the role of institutions in social systems, see T. Parsons, *The Social System* (Glencoe, 1951), pp. 36-58, 204-205.

present in the minds of those empowered to make relatively major decisions regarding how a society's scarce resources are to be employed. The choice of institutional instruments and administrative arrangements, on the contrary, largely reflects the state of technical information bearing upon the comparative adaptability of alternative means to given ends. As will be noted later, competent social theory illuminates policy as defined whereas ideological considerations tend to reduce its effectiveness.

It is necessary, for analytical purposes, to distinguish between state (or political system) and economy, since the rate of economic growth is conditioned by what the state does or tolerates, even though the efficiency of the apparatus of state usually is of about the same relative order as that of the private economy.[13] In the nineteenth century and in much of the present century economic growth was largely the result of what took place in the private sector, with the efforts of the state confined largely to establishing a milieu favorable to growth and to supplementing private activities here and there. In earlier centuries, by contrast, and even more recently in backward lands, the state often retarded economic development by frustrating business enterprise and by wasting much of the surplus value whence growth might be supported. In many if not all of the underdeveloped countries of the present-day world, however, the state has assumed, or is attempting to assume, considerable responsibility for the support, the direction, and the fomenting of economic development. This tendency reflects, as is shown later, various contemporary beliefs, conditions, and suppositions: e.g., lack of confidence in the morality or in the capacity of a free-enterprise system; the supersession of nineteenth-century anti-state ideology by twentieth-century pro-state ideology;[14] the

[13] This statement is far more applicable to a Western than to (say) an Asian type of society in which the state is not very powerful and efficient and in which the claims of smaller social units (e.g., joint family, religious order) are very strong and significantly affect political, entrepreneurial, and related behavior. However, as E. C. Banfield has shown, even the nuclear type of family may behave in a way unfavorable to economic development. See *The Moral Basis of a Backward Society* (Glencoe, 1958), p. 10.

[14] Even in the United States, as Milton Friedman points out, a widespread verbal endorsement of freedom of enterprise conceals "the implicit acceptance of many views that derive from the socialist orientation of intellectual thought in past decades, views that have been further strengthened by the success of the communist world in politics, their achievements in the production of military weapons, and their claims of great economic accomplishments." This acceptance is reinforced

assumption that the formation of capital will proceed too slowly if left to private decision; the supposition that domestic private enterprise may be too poor to create required social and economic overhead capital, or to undertake massive change and investment; the realization that there cannot be much growth until enterprise finds itself in a suitable milieu; and so on.[15]

The success of an economy, whether public or private, in accomplishing assigned objectives depends in part upon the sensitivity of its feedback system. When decision-makers operating in the private sector find that a policy-objective is not attainable, or is not attainable through use of the methods chosen, they modify the objective or fall back upon different methods. They are interested in realizing satisfactory profits and in continuing the life of their businesses, and they cannot accomplish these purposes unless they discover failures quickly and take corrective action promptly. Decision-makers in the public sector, on the contrary, are less likely to discover failure, both because they tend to employ less sensitive indicators or feed-back mechanisms and because they are less anxious to discover failures; furthermore, when they become aware of failures, they are not so disposed or so free as are private operators to take adequate action. Moreover, insensitivity of psychological or organizational or mechanical origin is far more prone to be accentuated by ideological considerations in the public than in the private sector. Even in the realm of policy as such, therefore, what I have called content of the mind may prove quite significant.

III. The Role of Theory

Discussions of theory and its role may be carried on at a quite general or macro-theoretical level, or at a particularistic or micro-

by the "conservative" bent of the American people which prompts them to view as necessary all the governmental intervention that has already taken place. At the same time American foreign economic policy serves to increase the strength of the public sector at the expense of the private in most parts of the world, thereby denying the validity of the very private-enterprise philosophy it purports to support. See Friedman's essay in Committee for Economic Development, *Problems Of United States Economic Development* (New York, 1958), I, 253-254, also 257.

[15] On the roles the state may assume, see W. A. Lewis, *The Theory of Economic Growth* (London, 1955), chap. vii, and P. T. Bauer and B. S. Yamey, *The Economics of Under-developed Countries* (London, 1957), Part II.

theoretical level. The discussion in this section is carried on at the micro-theoretical level. Northrop's work suggests, however, that the existence of a macro-theoretical level of discussion should be recognized. For he distinguishes a number of ways in which nature may be conceived, of which the Asian and the Western types are major instances. The former consists in the "naive observation of nature"; the latter, in "deductively formulated scientific theories of nature which require every fact to be seen as an instance of a determinate universal law." The former approach is incompatible with some of the prerequisites to economic development; it is defective, among other things, in terms of particularistic theory.[16]

Turning now to theory at the micro-theoretical or particularistic level, we may say, with J. M. Keynes, that theory, be it economic or otherwise, "is a method rather than a doctrine, an apparatus of the mind, a technique of thinking, which helps its possessor to draw correct conclusions."[17] Its function is an analytical one. Practical applications need not be made of its findings. As a rule, however, its findings, when deemed relevant, eventually are put to practical use. For, as will be noted, theory makes possible the selection of effective means to preconceived ends, and it may even facilitate careful definition of an end and its sequestration from other ends or objectives in the complex of ends and quasi-ends that channel man's behavior.

In the present discussion theory is viewed as an analytical instrument and as a source of findings applicable in the realm of developmental policy. We are particularly interested in theory that enables us to discover and assess the comparative importance of the antecedents and the concomitants of political and economic development, that discloses how development may be accelerated, and that isolates the benefits, costs, and less conspicuous side-effects of alternative accelerative measures. We are interested, therefore, in economic theory, in political-behavioral theory, and in relevant sociological, social-psychological, and anthropological theory. We are interested particularly in theory suited to analyze the genesis of the con-

[16] See F.S.C. Northrop, *The Taming of the Nations*, chap. vii; also his *The Meeting of East and West* (New York, 1946), in which the differences between Asian and Western theory are examined in detail.

[17] E.g., see his introduction to E.A.G. Robinson, *The Structure of Competitive Industry* (New York, 1932), p. iii.

tent of men's minds, together with the means available for its modification. For illustrative purposes, however, our discussion will center upon economic theory, upon what such theory is and does, and upon its distinction from ideology which may masquerade as theory and which always interferes with its optimal application. There is not space, of course, in which to discuss the many methods of which the theorist may make use, or the manner in which the analysis and solution of large problems may be accomplished by breaking them into many smaller ones, each of which may then be dealt with initially in isolation from the others.[18]

When one assigns both an applicatory role and an analytical role to a science, one must observe J. N. Keynes's conclusion that a science may have three departments, to each of which certain kinds of enquiry may be referred. For a science may be concerned with what is, or with what ought to be, or with the achievement of what ought to be, and each concern must be sharply distinguished from the others.

A *positive science* may be defined as a body of systematized knowledge concerning what is; a *normative* or *regulative science* as a body of systematized knowledge relating to criteria of what ought to be, and concerned therefore with the ideal as distinguished from the actual; an *art* as a system of rules for the attainment of a given end.[19]

A positive science, or a science in its positive guise, is, as Friedman points out, "in principle independent of any particular ethical position or normative judgments."[20] Its ultimate goal is not what ought to be, or how to achieve what ought to be; it is instead "the

[18] E.g., one may distribute analytically among supposedly unrelated sets various concrete elements which are in fact interrelated. Decomposition of large problems into manageable components is emphasized in the literature of "operations research." See C. W. Churchman, *et al.*, *Introduction to Operations Research* (New York, 1957), chap. v.

[19] *The Scope and Method of Political Economy* (4th ed.; London, 1917), pp. 34-35. Although Keynes was writing about political economy, what he said is equally applicable to other social sciences. It is essential, however, to keep in mind Northrop's observation that the philosophical method of inquiry suited to "normative" science is not the same as that suited to positive science. See his *The Meeting of East and West*, pp. 256-261, and *Ideological Differences and World Order* (New Haven, 1949), pp. 423-427. See also Mathilde Holzman, "Theories of Choice and Conflict in Psychology and Economics," *Journal of Conflict Resolution*, II (1958), 310-320.

[20] M. Friedman, *Essays in Positive Economics* (Chicago, 1953), p. 4.

development of a 'theory' or 'hypothesis' that yields valid and meaningful predictions about phenomena not yet observed." In an absolute sense, therefore, the positive role of a science is of greater fundamental importance than is its normative or its artistic role. For a science in its positive guise is functionally independent and self-sufficient, whereas the capacity of the normative or of the artistic branch of a science to function effectively depends upon the effectiveness with which its positive branch functions. In the absence of the solidly established findings of positive science, it is not possible to lay down acceptable criteria regarding what ought to be, or to select and systematize the rules best suited to attain ends that have been agreed upon. For "a policy conclusion necessarily rests on a prediction about the consequences of doing one thing rather than another, a prediction that must be based" on positive scientific findings. Moreover, inasmuch as policy differences flow largely from disagreement respecting the consequences of taking given actions, such differences reflect inadequate prior recourse to positive science. Development of consensus regarding what is "correct" policy thus depends greatly upon the progress of positive science "in yielding conclusions that are, or deserve to be, widely accepted."[21]

Having noted the nature of the relation of positive science to policy, I shall touch more specifically upon this relationship, before describing the nature of positive science. While positive science can reduce lack of consensus respecting what is "correct" policy, it cannot establish complete consensus. For policy recommendations necessarily reflect both the findings of positive science and value premises. Furthermore, a positive approach may temporarily make even more difficult the attainment of workable compromises. It may make apparent undesirable as well as desirable effects, both of policies and of recourse to particular kinds of social mechanisms. It may also, by making value premises explicit, reveal underlying conflicts among the values sought. Even so, it is probable, at least in a democratic society, that a working compromise arrived at in the light of all the evidence attainable regarding policy consequences and value conflicts would prove more durable than one based upon incomplete evidence and neglect of disharmonies in need of com-

[21] *Ibid.*, pp. 3-7.

position; for it would very likely fall within that portion of the area of acceptance in which stability is to be found.[22]

No account has been taken, in the preceding paragraph, of the extent of economic or political change that the introduction of a new policy may entail. If the change is small, the contribution that positive theory can make is small. For, as a rule, the effects of small changes are relatively easy to predict, and if they do not materialize, small corrective changes in policy are easily made. When, however, the contemplated change is large, it is essential that its probable consequences be anticipated and carefully assessed, since it is not so easy to reverse or compensate a major change once it is initiated.[23] This distinction between policies that produce small changes and policies that produce large changes is particularly important in respect of politico-economic development. For very frequently in an underdeveloped country a new development-oriented policy entails large-scale changes, whereas, in a developed country in non-crisis times, a new policy usually entails only change in the small. Accordingly, when a policy designed to produce large-scale changes is under consideration, it is important that the bargaining which precedes its adoption, among both governmental agencies and interested non-governmental groups, eventuate in a fairly durable compromise; for otherwise, should the policy not prove successful, the political repercussions might prove quite unfavorable to economic development.

Friedman's conception of economic theory illustrates nicely what is to be expected of social theory in its positive guise.[24] He describes

[22] On the area of acceptance, see H. A. Simon, *Models of Man,* pp. 75, 189, 193. See also P. Streeten, "Economics and Value Judgments," *Quarterly Journal of Economics,* LXIV (1950), 583-595, and "Programs and Prognoses," *ibid.,* LXVIII (1954), 355-376; H. Tyszynski, "Economic Theory as a Guide to Policy: Some Suggestions for Re-appraisal," *Economic Journal,* LXV (1955), 195-215. The contributions that positive economics has made to the establishment of criteria for judging alternative ends are well illustrated in the literature of welfare economics. E.g., see I.M.D. Little, *A Critique of Welfare Economics* (2d ed.; Oxford, 1957), and J. de V. Graaf, *Theoretical Welfare Economics* (Cambridge, 1957); also S. K. Bailey's observations in R. D. Calkins, ed., *Research Frontiers in Politics and Government* (Washington, 1955), pp. 18-22.

[23] E.g., see C. E. Lindblom, "Policy Analysis," *American Economic Review,* XLVIII (1958), 298-312; also J. E. Meade, *Trade and Welfare* (London, 1955), pp. 6-9.

[24] I use economic theory for illustrative purposes because economic theory is the most highly developed of the social-science theories and because other branches of social theory have been influenced by economic theory (e.g., see works of Parsons

economic theory "as a filing system for organizing empirical material and facilitating our understanding of it," together with a "body of hypotheses designed to abstract essential features of complex reality." Inasmuch as many hypotheses are consistent with any given set of facts, and as economics consists in "a body of tentatively accepted generalizations about economic phenomena that can be used to predict the consequences of changes in circumstances," it becomes necessary in any case to choose the best of the hypotheses available. That hypothesis is to be preferred which has the greatest predictive power, and which, when several have similar predictive power, is the most simple and fruitful.[25] The hypotheses in question may be general or special, though a special hypothesis intended to explain a unique event or situation usually involves recourse to general hypotheses and detailed empirical study.[26] Verification of an hypothesis, in the sense of inferring a set of conclusions reconcilable with the observed data, does not definitely confirm it; verification can merely *not disconfirm* an hypothesis, since it might not survive an additional test.[27]

Friedman's approach avoids the kind of controversy in which exponents of (respectively) aprioristic and ultra-empirical economics sometimes engage. The former reason deductively from postulates regarding man's behavioral tendencies, and they find confirmation of these postulates in the general congruence of observed with deduced "economic" behavior. The aprioristic economists count upon intro-

---

and Simon, cited earlier). Moreover, economic theory is more explicit and more quantitative than much of the remainder of social theory, though this difference has been diminishing in recent years. Use of a variety of methods is compatible with dependence upon alternative bodies of theory. It is perhaps well to remember that much of what is treated in so-called histories of branches of social theory belongs to the realm of ideology rather than to the realm of theory. On the comparative maturity of the social-science disciplines, see C. A. Anderson, "The Striving for Cooperative Autonomy," *Social Forces*, XXIX (1950), 8-19.

[25] See Friedman, *Essays*, pp. 8-10, 33, 39. On the general problem of testing an hypothesis for simplicity, see N. Goodman, "The Test of Simplicity," *Science*, CXXVIII (Oct. 31, 1958), 1064-1069. For an empirical illustration of Friedman's approach, see his "Price, Income and Monetary Changes in Three Wartime Periods," *American Economic Review*, XLII, No. 2 (1952), pp. 612-625. His conclusion is that the quantity theory of money is superior to the Keynesian income expenditure theory for the purpose of explaining price and income changes in wartime.

[26] See F. Machlup, "The Problem of Verification in Economics," *Southern Economic Journal*, XXII (1955), 2-3.

[27] *Ibid.*, pp. 4-5; also K. R. Popper, *The Logic of Scientific Discovery* (New York, 1959), chap. x.

spection to inform them how men tend to behave economically, and they conceive of men as inclined to act sensibly and in accordance with what Schuetz calls the "common-sense experience of social reality."[28]   This approach is attacked by exponents of ultra-empiricist economics on the ground, among others, that the postulates in question do not correspond closely enough with "reality."[29]   They thus overlook the fact, emphasized by Friedman, that since a major purpose of theory is to explain "much by little," its assumptions (other than that of a great deal of underlying regularity) cannot be realistic in the sense of aping reality closely.[30]

I have dealt thus far with the nature of a positive science, using economics as an exemplar.   I have not dealt with the substantive content of social science, nor with the significance of the difference between social-science and natural-science data.   Regarding the substantive content of social science, there is space only in which to remark that the phenomena involved in politico-economic development embrace scarcity and power as well as interactionist, organizational, cultural, and other phenomena of particular concern to economics, politics, sociology, anthropology, etc., and that therefore each of these branches of social science has something to contribute to the analysis and the fomenting of politico-economic development.   But what each science's contribution is, lies outside the purview of this paper.   This contribution can be made most effectively, however, only if the practitioners of each of the social sciences distinguish

[28] See A. Schuetz, "Common-Sense and Scientific Interpretation of Human Action," *Philosophy and Phenomenological Research*, XIV (1958), 41; also Machlup, *op. cit.*, pp. 5-7.   On reasoning from postulates, see also F.S.C. Northrop, *The Logic of the Sciences and the Humanities* (New York, 1947), pp. 107-110, 116 ff., 235-254, 261; also J. R. P. French, Jr., "A Formal Theory Of Social Power," *General Systems Yearbook*, II (1957), 92-101.

[29] See Machlup, *op. cit.*, pp. 7-8, 17 ff; also M. N. Rothbard, "In Defense of 'Extreme Apriorism,' " *Southern Economic Journal*, XXIII (1957), 314-320.

[30] See Friedman, *Essays*, p. 14.   Somewhat different is the approach of A. G. Papandreou.   He observes that economists do not construct theories that are susceptible of refutation.   Instead they devise models, that is, "deductive systems whose constituent statements are capable of confirmation but not of rejection."   The function of these models is explanatory; they "provide explanations of economic behavior in those instances in which they are confirmed."   While such models may be used as foundations for predictions, what model is selected for this purpose depends upon the "state of mind" of the selector and his opinion respecting the relevant future.   See "Explanation and Prediction in Economics," *Science*, CXXIX (1959), 1098-1099, and *Economics as a Science* (New York, 1958), chaps. i-ii, vi-vii.

sharply between its positive and its other branches, and rest its applicatory department upon findings reported in its positive department.

Regarding differences between social-science and natural-science
data, it is to be noted that the analytical and applicatory effectiveness
of social as of other theory is conditioned by the extent to which it
is adapted to the kinds of data with which it is concerned. While
there is far less scope for controlled or directed experiment in the
field of social science than in that of natural science, there is nearly
as much scope for the use of quantitative methods, for the construction and application of models, for the employment of mechanistic
and organic concepts, for the avoidance of ambiguity through recourse to operational definition, for the application of logic, and for
recourse to theory. But there are also differences. The social scientist
is interested in making use of those models which afford him the
requisite amount of pertinent information,[31] and in establishing
theorems which are subject to refutation.[32] Yet he would hardly
reason, as does the natural scientist, that how good a model or a
theory or frame of reference is depends upon how "isomorphic" it
is with "the world of observed phenomena";[33] for, as he utilized a

[31] E.g., see H. A. Simon's account of the comparative merits of profit-maximiz-
ing and of organization-theory models when used to account for the behavior of
firms, in *op. cit.*, pp. 170-182.

[32] E.g., see P. A. Samuelson, *Foundations of Economic Analysis* (Cambridge,
1947), pp. 4-5, 21 ff.; also A. Schuetz, "Concept and Theory Formation in the
Social Sciences," *Journal of Philosophy*, LI (1954), 257-273. One may also, with
R. B. Braithwaite, make the acceptability of a system turn on the verifiability of
facts deduced from the concepts and the concept-connecting axioms or laws composing
that system. See his *Scientific Explanation* (Cambridge, 1953), pp. ix, 22 ff. This
approach, F.S.C. Northrop suggests, is characteristic of Western scientific and
philosophical thought but not of Eastern thought. See *The Meeting of East and
West*, chaps. viii, x.

[33] E.g., see N. Rashevsky, "Is the Concept of an Organism as a Machine
a Useful One?," *Scientific Monthly*, LXXX (1955), 32-35. M. J. Walker em-
phasizes capacity for quantitative prediction in "An Orientation toward Modern
Physical Theory," *ibid.*, LXXXI (1955), 27-37. For other opinions see L. R. Dice,
"What Is Ecology?," *ibid.*, LXXX (1955), 346-351; A. C. Moulyn, "The
Limitations of Mechanistic Methods in the Biological Sciences," *ibid.*, LXXI (1950),
44-49; S. S. Stevens, note 107, below; W. Weaver, "Fundamental Questions in
Science," *Scientific American*, CLXXXIX (September, 1953), 47-57; R. E. Peierls,
"The Atomic Nucleus," *ibid.*, CC (January, 1959), 75-82. The uses and limitations
of operationalism have been treated by H. Margenau and others in a symposium on
"The Present State of Operationalism," in *Scientific Monthly*, LXXIX (1954), 209-
231; see also P. W. Bridgman, "Science and Common Sense," *ibid.* (1954), pp. 32-

theory to explain much by little, he would often find that marked isomorphic correspondence with a detail-ridden social world permitted the ephemeral to blot out the fundamental. Of greater importance, the social scientist deals with data that are more subjective and hence more mutable than are the data with which the natural scientist deals, a matter of particular significance for a discussion focused, as is the present one, upon the content of the mind. The natural scientist has to do with data which are ultimately objective, with data which are independent "of what men think or do about them." The social scientist, on the contrary, has to do largely with subjective data, with "what men think and do" or allegedly intend to do,[34] with a reality that is psycho-social rather than physical,[35] with objective manifestations that may have a different meaning for an actor from that which it has for an observer, with actions that are understandable in the sense that sensible men would act thus in the situations under consideration, etc.[36] The methods employed by social scientists must allow for the subjectivity of their ultimate data, and for the fact that their data are more prone than natural-science data to become affected with the subjectivity of the enquirer. Of significance too is the fact that frequently the carrying out of development-oriented policy entails changes in subjective rather than in objective data.

39. On scientific method in general, see P. F. Schmidt, "Some Merits and Misinterpretations of Scientific Method," *ibid.*, LXXXII (1956), 20-24.

[34] See James Tobin, "On the Predictive Value of Consumer Intentions and Attitudes," *Review of Economics and Statistics*, XLI (1959), 1-16.

[35] See Hayek, *The Sensory Order*, pp. 170-171, 193-194; also P. W. Bridgman's recognition of this point in *The Ways Things Are* (Cambridge, 1959).

[36] See Hayek, *The Counter-Revolution of Science*, chaps. ii-iv, esp. pp. 23, 33, 39; see also F. Machlup's emphasis on the subjective aspects of a price-maker's behavior in his *The Economics of Sellers' Competition* (Baltimore, 1952). See Nagel's criticism of Hayek's views, in *Logic without Metaphysics* (Glencoe, 1956), pp. 361-368, also 371-375, and the somewhat similar views of A. Grünbaum "Science and Ideology," *Scientific Monthly*, LXXIX (1954), 13-19. See also Schuetz's evaluation of Nagel's approach and Schuetz's own views in "Concept and Theory Formation . . .," *loc. cit.*; also Machlup, "The Problem. . .," *loc. cit.*, pp. 5-7, 16-17, and Parsons, *Social Systems*, pp. 543-545. Natural scientists often deal quite indirectly with what are for them ultimate data; hence their indicators of these ultimate, referent data may include a subjective component. Furthermore, as M. Black points out, "The more advanced the science, the greater the part played in its theories by unobservables" ("The Definition of Scientific Method," in R. C. Stauffer, ed., *Science and Civilization* [Madison, 1949], p. 90). Still, the ultimate data are in themselves relatively objective whereas the ultimate, referent data of social science usually are relatively subjective.

IV. WHAT KIND OF SOCIAL UNIVERSE

It is essential that the nature of the social universe under consideration be correctly apprehended by both theorist and policy-maker.   The models and other analytical techniques which the theorist uses must fit the nature of the social universe under study; otherwise the value of his findings and their usefulness for purposes of policy will be quite limited.[37]   The effectiveness of a policy thus turns in large measure, as does the validity of a theory, upon its fitting the situation in which it is applied.   It is not necessary, of course, that the theorist or the policy-maker rest his conception of the social universe upon some cosmic or other principle, such as faith in the uniformity of nature.[38]   Any such principle is but an hypothesis in an infinite regress of hypotheses;[39] it cannot reveal the manner in which events or societal variables are interrelated inasmuch as such information is obtainable only through appropriate empirical inquiry.[40]   Even so, such principles or hypotheses may at one time have operated heuristically to contribute greatly to the progress of scientific inquiry.[41]

The societal universe to which the scientist responds reflects, as does the policy-maker's, the contents of his mind.   M. Ginsberg writes:

[37] In the social universe, for example, the randomness on which the frequency theory of probability rests may be even less fully realized than it is in other universes.   On the alleged absence of randomness in general, see G. S. Brown, *Probability and Scientific Inference* (London, 1957).   See also L. Hogben, *Statistical Theory* (New York, 1957), chap. xix.   It is now possible, with electronic computers, to simulate sequences of events, and thus get a more reliable representation of relevant universes.

[38] Of course, unless the phenomena analyzed are connected in some orderly and relatively stable manner, policy-oriented theorizing is difficult if not impossible.

[39] E.g., see Popper, *The Open Society*, II, 8-13, 275-280.

[40] See Ernest Nagel, *Logic without Metaphysics*, pp. 15-16.

[41] It may be argued that the introduction of the concept of utility (now considered unnecessary) into economic analysis hastened the development of consumption and demand theory.   It is probably true, as A. N. Whitehead (*Science and the Modern World* [New York, 1925], chap. i) has suggested, that belief in an Order of Nature under the governance of the laws of Nature greatly fostered the growth of modern science.   Needham, in his account of the failure of science to develop in China as in the West, remarks: "But historically the question remains whether science could ever have reached its present stage of development without passing through a 'theological' stage."   See *op. cit.*, II, 543, 564, 579.   Similarly, as Cassirer suggests, the development of modern international law was initially facilitated by the revival of Platonic conceptions of natural law.   See E. Cassirer, *The Philosophy of the Enlightenment* (Boston, 1955), p. 240.

Those who start with an atomic conception of nature, of things externally related to each other [,] are likely to form an 'individualist' conception of the social order and to conceive of law as imposed or externally related to individuals.   On the other hand, those who stress the interdependence of things are likely to form an 'organic' conception of society and to think of juridic law as immanent in society.[42]

And Edward Shils observes:

The political conceptions which are expressed in the prevailing notions of economic . . . development rest on a deep-lying image of the nature of society and of the right ordering of life.   It is an image of the concentration of charisma in those who rule the nation.   One of the central features of the dominant conception of economic development is that autonomous movement of the economic system is thought to be undesirable, even if possible.   What are called "economic motives" are distrusted because it is believed that no intrinsic value resides in the economic sphere—in the way in which the religious and political spheres possess the intrinsic value connected with sacred things.   The only truly respected motives are those generated by authority, the exercise of that sovereignty, religious or political, which entails communion with the sacred.[43]

He then shows how this image affects public policy in underdeveloped countries in which there is no esteemed, private-entrepreneurial class, and sentiments are predominantly antibourgeois.   In these countries the only modern class present is committed to achieving economic development almost entirely through the joint efforts of politicians and civil servants, with the result that little reliance is placed in the activity of creative entrepreneurs such as played a great role in the West.[44]   The image which Shils describes has been enabled to persist by emphasis upon humanistic and (especially if legal or theological training is prized) casuistical education and values rather than upon empirical subject matter in educational and related institutions in underdeveloped countries, in part be-

[42] M. Ginsberg, "The Concepts of Juridical and Scientific Law," *Politica*, IV (1939), 15.   See also K. Pribram's papers cited in note 100 below.
[43] See "The Concentration and Dispersion of Charisma: Their Bearing on Economic Policy in Underdeveloped Countries," *World Politics*, XI (1958), 2.
[44] See *ibid.*, pp. 6 ff., also Shils, "Intellectuals, Public Opinion, and Economic Development," *World Politics*, X (1958), 232-255.

cause such education is cheaply produced, is compatible with being idle, and may possibly be of use in politics.[45]

What the social scientist can discover depends, even as does what the policy-maker can accomplish, upon the degree to which his conception of the social universe corresponds to the real, underlying social universe. Of great importance, therefore, is the nature and the extent of the interrelations which connect the activities of individuals or those of identifiable and somewhat autonomous groups. For example, one cannot effectively use multiple regression analysis to study the behavior of fertility if the fertility correlates under analysis are interdependent; for it can be proved, if interdependence is present, that least square parameter estimates are biased, and that, therefore, some other estimating techniques should be used. Similarly, the extent to which changes originating outside a society, or in some sector of it, tend to be propagated among that society's members is conditioned by the manner in which the behavior of given members is related to that of other members. The realizability of policy-objectives is conditioned in like fashion: if policy-objectives are interdependent they must be dealt with as a kind of totality whereas, if they are independent, it becomes possible to use given instruments and to seek given objectives in isolation.[46]

The determinants of politico-economic development may be variously classified. For present purposes we shall employ a twofold classification. First, we shall divide the actions of individuals into those which are describable as political or economic and those which do not fall within the politico-economic category; then politico-economic development is a consequence primarily and immediately of politico-economic actions and secondarily of other actions, together with the constraints imposed by the nonsocial environment

[45] E.g., see Ralph Braibanti's illuminating account of the education of civil servants in "The Civil Service of Pakistan: A Theoretical Analysis," *South Atlantic Quarterly*, LVIII (1959), 274-283, also 283 ff. on effects of this educational emphasis. See also Northrop, *The Meeting of East and West*, pp. 258, 390, ff., 430-435.

[46] See J. Tinbergen, *On the Theory of Economic Policy* (Amsterdam, 1952), chap. ix. Tinbergen emphasizes the great importance of the interdependence of economic variables for policy purposes. He argues in particular that a policy solution is attainable only if the number of "targets" (i.e., objectives of policy decisions) is equal to the number of "instruments" (i.e., variables subject to direct control by policy-makers). See *ibid.*, chaps. iv-v.

in which all action is taking place. Second, we may divide the determinants into those which are endogenous to the politico-economic world and those which are exogenous to it. In the latter category we place changes in elements (only some of which are variable in the short-run) which condition or affect variables included in the political and the economic systems of variables but which supposedly are affected only negligibly or not at all by changes in politico-economic variables; in the former we place the politico-economic variables, changes in any one of which occasion reactions in various other such variables. Accordingly, when we are concerned with politico-economic development, and particularly in the short run, we include political and economic variables in the endogenous category, and non-politico-economic variables, together with elements composing the nonsocial environment, in the exogenous category. If, as is necessary when economic or political analysis is being carried on, we distinguish between economic and political variables, we must place the political (economic) variables in the exogenous category when making an economic (political) inquiry.[47]

The causal consequences of changes in exogenous variables or conditions are not wholly identical with those of changes in endogenous variables. Changes in exogenous variables are more likely to produce a unidirectional causal influence. For example, changes in variables or environments exogenous to the economic system produce an effect in the economic system proper, but this effect is not always and immediately accompanied in turn by significant repercussions in the world made up of exogenous variables and environments. Changes in endogenous variables, however, produce a multidirectional causal influence; these changes are communicated to the variables making up the endogenous system and then in turn undergo modification until a new equilibrium is established. Endogenous

---

[47] What is said in this paragraph and in the next paragraph has been much influenced by K. J. Arrow's "Mathematical Models in the Social Sciences," in D. Lerner and H. D. Lasswell, eds., *The Policy Sciences*, chap. viii, and by G. H. Orcutt, "Toward Partial Redirection of Econometrics," *Review of Economics and Statistics*, XXXIV (1952), 195-200, 211-214, and "Actions, Consequences, and Causal Relations," *ibid.*, pp. 305-313. See also H. Wold, "Causality and Econometrics," *Econometrica*, XXII (1954), 162-177; J. Tinbergen, *Econometrics* (New York, 1951), pp. 193-214; R. Bentzel and B. Hanson, "On Recursiveness and Interdependency in Economic Models," *Review of Economic Studies*, XXII (1954-55), 153-168; T. Koopmans, "Statistical Estimation of Simultaneous Economic Relations," *Journal of the American Statistical Association*, XL (1940), 448-466.

variables thus resemble, as Marshall remarked, balls "lying in a bowl": "they mutually govern one another's positions," with the result that a change in the position of one produces changes in the positions of the others.[48]

In view of what has been said, economic and other inquiries are subject to several sorts of error. On the one hand, inadequate account may be taken of the fact that the variables composing the system under analysis are interdependent, with the result that causation is multidirectional instead of unidirectional. On the other hand, it may be incorrectly assumed that the system of variables selected for study is virtually a closed system and hence subject to little external influence, even in the longer run.[49] As a result, the analyst must give care to determining whether he may safely proceed on the supposition that causation is essentially unidirectional in the situation under analysis, and whether, given the time dimensions of the inquiry, exogenous elements may be disregarded. Even if errors of the sort just described are avoided, related errors will result if the tendency to change in the societal world is incorrectly apprehended. For, it is unrealistic to infer that the state of any system of variables found within a society of systems will become one of permanent rest; new ideas and other sources of novelty always operate somewhere in a society to produce change and eventually to modify the conditions of equilibrium in other systems.[50] At the same time, as Sorokin concludes, potentialities for change are limited, with the result that rhythms, periodicities, and fluctuations and related factors tend to characterize social phenomena.[51]

[48] A. Marshall, *Principles of Economics* (London, 1920), p. 526. On interdependence, see also L. J. Henderson, *Pareto's General Sociology* (Cambridge, 1935).

[49] S. Schoeffler traces many of the errors of empirical economic analysis to "the penchant of economists to treat the economic system and its various subsystems" as "closed" even though "any economic system . . . is always an essentially open system." See *The Failures Of Economics: A Diagnostic Study* (Cambridge, 1955), pp. 49-54, 155-156.

[50] See Whitehead, *op. cit.*, pp. 269, 289 ff., and *Adventures of Ideas* (New York, 1933), pp. 10-110-126; 272-273; also Joseph J. Spengler, "Generalists versus Specialists in Social Science: An Economist's View," *American Political Science Review*, XLIV (1950), 362-364. On the shortcomings of equilibrium analysis as applied in the study of the social system, see David Easton, "Limits of the Equilibrium Model in Social Research," *Behavioral Science*, I (1956), 96-104.

[51] See P. A. Sorokin, *Social and Cultural Dynamics*, IV (New York, 1941), chaps. xiv-xvi.

As has been indicated, correctness of policy formulation turns on the correctness with which inter-variable relations are apprehended. Let us describe as stategic any variable which is both subject to effective manipulation and is so connected directly and indirectly with other variables that significant changes may be produced in the latter by modifying the supposedly strategic variable. Whether such variable is strategic, even though it be manipulatable, depends upon the closeness of its connections with other variables.

It is probable that there is much more play in many of the systems of variables encountered in a society than is sometimes supposed or implied. There apparently is more play also in advanced societies than in backward societies whose cultures are more homogeneous and less pluralistic than are those found in advanced societies. To illustrate: we may gather the variables encountered in a societal system into a number of lesser systems, into each of which are introduced those variables with a greater affinity for each other than for variables belonging to other such systems. Thus we may assemble economic variables into one system, political variables into another, and so on. Yet, even when this has been done, many of the variables which are included in some one of these systems may be only weakly connected with many of the others found therein. It usually is possible, therefore, to break up such a system into subsystems in each of which are assembled variables relatively closely connected with one other. Each such subsystem may then be studied in comparative isolation from other subsystems.[52] For the economists a firm or market may be such a subsystem; for the political scientist, a local government area. Such a subsystem is likely to be relatively immune to minor changes occurring in other subsystems and systems, but sensitive to various major changes taking place therein. In so far as this is true, therefore, social change must often be of the order of the large if such change and its effects are to be permanent; change of the order of the small, though deemed adequate by Marshall and others (perhaps under the influence of Darwin, or the differential calculus),

[52] Even the industrial system, T. Veblen remarked, "has not yet reached a fatal degree of close-knit interdependence, balance, and complication; it will still run along at a very tolerable efficiency in the face of a very appreciable amount of persistent derangement." See *The Engineers and the Price System* (New York, 1944), p. 57.

may not suffice. Of this we have evidence in the fact that cultures often are able to absorb, without much institutional change, even a significant institutional innovation;[53] that economic changes prove less disturbing than one might have anticipated on the basis of an interdependent price system or of a Leontief input-output system; and that various backward countries have remained so despite many decades of exposure to minor politico-economic stimuli of external origin.

Should there be as much play in the social universe and its systems and subsystems as has been suggested, certain conclusions follow in respect of theory and policy. Organismic and highly integrated functionalist conceptions of the social universe tend to exaggerate the extent to which a society's parts are interdependent much as does the approach associated with dialectical materialism. The generation of social change may call for heavy jolts instead of light stimuli; thus, according to H. Leibenstein, only a critical minimum effort can release the population of many an underdeveloped country from the Malthusian trap in which it now is caught.[54] Further inquiry is indicated into the causes of the empirical clustering of institutions and practices reported by Parsons.[55] It remains to be discovered also to what extent observed interconnections between variables are the result of the contents of men's minds, and to what extent these interconnections are relatively variable because they are mental instead of mechanical or otherwise non-mental in character. Should these interconnections be largely mental and hence variable, it would follow that the impact of an ideology unfavorable to economic development would be more adverse than if these connections were (say) mechanical and hence relatively immune to changes in mental phenomena.

The nature of the underlying social universe is of relatively less concern to the historian than to other social scientists. His emphasis is upon singular events, upon the connections obtaining between

[53] See S. Morgenbesser, "Role and Status of Anthropological Theories," *Science*, CXXVIII (1958), 287; also criticisms of functionalism by Rose, *op. cit.*, pp. 13-26; Nagel, *Logic without Metaphysics*, pp. 247-286; and J. Henry, "Homeostasis, Society and Evolution: A Critique," *Scientific Monthly*, LXXXI (1955), 300-309.

[54] See his *Economic Backwardness and Economic Growth* (New York, 1957), chaps. viii, xii.

[55] *Social System*, chap. v. See also J. R. Caldwell, "The New American Archeology," *Science*, CXXIX (1959), 306.

specific occurrences, upon the discovery of the comparative importance of the circumstances which have operated in combination to
produce specific historical events. His approach is not entirely
idiographic, however; it also includes a nomothetic component. He
must make use of assumed laws and statements regarding initial
conditions. In consequence he is not without concern respecting
the nature of the underlying social universe, and this concern has
often been manifest in his approach and analysis, even though it has
remained essentially anthropomorphic.[56]

V. IDEOLOGY AND THE NON-RATIONAL

In Section I a distinction was made between contents of the
mind having to do with theory and the rational selection of means
to ends and contents left over and forming a residuum. Within this
residuum, it was implied, were to be found contents bearing upon
the choice both of ends to be pursued and of means to be employed
in this pursuit. In the present section we deal primarily with
ideological and secondarily with other non-rational or non-logical
determinants of politico-economic development. Parsons' conception
of action (or of human social action) is employed.

Parsons' scheme of action embraces actors, ends, means, conditions, and norms. The actor expends energy or puts forth effort.
He does this in order to achieve an end, or objective, or "anticipated state of affairs." He puts forth this effort in a situation which
includes both environmental and hereditary elements that he cannot
modify to suit his purpose, and elements that, being variable, are
subject to his control; the former set of elements—i.e., the "conditions"—amounts to a set of constraints upon the actor's action whereas the latter set comprises the "means" from among which he may
choose instruments supposedly suited to realize his end. His choice

[56] See Ernest Nagel, "Some Issues in the Logic of Historical Analysis," *Scientific Monthly*, LXXIV (1952), 162-169; also Cassirer, *An Essay on Man*, pp. 235-236, 241-242. Popper declares that history "has no meaning," that none of its interpretations can be "final." See *The Open Society*, II, chap. xxv, esp. pp. 255-256. But cf. H. Meyerhoff's comments in his anthology, *The Philosophy of History in Our Time* (Garden City, 1958); also R. G. Collingwood's criticism of the idiographic-nomothetic dichotomy, in *The Idea of History*, New York, 1956), pp. 166-176.

of means is not free of restriction, however; it is subject to regulation by norms which may be variously sanctioned and which may
or may not permit the selection of those means which are best
adapted to realization of the end or ends in view.[57] This choice
is greatly influenced, as are cognitive and eudemonic standards, by
the value-orientations regnant in a society, much as the selection of
ends to be sought is greatly influenced by the system of values
dominant in a society; for these value-orientations and values get
incorporated within individuals and are reinforced by the various
goal-oriented arrangements whereunder individuals interact.[58]

It should be noted once again that, although economic or political development is treated as an end in this paper, its position in
the means-ends chain underlying human action is not that of end,
for economic development and (in very large measure if not wholly)
political development are means to higher purposes. Development
is sought because it supposedly serves the ultimate and quasi-ulti-
mate purposes and values men prize and set store by; it will be
sought only in proportion as it is deemed, especially by the elite, to
serve these purposes or values. These purposes or values are non-

[57] See Parsons *et al., Toward a General Theory of Action,* Parts I-II; also
Parsons, *Social Systems,* esp. chap. i and *The Structure of Social Action,* all previously cited. For a more precise description of the components of an action scheme,
see M. Kochen and M. J. Levy, Jr., "The Logical Nature of an Action Scheme,"
Behavioral Science, I (1956), 265-289. See also W. J. Baumol's defense of the
practice of taking the existence of distinct ends for granted at a given time even
though it is true that goals may be modified in the course of their being sought.
See *Welfare Economics and the Theory of the State* (Cambridge, 1952), p. 121 n.
According to V. Valvanis, the locus of ethical decision is much narrower than is
usually assumed. See "The Resolution of Conflict when Utilities Interact," *Journal of Conflict Resolution,* II (1958), 156-169.

[58] "A value-orientation" is "a generalized and organized conception, influencing
behavior, of nature, of man's place in it, of man's relation to man, and of the
desirable and nondesirable as they may relate to man-environment and interhuman
relations." See *Toward a General Theory,* p. 411, also p. 60 on the relation of
the individual's value-orientation to his norms and standards. "A value is a
conception . . . of the desirable which influences the selection from available modes,
means, and ends of action." It is "a preference which is felt and/or considered
to be justified"; it instigates and somewhat canalizes behavior. See *ibid.,* pp. 395,
396; Joseph J. Spengler, "Sociological Value Theory, Economic Analyses, and
Economic Policy," *American Economic Review,* Vol. XLIII No. 2 (1953), pp. 340-
349. See also W. R. Catton, Jr., "A Theory of Value," *American Sociological Review,* XXIV (1959), 310-317; A. L. Kroeber, ed., *Anthropology Today* (Chicago,
1953), pp. 668-699. See also H. Vaihinger's, *The Philosophy of "As If"* (New
York, 1935), p. xxx, where he enunciates his "Law of the Preponderance of the
Means over the End," according to which "an original means" tends to "acquire independence and to become an end in itself."

rational or irritational much as are the value-orientations underlying ideology as we define it below. Ultimately, therefore, the extent to which economic or political development takes place depends very largely upon the orientations of the elements situated
in the non-rational world of values and value-orientations—a world
existing in the minds of men; thereupon depend what men seek
and how they seek it.

In the past the shape and the pace of politico-economic development in given societies has been greatly affected by the values,
value-orientations, and value-attitudes dominant therein, and particularly by those regnant among the elites by whose members are
made the most important decisions respecting the use of scarce
resources. The choice of objectives to be sought as well as the selection of means to attain such objectives has always been dominated
by the values and value-orientations dominant in societies. For
example, values which conduced to war and emulative waste not
only made for the destruction of that very surplus whence a nation's politico-economic growth might have been supported. They
also depreciated activities suited to give man increasing "control
over nature," by playing up otherworldly objectives, by playing
down the importance of material things, and in general by generat-
ing aspirations that were unfavorable to economic growth. They
thus retarded economic and related development by delaying the
progress of positive science, since policies suited to give rise to such
development are most likely to be formed, selected, and effectively
applied when social and other theory is positive and designed to
reveal functional and causal relations unambiguously.[59] At no time,

---

[59] E.g., it has been suggested that epistemological realism was far less favorable
to the rise of capitalism than was epistemological nominalism, the development of
which supposedly was essential to the supersession of the *Gemeinschaft*-type of social
relationship by the *Gesselschaft*-type. See Stark, *Sociology of Knowledge*, pp.
39-41, 81; on the two types see Parsons, *Structure of Social Action*, pp. 686 ff.
The rise and spread of nominalism was long retarded by the predominance of
scholastic modes of posing questions. See W. Windelband, *A History of Philosophy*
(New York, 1901), pp. 343-344. On modern nominalism see A. Pap, "Mathematics, Abstract Entities, and Modern Semantics," *Scientific Monthly*, LXXXV
(1957), 29-40. It is not always easy to foresee or to estimate the net impact
of new ways of evaluating human activities. For example, mysticism is extremely
unfavorable to economic development; yet its rise in the medieval world, insomuch
as it undermined authority, must have facilitated the rise of nominalism. On
circumstances affecting the disposition of the surplus in primitive societies, see
M. J. Herskovits, *Economic Anthropology* (New York, 1952), Part V.

however, has science been used as effectively as it might be; for many a person's apprehension of causal and functional relations has been blurred or distorted, as has his choice of means to ends, by illusions, delusions, biases, etc., by what Francis Bacon called the "idols which beset men's minds."[60]

Because values differ in respect of their favorableness to politico-economic development and because a given end may often be accomplished in a variety of ways, it is not easy to specify *empirically* that set of concrete conditions which is more conducive to such development than any alternative set of concrete conditions. Specification becomes more difficult, furthermore, when it is impossible to define the content of development in precise, relatively non-arbitrary, and empirical terms. Some of the difficulties may be avoided if development is quite arbitrarily defined—for example, if it is defined in terms of economic means and of economic objectives free of implications respecting the distribution of the results. We might then say that economic development tends to proceed most rapidly when, hereditary and physical-environmental conditions being given, a people's system of values is most favorable to the selection of development-oriented ends, and when its value-orientations are most favorable to the selection of means optimally suited to realize these ends. It is rarely possible, of course, to select the uniquely best of the "logical"[61] means available in given situations, either because the means have not yet been carefully ordered in terms of their efficacy, or because, even if they have been ordered on the basis of certain past experience, the current situation is somewhat unique and therefore not one to which an ordering based on past experience is necessarily applicable.

Ideology, as defined in this chapter, retards both economic development and political development (insofar as the latter is

---

[60] See *Novum Organum*, Bk. I, secs. xxviii ff.

[61] One may (with Kochen and Levy) put into a set of "logical" means all those which are suited to produce a given end, and then define as "rational" that one of these means which is optimal in terms of some arbitrary criterion. Given development, suitably defined, as the objective, every means conducive thereto is "logical," but only that means is rational in an economic sense which minimizes composite input per unit output of development. On the logical and rational aspects of action, see Kochen and Levy, *op. cit.*, pp. 279-284. See also J. G. March and H. A. Simon, *Organizations* (New York, 1958), chap. vi, esp. pp. 136-142, 169-171; also Karlsson, *op. cit.*, pp. 11-16. See also S. Schoeffler, "Toward a General Definition of Rational Action," *Kyklos*, VII (1954), 246-270.

not defined to include ideological values). We define ideology
to include those values which operate, directly or indirectly, (1)
to prevent the selection of means which are relatively optimal, and/
or (2) to obscure and hence to foster neglect of inter-end conflict
susceptible of composition. Effects (1) and (2) may also be accompanied by a corollary development-retarding effect, the homogenizing of expression, if the presence of the underlying ideological
values unduly reduces heterogeneity of expression. Values present
in value-systems give rise to effect (1) indirectly, as when they
make for ignorance respecting what means are relatively best, or
directly, as when they prompt the selection of means which are
recognized as falling quite short of optimal. In practice, of course,
it is not always easy to determine if effect (1) is a direct or an indirect outcome of regnant values; and this difficulty is accentuated
by the fact that usually one can at best isolate means in the neighborhood of the optimum, but without being able to identify the
optimum as such. It is even more difficult to determine whether
regnant values are giving rise directly and/or indirectly to effect
(2). For it is seldom easy to specify with precision either the nature
of inter-value conflict, or the alternative ways in which such conflict may be composed, given the complexity of the complementary
and the competitive relations apparently present in the collection
of more or less ultimate values, together with the fact that many
individuals fail to settle or equilibrate their own private positions.

Intervalue conflicts are of two sorts, those resting on cost and
hence susceptible of being balanced, and those which do not rest
on costs and may or may not be resolvable. Suppose, as illustrative of the first, i.e., of conflict based on costs, two values V_1 and
V_2, the side-relations of which may be neglected. Suppose further
that realization of the specific objectives to which these values give
rise entails resource costs of c_1 and c_2, respectively, with the amount
of cost depending on the extent to which either value is objectively
realized. Under these circumstances, the conflict between V_1 and V_2
can be resolved by appropriately distributing between them the
scarce resources to be absorbed in the form of costs c_1 and c_2. Let
us suppose next that we have two values V_a and V_b, the objective
realization of which does not entail absorption of scarce resources.
Between these two values there may be no conflict, or there may be

only conflict of the sort that can be resolved by persuasion, by appeals to tolerance, by resort to methods of satisfaction whereunder V_a-oriented persons are sequestered from V_b-oriented persons when satisfying these values, and so on. There may be some values V_a and V_b, however, which may not be able to co-exist, if their realization is sought; they may, in Leibnizian terms, not be *compossible*, with the result that one or the other must give way. Ideological considerations may hide the true nature of the intervalue conflict involved and thus interfere with its resolution, given that such resolution is possible.[62]

What has been said respecting ideology may be summarized. Ideological values, present among the contents of men's minds and to be found in some measure in every culture, retard economic development. They do this because they make for scientific non-objectivity and because they may be unfavorable to the persistence of heterogeneity of outlook. For non-objectivity interferes with both the resolution of inter-value conflicts and the selection of optimal means, thus impairing inquiry and policy-formation; while a homogenizing of the contents of the mind consequent upon a non-objective approach to the study of means and ends reduces that diversity whence potentially salutary change issues.[63] The extent to which ideological values can produce adverse effects of the sort noted depends, *ceteris paribus*, however, upon the degree to which they are organized and institutionalized as well as upon the degree to which countervailing social forces are organized and institutionalized.[64]

[62] Leibniz used the term "compossible" in respect of actual and possible species and worlds, and not in respect of values as such. See Bertrand Russell, *A Critical Exposition of the Philosophy of Leibniz* (Cambridge, 1900), pp. 66-67, 223. On the impact of government and of vote-maximizing upon the likelihood of a society's balancing costs suitably, or of attaining a Paretian optimum, see A. Downs, *An Economic Theory of Democracy* (New York, 1957), chap. x.

[63] On the dependence of progress upon the persistence of diversity see C. Russell and W. M. S. Russell, "An Approach to Human Ethology," *Behavioral Science*, II (1957), 197, and Karl Popper, "The Poverty of Historicism, III," *Economica*, XII (1945), 88.

[64] Popper (*Ibid.*, p. 87) argues that, because science tends to be institutionalized and thus to be "public" in character, each individual scientist finds himself under mental discipline and (hence) under pressure to be scientifically objective and therefore disposed to resist the adverse influence of ideological and related factors. This argument, while valid if appropriately restricted, overlooks the fact that ideological biases may also be institutionalized with the result that individuals who are disposed to be wholly objective may find it difficult to be so. Witness the impact of Lysenkoism in the Soviet Union, or the failure of economists in various

The meaning we have assigned ideology differs from the meanings usually assigned this term; it is compatible in spirit though not in substance with the intent of the ideologues whose views (which incurred the wrath of Napoleon) had to do primarily with ideas (i.e., sensations, memories, judgments, and desires) from an essentially physiological point of view.[65]   It is narrower than L. H. Garstin's notion when he defines ideology in this wise:

All ideologies contain four basic elements.   Ideologies in the true sense of the term include in their schemes a philosophy of history, an analysis of the present stage of man's development in the light of that philosophy, a projection of the analysis into the future, and an analysis of the human actions necessary to hasten the inevitable outcome predicted in the projection of events into the future.[66]

It is not wholly compatible with Clyde Kluckhohn's definition when he treats ideology as a "system of ideas," based sometimes on "the special interests" of a minority within a society and "sometimes upon a supernatural revelation" or upon a "nonempirical, nonscientific norm," and describes it as having a "somewhat pejorative sense which does not attach to value"; or when he limits its impact by arguing that "ideologies determine the choice between alternative paths of action, which are equally compatible with the underlying values."[67] Its emphasis is not the same as that of definitions which assign to ideology a functional, organizing, unifying, and purposive role (e.g.,

---

Moslem lands to discuss the function of loan interest freely and objectively.   In general, as Edward Shils has shown, when great obstacles exist "to the emergence and effectiveness of responsible criticism of governmental policies in the new countries" (e.g., because of a dearth of detached factual research on public issues, because of a shortage of well-trained intellectuals, because of the lack of a responsible press and independent civic associations, etc.), the tendency to correct intelligently error incorporated in public policy is weak and development is retarded accordingly.   See "Intellectuals, Public Opinion, and Economic Development," *loc. cit.*   C. Zirkle discusses Lysenkoism in his *Evolution, Marxian Biology, and the Social Scene* (Philadelphia, 1959).

[65] See G. Chinard's introduction to Emile Caillet's *La tradition littéraire des idéologues* (Philadelphia, 1943), and *ibid.*, chaps. v-vii; also George Boas, *Dominant Themes of Modern Philosophy* (New York, 1957), chap. xii; F. A. Hayek, *The Counter-Revolution of Science* (Glencoe, 1952), pp. 113-116. "It was the misfortune of the *ideologues*, as they called themselves, that their very name should be perverted into a catchword describing the very opposite from what they stood for. . . ."   See *ibid.*, p. 113.   Writers who emphasized sensations must, however, be included among the forerunners of the sociologists of knowledge.

[66] *Each Age Is A Dream: A Study In Ideologies* (New York, 1954), p. 3.

[67] See Parsons *et al.*, *Toward a General Theory*, pp. 432-433.

that of obtaining votes; that of preserving the rationale of a political system against erosive forces; etc.).[68]   It does, however, resemble somewhat Stark's conception of ideology as a non-objective and relatively illogical mode of thinking.[69]

When ideology is given a broad meaning, as in Garstin's definition, it not only affects development adversely by subordinating it to a rigid conception of the course it will follow;[70] it also includes values which may focus effort upon certain developmental objectives and sometimes generate emotional drive favorable to their realization.[71]   My narrower definition of ideology averts this conflict in effects.

Even when one defines ideology as narrowly as I have, one still

[68] E.g., see K. Mannheim, *Ideology and Utopia* (New York, 1937), chap. vii; Downs, *op. cit.*, pp. 96-141; A. B. Ulam, "Soviet Ideology and Foreign Policy," *World Politics*, XI (1959), 171-172; F. S. C. Northrop, *The Meeting of East and West*, pp. 256 ff.; L. Dion, "Political Ideology as a Tool of Functional Analysis in Socio-Political Dynamics: An Hypothesis," *Canadian Journal of Economics and Political Science*, XXV (1959), 47-59.   A variety of meanings assigned to the term "ideology" are listed or discussed by A. Naess, *Democracy, Ideology And Objectivity* (Oxford, 1956), pp. 162-172.   The history of the concept is dealt with in *ibid.*, pp. 148-153; and by J. S. Roucek, "A History of the Concept of Ideology," *Journal of the History of Ideas*, V (1944), 479-488.   On the use of "positivism" to dissipate "colonial Spirit" in Latin America, see Leopold Zea, "Positivism and Porfirism in Latin America," in F. S. C. Northrop, ed., *Ideological Differences and World Order*, pp. 166-191.   On the place of ideology in nineteenth-century philosophy, see H. D. Aiken, *The Age of Ideology* (New York, 1956).

[69] *Op. cit.*, pp. 48-49, 80 ff.   Stark attributes this nonobjectivity to an individual's entertaining "ideas in the psychological origin of which some selfish or sectional interest or desire has played a part."   See *ibid.*, p. 48.   See also Mannheim, *Ideology and Utopia*, chap. ii, sec. 1; also R. Bendix's treatment of ideology as a self- or group-justifying argument, in his *Work and Authority in Industry: Ideologies of Management in the Course of Industrialization* (New York, 1956). Respecting Stark's emphasis upon the psychological influence of a special "interest," it may be said merely that such interest tends to give rise to *ex parte* testimony, but that it need not make for non-objectivity in the ascertainment and analysis of relevant data.

[70] That historical method can yield valid historical prediction is criticized by K. Popper in a three-part paper, "The Poverty of Historicism," *Economica*, XI-XII, (1944-45).   See also Isaiah Berlin, *Historical Inevitability* (New York, 1957), and Collingwood, *op. cit.*, p. 220 and *passim*; but compare H. Meyerhoff, ed., *The Philosophy of History in Our Time*.

[71] E.g., S. H. Clough, in his account of the movement of civilization, assigns great importance to what he calls "the controlling ideologies of a culture," to the "goals, intellectual standards, art forms, and technological attitudes" that become "differentiated and specialized" when a culture is coming into being. See his *The Rise And Fall of Civilization* (New York, 1951), pp. 9-11.   But he includes under ideology all of the norms and goals present in a culture and so makes ideology, instead of growth-oriented values, foster development.

finds it difficult at times to separate ideological sources of non-objectivity completely from other non-rational values which may affect analysis adversely. Here it is possible only to cite varied evidence of the impact of ideological values in the field of social science.

Ideology manifests itself in various ways in economics, in part because particular decision-makers (e.g., trade-union leaders, industrial price-makers, governmentally created price-fixers) stand to benefit by endorsing certain ideological manifestations. Paramount among these manifestations is a persistent refusal or inability to appreciate that a flexible price system is both the most economical and the most unbiased of the computing and coordinating mechanisms that man has devised.[72] One might cite statements made in countless popular and semi-popular papers as well as those occasionally expressed in technical essays. One may turn to Soviet economics and practice for evidence of distorting and wasteful impact of this sort of ideology, for Soviet administrators and economists remain under pressure, though in decreasing measure, to make use of a labor theory of value instead of a flexible price system and associated indicators.[73] One may turn also to thought and practice in Moslem lands as one could at one time turn to that found in Christian communities; for here the use of interest to stimulate saving and to facilitate the appropriate allocation of capital is still deemed contrary to religious and/or ecclesiastical sanction.[74] The presence of ideological elements has been noted by scholars in modern as well as in classical discussions of a variety of economic sub-

[72] E.g., see R. H. Coase's nice comparison of the role of the firm with that of the free market or price mechanism, in "The Nature of The Firm," *Economica*, IV (1937), 386-405.

[73] E.g., see G. Grossman, "Scarce Capital and Soviet Doctrine," *Quarterly Journal of Economics*, LXVII (1953), 341-342; A. Nove, "The Problem of 'Success Indicators' in Soviet Industry," *Economica*, XXV (1958) 1-13. See in general R. L. Ackoff, "Scientific Method and Social Science—East and West," *Scientific Monthly*, LXXV (1952), 155-160; B. Moore, Jr., "Influence of Political Creeds on the Acceptance of Theories," *ibid.*, LXXIX (1954), 146-148; symposium on "Ideology and Reality in the Soviet System," in *Proceedings* of the American Philosophical Society, XCIX (1955), 1-38; H. Smith, "The Economics of Socialism Reconsidered," *Economic Journal*, LXV (1955) 414 ff.; S. Hook, "Socialism and Democracy," *The New Leader*, XLI (Nov., 1958), 17 ff. On ideology in the psychosocial sciences, see G. Razran, "Soviet Psychology and Psychophysiology," *Science*, CXXVIII (1958), 1193. See also note 90 below.

[74] E.g., see A. I. Qureshi, *Islam and the Theory of Interest* (Lahore, 1946); J. T. Noonan, Jr., *The Scholastic Analysis of Usury* (Cambridge, 1957).

jects.[75] Such manifestations seem to be relatively more frequent or pronounced when economists are not in agreement concerning either theoretical findings or policy objectives, or when prognosis is involved. For example, ideological considerations have entered into discussions of governmental debt and budget-balancing, of trade theory and policy, and of egalitarianism in advanced countries where the need for capital is less acute than in backward lands; and they tend to be present in discussions relating to economic development concerning aspects of which opinions differ widely.[76] They emerge when analytical concepts are given an evaluative role and made to subserve political instead of scientific purposes.[77] They tend to emerge also when so-called human-rights-oriented policy objectives (e.g., fullness of employment; use of a rationing system as a guide to factor allocation) are under consideration.[78]

[75] E.g., see O. H. Taylor, "Economic Science Only—or Political Economy," *Quarterly Journal of Economics*, LXXI (1957), 14-18; G. H. Sabine, "Beyond Ideology," *Philosophical Review*, LVII (1948), 1-26. See also the suggestion of E. Kuh and J. R. Meyer that insistence on long-run considerations may act as an ideological factor, in "Keynes and the Forces of History," *Quarterly Journal of Economics*, LXVI (1952), 456-457. P. Lambert asserts that the "ideological overtones" of Malthus's critique of Say's Law of Markets contributed greatly to the rejection of Malthus's theory. See "The Law of Markets Prior to J. B. Say and the Say-Malthus Debate," *International Economic Papers*, VI (1956), 22. See also W. Stark, *The Ideal Foundations of Economic Thought* (London, 1958), *passim*; Manuel Gottlieb, "The Ideological Influence in Schumpeter's Thought," *Zeitschrift fur Nationalökonomie*, Band XIX, Heft 1-2 (1959), pp. 1-42; and J. A. Schumpeter, "Science and Ideology," in R. V. Clemence, ed., *Essays of J. A. Schumpeter* (Cambridge, 1951), pp. 267-281.

[76] E.g., see J. Burkhead, "The Balanced Budget," *Quarterly Journal of Economics* LXVIII (1954), 210-216; H. Myint, "The 'Classical Theory' of International Trade and Underdeveloped Countries," *Economic Journal*, LXVIII (1958), 316-321, 334-337; R. J. Lampman, "Recent Thought on Egalitarianism," *Quarterly Journal of Economics*, LXXI (1957), 234-266; Streeten, "Programs and Prognosis," *loc. cit.*, pp. 368-376; F. Machlup, "Disputes, Paradoxes, and Dilemmas concerning Economic Development," reprinted from *Revista Internazionale di Scienze Ecomiche e Commerciali*, IV (1957), No. 9. "The polymorphism of human thought generates rival diagnoses concerning the sources of human affliction" —Grünbaum notes (*op. cit.*, p. 13).

[77] See F. Machlup, "Equilibrium And Disequilibrium: Misplaced Concreteness and Disguised Politics," *Economic Journal*, LXVIII (1958), 2, 12-14, 23-24; W. H. Nicholls, "Social Biases and Recent Theories of Competition," *Quarterly Journal of Economics*, LVIII (1943), 1-26.

[78] Ideological elements are touched upon by G. Myrdal in *The Political Element in the Development of Economic Theory* (London, 1953). In his preface to this translation Myrdal recognizes that in economics as in all science there "is an inescapable *a priori* element" which reflects individual or collective valuations. How the economist's psychological mechanisms and needs shape, or may shape, his formation of concepts, etc., is discussed by W. A. Weisskopf in "Psychological As-

Ideology is present in discussion in fields outside economics. It appears to be more common in history, however, than in other branches of the social studies, perhaps because history makes relatively little use of explicit theory, because it so frequently serves as a handmaiden to politics, and because it sometimes views as inevitable what is not or may not have been inevitable at all.[79] Ideological influences have sometimes colored American sociological theory.[80] They have also manifested themselves in political science. Here in particular one encounters vestiges of that Natural Law which its exponents, purporting to know the purposes (hidden and otherwise) of things and their physical processes, have frequently utilized in ways that hinder politico-economic development; thus Natural Law was long used to bolster the so-called case against interest-taking, and it is still used to retard the introduction of effective modes of contraception, lack of which makes progress in average material welfare very difficult if not impossible in many parts of the world.[81] The relatively great prominence of ideological ele-

pects of Economic Thought," *Journal of Political Economy*, LVII (1949), 304-314, in "Hidden Value Conflicts in Economic Thought," *Ethics*, LXI (1951), 195-204, and in *The Psychology of Economics* (London, 1955), *passim*. For a critique of praxeological and related approaches to economics and for arguments favoring the use of an alternative set of *a priori* elements, see K. W. Kapp, "Economics and the Behavioral Sciences," *Kyklos*, VII (1954), 205-224.

[79] See Stark, *Sociology of Knowledge*, pp. 67 ff.; J. C. Manlin, *On The Nature of History* (Ann Arbor, 1954), pp. 284-288, also pp. 88, 101, 254-261; I. Berlin, *Historical Inevitablity*; Popper, *The Open Society*, II, chaps. xxii, xxv. As Nagel has pointed out, however, historians can avoid ideological distortions ("Some Issues in . . . Historical Analysis," *loc. cit.*). See also T. S. Ashton's comments on the use of theory, in *Economica*, XIV (1947), 226-227. Problems arising from the involvement of the historical observer with that which is observed are discussed by I. D. London and N. P. Poltoratzky, "The Problems of Contemporary Analysis in History and Psychology," *Behavioral Science*, III (1958), 269-277. On various approaches to history, see also Simkhovitch, *op. cit.*, *Political Science Quarterly*, XLIV-XLIX, (1929-1934); H. Butterfield, *The Englishman and His History* (Cambridge, 1944); and H. Meyerhoff, ed., *The Philosophy of History in Our Time.*

[80] E.g., see C. W. Mills, "Methodological Consequences of the Sociology of Knowledge," *American Journal of Sociology*, XLIV (1940), 328-330.

[81] When the term Natural Law merely denotes a so-called law of nature, such as that of falling bodies, the above comment does not apply. On the role of Natural Law in anti-usury literature, see Noonan's excellent account in his *The Scholastic Analysis of Usury*. V. Pareto, who was much concerned with the ideology problem (see Parsons, *Structure of Social Action*, pp. 269 ff., 283 ff.), touched upon the use of the supposed entity, "Natural Law," to support that which its exponents favored. See *The Mind and Society* (New York, 1935), I, pars. 401-462. See

THEORY, IDEOLOGY, AND NON-ECONOMIC VALUES

ments in the literature of political science may be due also to its emphasis upon ends rather than upon positive analysis,[82] and to its frequent recourse to approaches of the sort found in the study of law.[83]

Having commented on the presence of ideological elements in contemporary social-science literature, I shall close this section by touching upon the adverse influence exercised by ideology in the past upon scientific progress and hence upon political or economic development. In general, an ideology will be unfavorable to scientific progress in so far as the metaphysical attitude permeating this ideology is competitive with that characteristic of science, as when explanations based upon Genesis experienced competition from Darwinian explanations in what amounted to a contest for the allegiance of men's minds.[84]

In the Western world, the long-run history of concepts suggests, ideological as well as related values have usually been quite unfavorable to scientific progress. Even among the Greeks, creators of demonstrative mathematics and modern science,[85] the progress of science always was hindered and eventually was checked by superstition and the prevalence of values unfavorable to economic

---

also Nagel, *Logic without Metaphysics*, pp. 3-18, on the account of the world given by exponents of "naturalism." See E. Cassirer's account of changing concepts of natural law in his *The Philosophy of Enlightenment*, chap. ii.

[82] A. S. Kaufman contends that "political theory should be a guide to action." See his "The Nature and Function of Political Theory," *Journal of Philosophy*, LI (1954), 1.

[83] Careful inquiry would probably reveal that the casuistic approach of legal students to their subject matter is very inferior to that of the economist or that of the engineer in so far as the fostering of economic development is concerned.

[84] See J. R. Newman's review of E. Schrodinger's *Nature and the Greeks* (1954), in *Scientific American*, CXCI (July, 1954), 84-88. This type of conflict did not exist among the Greeks (*ibid.*, p. 84). Mannheim sought to show that the desire of groups for power and advantage had shaped their approaches to the solution of problems and had generated continuous competition among divers approaches to social science (*Essays*, pp. 195-197, 228). In his "Approaches to History II," *Political Science Quarterly*, XLV (1930), 491-504, V. G. Simkhovitch implied that whether there will be a conflict or not turns on the attitudes of scientists and ideologues. Compare L. F. Koch, "Vitalistic-Mechanistic Controversy," *Scientific Monthly*, LXXXV (1957), 245-255.

[85] E.g., see J. F. Scott, *A History of Mathematics*, (London, 1958) but see also O. Neugebauer, *The Exact Sciences in Antiquity* (Providence, 1957), chap. vi. Greek emphasis upon pure mathematics entailed a cost, neglect of the applicability of elementary mathematics. See Needham, *op. cit.*, (Cambridge, 1959), III, 151.

development.[86] That ideology was unfavorable to scientific progress is supported by the history of the concepts of force and space, with which extra-scientific notions long were mingled,[87] as well as by the ancient and the medieval world's persistence in not abandoning its homocentric, two-sphere view of the universe for a more accurate heliocentric one, which, however, demoted man;[88] and it may perhaps be supported by the slowness with which man developed the concept of electric charge.[89]   If, however, we look only at the relatively recent history of concepts, we may infer that their formation and development eventually became comparatively free of ideological, as well as of other extra-scientific considerations, in part because of the rise of a secular point of view, and in part because the problems studied have become more and more detailed and technical (e.g., in the Soviet Union administrative requirements

[86] E.g., see B. Farrington, *Science and Politics in the Ancient World* (London, 1946) and *Greek Science* (London, 1949).   Some Greek concepts respecting nature had their origins, as apparently did some Chinese concepts, in notions concerning human relations.   The Greeks initially held the "structure and behavior of the world to be continuous with—a mere extension or projection of—the structure and behavior of human society." See F. M. Cornford, *From Religion to Philosophy* (New York, 1957), chap. ii, sec. 24; also H. Kelsen's account in *Society and Nature* (Chicago, 1943), chap. v, of the evolution of the Greek notion of causality out of a primitive notion of retribution and conception of nature patterned after an order-maintaining authoritarian community; and Eisman's psychological description of "cause" as a "predisposition of thought" (*op. cit.*, p. 259).   See also P. M. Schuhl, *Essai sur la formation de la pensée Grecque* (Paris, 1949).   On Chinese concepts, see Gerard De Gre, *Society and Ideology* (New York, 1943), pp. 56-59; M. Granet, *La pensée chinoise* (Paris, 1934); J. Needham, *op. cit.*, II, 337, 527-528.

[87] See Marx Jammer, *Concepts of Space* and *Concepts of Force*, both published in Cambridge in 1957.

[88] See J. R. Newman's comments, based upon T. S. Kuhn's *The Copernican Revolution*, in the *Scientific American*, CXCVII (October, 1957), 156 ff.   Even so, ideological considerations may have contributed to the adoption of Copernicus' view of the universe in that its discovery inspired the belief that simple, mathematical regularities might be found to dominate nature (*ibid.*, p. 158), a belief further fortified when Newton made light where theretofore, in Pope's words, "Nature and Nature's laws lay hid in night."   But see Neugebauer, *op. cit.*, pp. 183, 204-206, on the impact of accumulated empirical data.   See also H. Dingle, "Cosmology and Science," *Scientific American*, CXCV (September, 1956), 224-236; P. Frank, "The Logical and Sociological Aspects of Science," *Proceedings* of the American Academy of Arts and Sciences, Vol. LXXX, No. 1 (1951), pp. 19-25; and F. E. Hartung, "Sociological Foundations of Modern Science," *Philosophy of Science*, XIV (1947), 72-75 and 76 ff. on the decline of the medieval view that man and nature were decaying.

[89] See D. and D. H. D. Roller, *The Development of the Concept of Electric Charge* (Cambridge, 1954).

are resulting in the replacement of the Marxian law of value by linear programing).[90]

VI. Content of the Mind: Genesis

We have merely been treating theory, ideology, and development-affecting, non-rational values as contents of the mind. We have thus left largely untouched three problems of great concern to students of politico-economic development, given that contents of the mind may be thought of as a strategic vantage from which to approach the subject of development. First, mind must be dealt with in terms that assign it a role which is significantly determining and yet selectively responsive to external stimuli. For this purpose a theory as good as any seems to be Hayek's respecting how events in the external world get linked in the higher nervous centers and so give rise to a kind of semi-permanent "map" or "semi-permanent structure" which evaluates impulses, etc., and affects decisions accordingly. This map or structure, amounting to an "apparatus of classification," provides "a sort of inventory of the kind of things of which the world is built up, a theory of how the world works rather than a picture of it." It may and does undergo change, but significantly under its own guidance, with the realm of "mind" remaining "forever a realm of its own." Accordingly, while changes in "mental phenomena" and associated "human decisions" may and do accompany changes in "physical events," one cannot infer, as would some expounders of sociology of knowledge, "which are the

---

[90] "Social causation largely ceases to apply as soon as a problem becomes detailed and technical." See Bertrand Russell, A History of Western Philosophy (New York, 1945), p. 786, also pp. 786-788 for illustrations. Concept changes are illustratively discussed also in the following: a symposium on "Psychoanalysis and Scientific Method," Scientific Monthly, LXXIX (1954), 293-310; R. B. Lindsay, "Concept of Energy in Mechanics," ibid., LXXXV (1957), 188-194; G. Hardin, "Meaninglessness of the Word Protoplasm," ibid., LXXXVI (1958), 112-120; H. E. Landsberg, "Trends in Climatology," Science, CXXXVIII (1958), 749-758; P. F. Lazarsfeld, Mathematical Thinking in the Social Sciences (Glencoe, 1954), pp. 348-387. The development of various branches of science in medieval and later pre-nineteenth century times is described by A. C. Crombie, Augustus to Galileo: The History of Science A.D. 400-1650 (Cambridge, 1953), and by A. R. Hall, The Scientific Revolution, 1500-1800 (New York, 1954). These authors are not, however, particularly concerned with the impact of ideology upon the progress of science.

particular physical events which 'correspond' to a particular mental event."[91] Mind, therefore, while largely the product of cumulated past events, at any moment is possessed of great autonomy and hence of the content essential to dealing selectively and authoritatively with current events, stimuli, and situations.

How to modify the contents of the mind in a manner suited to get development under way and sustain it is the second problem; it is touched upon in the last section. The third task is that of reviewing in a general fashion ways in which some of the content of the mind has undergone change in the past. This task is the concern of the present section, wherein we touch upon the emergence of the subjective superstructures from the substructure of man's interaction with his fellows and with the constraints and opportunities present in his physical environment. For not even a philosopher endowed with Kant's categories could free himself of external influences.[92] Even so, there is lack of consensus respecting the impact of influences external or internal to bodies of theory or value.[93]

Unfortunately neither of the methods available for the study of the genesis of theory, ideology, and development-affecting values is adequate. (1) It is possible, through historical inquiry, to assemble considerable information respecting the origin and evolution

[91] See Hayek, *The Sensory Order*, chap. v, especially pp. 115, 130-131, but also pp. 145-146, 166 ff., 179 ff., 192-194; compare Stark, *Sociology of Knowledge*, pp. 140-150.

[92] S. K. Langer writes that every philosopher's "thought has developed amid certain problems, certain basic alternatives of opinion, that embody the key concepts which dominate his time and his environment and which will always be reflected, positively or by negation, in his own work." See P. A. Schlipp, ed., *The Philosophy of Ernst Cassirer* (New York, 1949), p. 381. See also O. L. Reiser's "Aristotelian, Galilean and Non-Aristotelian Modes of Thinking," *Psychological Review*, XLVI (1939), 153-155, in which the effect of substituting "an organismic conception" for the one underlying Aristotle's categories is examined.

[93] See Stark, *The Sociology of Knowledge*. See also Mannheim's *Essays*, and his *Ideology and Utopia*; Sorokin, *Social and Cultural Dynamics*; R. K. Merton, *Social Theory and Social Structure* (Glencoe, 1949); J. J. Maquet, *Sociologie de la connissance* (Louvain, 1949); B. Barber, *Science and the Social Order* (Glencoe, 1952); Hartung, *op. cit.* Karl Jaspers' account of the development of man's diverse conceptions of his role, in the immediately pre-Christian or axial period, is quite suggestive. See *The Origin and Goal of History*, Part I. Samples of the views of Karl Marx (who wrote at times as if the subjective superstructure were essentially an epiphenomenon) have been assembled by T. B. Bottomore and M. Rubel in *Karl Marx: Selected Writings in Sociology & Social Philosophy* (London, 1956). See also L. von Mises's critique of Marx's approach, in *Theory and History* (New Haven, 1957), pp. 122-142. On W. G. Sumner's notion of "ethos or group character," see *Folkways* (New York, 1940), chap. i, secs. 76-79.

of concepts and theories, their incorporation into a society's subjective-cultural heritage, their interrelations with politico-economic development, their passage from generation to generation and from country to country, and so on. It is possible also to discover how much human thought and inquiry are molded or channeled by theoretical and ideological and related categories already present in men's minds, by the nature and the malleability of the language in common use, by the extent and the orientation of current educational practice, by the values which govern what sorts of elite are held in high esteem, etc.[94] But it is not possible to make information of the various sorts described specific and complete enough. (2) It is possible through laboratory and related inquiry to assemble considerable detailed and specific information respecting the formation of concepts, the acquisition of opinions, etc., but it has not been possible to make laboratory conditions resemble real-life situations closely enough,[95] or to establish bases for generalizable propositions.[96]

In Section IV we dealt with the significance of the nature of man's social universe for the validity of his methods of inquiry and for the applicability of his developmental policies. In the West in particular his conception of this universe has undergone change a number of times, and this has affected his formulations of policy as well as his modes of inquiry and explanation. Initially he seems to have gotten his conception of the physical world from that of his social world,[97] but subsequently he sought to interpret his social world

[94] E.g., see De Gre, op. cit.; E. Durkheim, The Elementary Forms of the Religious Life (Glencoe, 1947); Talmon, op. cit.; K. E. Richter, The Development of the Concept Historic and Genetic (Lancaster, 1908), pp. 1-12; representative histories of economic, political, etc., ideas.

[95] See J. S. Bruner et al., A Study of Thinking (New York, 1957), and Ernest Nagel's comments in Scientific American, CXCVI (June, 1957), 153-158. The variegatedness of real-life situations is suggested by H. Elias' account (see "Discovery by Illustration," Scientific Monthly, LXX [1950], 229-232) of the manner in which the need to draw or illustrate body organs accurately led to new discoveries.

[96] Inquiry of the authors of scientific discoveries seldom sheds much light on the precise determinants or antecedents of specific discoveries. E.g., see R. Taton, Reason and Chance in Scientific Discovery (New York, 1957). See also studies such as the following: S. E. Asch's account of the genesis of opinions, attitudes, etc., in his Social Psychology (New York, 1952), chaps. xviii-xix, and in "Opinions and Social Pressure," Scientific American, CXCIII (November, 1955), 31 ff.; B. and J. Mausner, "A Study of the Anti-Scientific Attitude," ibid., CXCII (February, 1955), 35 ff.; W. Dennis, "Animistic Thinking among College and University Students," Scientific Monthly, LXXVI (1953), 247-249.

[97] See note 86 above.

in biological or in physical terms.   In the seventeenth century mechanical or social-physical conceptions of the social world or of its components became ascendant, though they did not entirely supersede biological conceptions.   In the eighteenth century and certainly in the nineteenth the importance attached to organic or biological conceptions increased even though the hold of the conception of the social universe in terms of mechanics and equilibration remained strong.[98]   In the twentieth century the social universe came to be conceived in stochastic terms as well as in terms of mechanical or biological equilibrium.[99]   These changes in conception of the social universe seem to have been much influenced but not dominated by progress in biology, mathematics, physics, and theoretical formulation and discovery in the physical world, or by the capacity of ascending conceptions to afford empirically more tenable conclusions respecting the social world than were supplied by earlier conceptions.   These changes thus appear to be attributable, in much greater degree than are parallel changes in the realm of physical science, to shifts in emphasis in the realm of non-rational value.[100]

Having dealt in a very general way with changes in man's conception of the social universe, together with factors fostering these changes, I shall touch illustratively upon the response of political theory to changing circumstances in the West and then contrast this response with that of economic theory.   The Greek concept of "polis,"

[98] See P. A. Sorokin, *Contemporary Sociological Theories* (New York, 1928); and also *Social and Cultural Dynamics*, II and IV; also note 86 above; also D. Hamilton, *Newtonian Classicism and Darwinian Institutionalism* (Albuquerque, 1958); Stow Persons, ed., *Evolutionary Thought in America* (New Haven, 1950); J. E. King, *Science and Rationalism in the Government of Louis XIV, 1661-1683* (Baltimore, 1949); Cassirer, *Philosophy of the Enlightenment*, pp. 19-20, 31-32.

[99] See E. Zilsel's essay in his and George de Santillana's *The Development of Rationalism and Empiricism*, International Encyclopedia of Unified Science, Vol. II, No. 8 (Chicago, 1941), esp. 60-64, 70-71; 78-94.   For recent economic discussions in biological terms, see A. A. Alchian, "Uncertainty, Evolution, and Economic Theory," *Journal of Political Economy*, LVIII (1950), 211-220; S. Enke, "On Maximizing Profits: A Distinction between Chamberlin and Robinson," *American Economic Review*, XLI (1951), 566-578; E. T. Penrose, "Biological Analogies in the Theory of the Firm," *ibid.*, XLII (1952), 804-819, and discussion in succeeding numbers.

[100] K. Pribram asserts that the organic, mechanical, and dialectical approaches to economic analysis reflect different philosophical approaches much more than they reflect changes in the realm of natural science.   See his "Prolegomena to a History of Economic Reasoning," *Quarterly Journal of Economics*, LXV (1951), 1-37, and "Patterns of Economic Reasoning," *American Economic Review*, Vol. XLIII, No. 2 (1953), pp. 243-258.

though Platonic rather than atomistic in philosophical orientation, referred to the whole of the Greek social system, and that of "constitution," to the totality of social relationships, political activity not yet having become sharply separated from private activity and power, as it was subsequently to become, first in the Hellenistic and Roman worlds and later in a church-dominated Christian world. The concept of "sovereignty" did not evolve and replace that of "dominion" (which associated political power with property), however, until urban civilization had re-emerged, ecclesiastical practice had exemplified the fundamental importance of bureaucracy in political as well as in church government, and internal and international divisions consequent upon the Reformation had facilitated the rise of individuals capable of using the apparatus of state to preserve order and assert the state's identity and autonomy. With the resulting differentiation of the state, together with its apparatus, from the underlying society or community, the concepts of society, state, and sovereignty gradually took on sharp outlines. Developments in the fields of biology and mechanics nonetheless made themselves felt as did revival of interest and confidence in Nature and her laws. Thus the concept of balance of power was introduced into the study of international relations in the seventeenth and eighteenth centuries, thereby giving articulate form to an idea that, Hume asserted, had influenced even ancient statecraft;[101] but the concept of interclass balance, present in Aristotle's formulation[102] of the Greek theory of the sequence of governmental forms, was not effectively dealt with until in the nineteenth century. Still, as Newton's (and his forerunners') "deep searching, saw at last the system dawn,"[103] so did that of social theorists find in society a self-regulating and harmony-producing social mechanism. Societal and state roles were modified accordingly. The role of society was increased. That of the state was constricted and made more residual (in consonance with a newly developed "modern" natural-law ideology that re-

[101] David Hume, "Of the Balance of Power," in *Essays, Moral, Political, and Literary*, ed. T. H. Green and T. H. Grose (London, 1882), I, 348 ff. Revival of emphasis upon intrastate checks and balances was probably prompted in part by the rise of mechanical theory.

[102] See F. Kort, "The Quantification of Aristotle's Theory of Revolution," *American Political Science Review*, XLVI (1952), 486-493.

[103] See James Thomson's poem, *A Poem Sacred to the Memory of Sir Isaac Newton* (1727). Cf. A. N. Whitehead, *op. cit.*, chap. i.

placed a "classical" or "medieval" predecessor natural-law ideology);[104] but this particular constriction proved temporary, for within a century the state's role expanded greatly, under the triple impact of repeated war, a rising *étatistic* ideology, and the emergence of needs supposedly beyond the capacity of private enterprise to supply.[105] Even so, private enterprisers were always counted upon to carry on most economic activities, among them nearly all of the activities whereon economic development depended.

Comparison of the development of economic theory with that of political theory lends some support to three tentative findings. First, during the past two or three centuries, conception, as distinguished from perception, has played a greater part in economics than in political science.[106] The statements of economists have reflected less closely referents existent in the real world. Economists have, of course, used ideas immediately apprehendable from referents present in the market place (e.g., prices, sales and purchases, functional incomes such as wages, business terms, items entering into the balance of payments); but they have put major stress upon ideas such as those signifying functional relationships (e.g., between variations in money supply and in prices, or between variations in prices and variations in quantities offered or demanded) and equilibrating prices (e.g., between supply and demand, or price and cost) that may be inferred from study of the behavior of referents present in the market place. Second, the progress of economic analysis was much more sensitive than was the progress of political analysis

[104] E.g., see V. Pareto, *The Mind And Society* (New York, 1935), esp. Vol. I, paragraphs 401-463; also Strauss's work, cited in note 105.

[105] This paragraph reflects in part observations made by Frederick M. Watkins in *The State as a Concept of Political Science* (New York, 1934). See also Joseph J. Spengler, "The Role of the State," in *The Tasks of Economic History* (which appeared as Supplement VII to *Journal of Economic History*, VII [1947], 123-143), and "The Problem of Order in Economic Affairs," *Southern Economic Journal*, XV (1948), 1-29; K. Freeman, *God, Man and State* (Boston, 1952); and B. F. Hoselitz's paper in Hugh Aitken, ed., *The State And Economic Growth* (Social Science Research Council, New York, 1959). On differences between classical and modern conceptions of natural law and natural rights, see Leo Strauss, *Natural Right and History* (Chicago, 1953), and E. Zilsel, "The Genesis of the Concept of Physical Law," *Philosophical Review*, LI (1942), 245-279. W. Stark contrasts the views of Plato and the atomists in *Sociology of Knowledge*, pp. 40, 171.

[106] This statement is true in much lesser degree of contemporary political science. E.g., see R. D. Calkins, ed., *Research Frontiers in Politics and Government*; also D. Lerner and H. D. Lasswell, eds., *The Policy Sciences* (Stanford, 1951).

to changes and improvements in certain natural sciences (e.g., physics, mechanics, and biology) and in certain "service-sciences" (particularly logic and mathematics). This second difference is in part at least a corollary to the first, since it is only at more general and less reality-bound conceptual levels that any given social science can draw on conceptual advances in other scientific areas. Third, whereas one would expect the two differences just described to enable economic science to improve more rapidly than political science, one finds this expectation confirmed only in part. For example, economists were slow to appreciate the allocative function of competition and economic decision-makers, the role of adjustments at the margin, the usefulness of macroeconomic models of the sort Quesnay introduced, and so on; they were slow also, despite suggestive eighteenth-century and early nineteenth-century examples, to describe economic interdependence mathematically or to incorporate available mathematical and statistical techniques into analytical models designed to describe or analyze economic reality.

The history of political and economic science in the West suggests also that concepts dealing with the social world originate in two ways, one of which is becoming ever more ascendant. Simple, primitive concepts arise quite directly from observation of their referents in the immediate politico-economic world whereas refined and rarefied concepts originate, as do the laws and axioms used to connect concepts with one another, in the minds of theorists. Accordingly, whereas the tenability of primitive concepts is conditioned primarily by their correspondence to their empirical referents, that of rarefied concepts is conditioned at least as much by their internal consistency as by the correspondence of their implications to observations made in the empirical world. Similarly, theories which connect variables in space and/or time reflect the contents, ideological and otherwise, of men's minds; and their coming into being is accordingly conditioned in far greater measure than is the emergence of primitive concepts by the propitiousness of ideological, theoretical, and related considerations.[107] Advancement in a social

[107] For example, ideas of social equilibrium were not derived from mechanics until the seventeenth century, even though they might have been suggested by thirteenth-century theories of mechanical equilibirum (described in Crombie, *op. cit.*, pp. 83-87). Scientific progress in the Middle Ages was greatly retarded, Whitehead believed, by the fact that the schoolmen emphasized classification instead of meas-

science involves the deprimitivization and refinement or rarefication of its concepts.   Hence, as a social science advances, its theoretical content becomes more subjective, more reflective of the contents of theorist's minds, more removed from variegated reality with which it purports to deal.   For this reason social theory tends in time to become self-generating and self-augmenting much as has invention.[108]

What has been said in the last two paragraphs is not applicable to the underdeveloped countries of Asia, in most of which ancient cultures are to be found, and in which, consequently, the content of men's minds differs both from that found in the progressive West, and from that found in backward countries whose culture, being tribal, is relatively easy to decompose and transform, or whose culture, remaining underdeveloped though containing much of European origin, is relatively more congenial to the absorption of practices that have worked in advanced countries.   As a result, in these Asian countries as in those of North Africa, how to get economic development under way is thought of quite differently than in the West.   In these countries, as Shils has noted, a predominantly religious intellectual tradition has persisted and with it "relative indifference toward the intellectual and practical mastery of nature" and its concrete description and analysis; this tendency to persist was reinforced, even in the absence of colonial status, by a lack of both personal incentives and institutional stimulants to develop a technological and engineering tradition, together with the scientific objectivity requisite thereto.   Furthermore, economic and political theory could not or at least did not develop as in the West.   It could not therefore undergird the rationale of political and eco-

urement. See S. S. Stevens, "Measurement and Man," *Science*, CXXVII (1958), 385.   Though men thought in terms of increments centuries before differential calculus was invented, incremental analysis was not utilized in economic analysis until in the eighteenth century.   Seneca (cf. *Benefits*, VI, 15) described what amounts to consumer's surplus when attempting to estimate the amount of "benefit" enjoyed by a beneficiary; yet the notion of consumer's surplus was not developed until the nineteenth century.

[108] "The greatest invention of the nineteenth century was the invention of the method of invention."   See A. N. Whitehead, *Science and the Modern World*, p. 141.   See also Lazarsfeld and Rosenberg, *op. cit.*, esp. pp. 1-12, and R. W. Gerard, "Units and Concepts of Biology," *Behavioral Science*, III (1958), 198-199.   On increasing subjectivity, see Hayek, *Sensory Order*, pp. 170-171.

nomic individualism, make clear how an essentially autonomous economic system works, clothe in esteem the private enterpriser and his role, and emphasize the essential irreplaceability of the motives animating this enterpriser or counted upon by him to get others to perform economic activities.   In consequence, as has been noted, the intellectual leaders in these countries now are counting upon the politicians and the civil service to supply the initiative and the populace "to carry out their schemes" within a socialistic framework of institutions.   They are giving far less scope than was given in the West to motives, values, etc., centered about the individual—far too little, some observers believe, than is essential if development is to get under way and persist.   They are underestimating costs and obstacles and overestimating the ease with which a populace may become disposed to work hard and intelligently for little pay.[109]

Regarding the origin and development of concepts and theories and (in lesser measure) of ideologies and systems of values, all of which are essentially subjective and hence govern interpretations of reality and responses thereto, a number of observations may be made. (1) Language habits and practices, together with the multiplicity and variety of words actually or potentially available, may condition a people's manner of classifying and interpreting perceptions and observations even as it may affect its precision of communication and its receptivity to salutary changes in mental phenomena (e.g., values, value-orientations, concepts, theories).[110] This

[109] This paragraph is based largely upon Shil's papers cited in notes 43 and 44 above. Sometimes, as in the Middle East, Lerner reports, the problem of motivation consists largely in providing the bulk of the areas's population "with clues as to what the better things of life might be." See *The Passing of Traditional Society*, pp. 411-412. Israel is of course an exception. There the problem is one of motivating the people to work whilst curbing their consumption sufficiently to permit the required amount of capital formation. See M. H. Bernstein, "Israel's Capacity to Govern," *World Politics*, XI (1959), 413-416. On the influence of problems upon the content of ideologies, see Mary Matossian, "Ideologies of Delayed Industrialization," *Economic Development and Cultural Change*, VI (1958), 217-228.

[110] E.g., see A. J. Bernatowicz, "Teleology in Science Teaching," *Science*, CCXXVIII (1958), 1402-1405; Granet, *op. cit.*; O. Temkin's account of the role played by metaphor in the formulation of biological views, in R. C. Stauffer, ed., *Science and Civilization*, pp. 169-196. F. L. Lucas remarks the importance of metaphor in the genesis of language in his *Style* (London, 1955), p. 193. But see E. Cassirer's critique of F. Max Müller's description of language as naturally and essentially metaphorical, in *An Essay on Man*, p. 142. On the classificatory role of language, see *ibid.*, pp. 262-263; and on the role of language generally,

circumstance is necessarily one of concern in underdeveloped countries in which "underdeveloped" languages are employed. (2) The progress of social science is conditioned in larger measure than is that of natural science by ideological and related non-rational values,[111] in part at least because natural science has been identified more closely with the world of means than with that of ends. (3) Herein may possibly be found an explanation of the fact that political science was slower than economics to take on the character of a science; for, whereas economics has always been viewed as being concerned solely with means, political science, as envisaged by many of its expounders, was long conceived of as dealing in some degree with ends or quasi-ends as well as with means. (4) Even though the formation of relatively primitive social-science concepts is markedly affected by conditions external to the theorist, their refinement, together with their interconnection in the form of theories or "laws," is accomplished at the mental level and hence becomes subject to the content of the theorist's mind. (5) It is necessary to distinguish between changes in an ideology or a body of theory that are of endogenous origin (i.e., arise from within)[112] and changes that are of exogenous origin (i.e., are occasioned primarily by changes occurring in the world external to the body of theory or ideology). (6) Questions with which scientists (and possibly also ideologists) concern themselves are determined in considerable measure by the nature of the problems that are seriously troubling important groups within a society,[113] but the manner in which these problems are analyzed and resolved is governed largely by the actual and the immediately potential state of knowledge in the relevant body of science at the time particular problems arise. (7) The circumstances governing the de-

---

Schlipp, *op. cit.*, pp. 379-442. For a quite different approach to the role and the development of language, see B. F. Skinner, *Verbal Behavior* (New York, 1957).

[111] E.g., see Stark, *Sociology of Knowledge*, pp. 164-173.

[112] E.g., Talcott Parsons writes: "It is no less probable that a considerable part has been played by an 'immanent' development within the body of social theory and knowledge of empirical fact itself." See *The Structure of Social Action*, p. 5, also pp. 597, 725-726; also P. A. Sorokin, *Society, Culture and Personality*, pp. 696-698. See also Shryock, *op. cit.*, pp. 221-230.

[113] The availability of tools serves in some measure, however, to generate or intensify awareness of particular problems to the solution of which the tools are oriented. See T. J. Koopmans, *Three Essays on the State of Economic Science* (New York, 1957), pp. 170 ff.

velopment and diffusion of an ideology are bound to differ significantly from those which govern the development and diffusion of a scientific theory or concept. Thus propagators of an ideology are more prone to make use of "persuasive definitions"[114] than are expounders of a scientific theory; and the spread of an ideology is likely to encounter different retarding and facilitating circumstances in social space from those encountered by a theory.[115] Even though it is evident that exogenous forces may play an important part in shaping a theory or an ideology, it is not possible to do all that is necessary in order to discover the degree of correspondence actually obtaining between changes in social space exogenous to a body of theory or ideology and changes in this theory or ideology, or supposing some correspondence has been established, to infer how this body of theory or ideology will respond to anticipated future exogenous changes.[116]

[114] "A 'persuasive' definition . . . gives a new conceptual meaning to a familiar word without substantially changing its emotive meaning"; it is used to change, "by this means, the direction of people's interests." See C. L. Stevenson, "Persuasive Definitions," *Mind*, XLVII (1947), 331.

[115] The metrical and topological properties of "social space" are not identical with those of geographical or nonsocial space. See A. Rappoport, "The Diffusion Problem in Mass Behavior," *Yearbook* of the Society for the Advancement of General Systems Theory, I (1956), 50; also P. A. Sorokin, *Sociological Causality, Space, Time* (Durham, N. C., 1943), chap. iii. One might examine the diffusion of ideological and scientific concepts in terms of the factors (together with the principles connecting them) employed in communication theory. These factors are: "(1) the *communicator* who transmits the communication; (2) the *stimuli* transmitted by the communicator; (3) the *individuals* who respond to the communication; (4) the *responses* made to the communication by the communicatee." See C. I. Hovland, "Social Communications," reprinted in B. Berelson and M. Janowitz, *Reader in Public Opinion and Communication* (Glencoe, 1950), p. 182. Even if the communicator of an ideological message were also a scientist, he would not couch this message as he would a communication having to do with his field of scientific specialization. Moreover, he would be addressing a different audience when communicating an ideological message than when communicating a scientific one. Furthermore, even if the audience were physically the same, its members would not be expected to behave similarly in the two situations. See also Ernest Nagel, "The Methods of Science: What Are They? Can They Be Taught?," *Scientific Monthly*, LXX (1950), 19-23; Karl Deutsch, "On Communication Models in the Social Sciences," *Public Opinion Quarterly*, XVI (1952), 386 ff. It is of interest to note that the philosopher Leibniz made use, in his *Monadology*, of phenomenal terms instead of more appropriate noumenal ones, because he believed that at that time phenomenal terms were more easily understood. See Homer H. Dubs, "The Misleading Nature of Leibniz's Monadology," *Philosophical Review*, L (1941), 515-516.

[116] Among the problems that must be solved the following may be noted: (*a*) it is essential to scale both the ideology or theory and each possible exogenous determinant; (*b*) it is essential to determine whether the influence exercised by each exogenous determinant is susceptible of being added to that exercised by other

VII. Content of the Mind: Manipulability

It has been argued thus far that the course and rate of politico-economic development in a country depends largely upon the contents or "elements" present in the minds of such country's inhabitants, and above all, upon the contents of the minds of the elite. There need to be present in the minds of many of the elite, for example, not only values or aspirations to the realization of which economic development is deemed to be absolutely essential,[117] but also beliefs, habits, etc., which prize change and presuppose its possibility,[118] which conduce to the formation of physical and personal (e.g., technical, professional, etc., training) capital, which make for the accumulation and application of development-oriented scientific knowledge, which augment the esteem in which innovators and enterprisers are held, and so on. Where these values prevail, economic development can proceed; where they are lacking, development is not realizable.

It should be noted parenthetically that limitations imposed by the physical environment have been ignored in this discussion. It should also be noted, however, that the values and mental attitudes favorable to economic development cannot flourish in the absence of sufficient progress in literacy, urbanization, and interindividual communication[119]. Changes in these conditions both accompany and contribute to change in the content of men's minds.

---

exogenous determinants, or whether the exogenous determinants are mutually interdependent; (c) it is essential to make allowance for the fact that some of the exogenous determinants may behave as constants in the short run though susceptible of variation in the longer run. Difficulties attendant upon defining social space carefully and locating therein the changing determinants of theories or ideologies make it hard to pass from a paradigm or classificatory stage of inquiry. Such a paradigm has been suggested by R. K. Merton in P. F. Lazarsfeld and M. Rosenberg, eds., *The Language of Social Research* (Glencoe, 1955), pp. 498-510. See also Merton's *Social Theory and Social Structure*, Parts III-IV; also Bertrand Russell, *A History . . ., passim.*

[117] The emphasis here is upon the supposition of essentiality, not upon the empirical tenability of this supposition; it is the supposition that foments the necessary activities, and it can do so as long as its empirical tenability has not been disconfirmed or otherwise undermined.

[118] Modern man, unlike pre-nineteenth-century man, believes in the susceptibility of man's conditions of life to rational control and salutary change. E.g., see Stark, *Sociology of Knowledge*, p. 138; Lerner, *The Passing of Traditional Society*, pp. 48-49.

[119] E.g., see *ibid.*

It has also been argued that the content of the mind is the fulcrum as well as the source of change, whether desirable or not. Change in underlying material conditions usually presupposes change in the contents of the mind, since material conditions are passive whereas mental conditions are potentially dynamic. Of primary importance therefore is the content of the minds of the elite, for changes in this are succeeded, whether through use of persuasion or of force, by appropriate changes in that of the underlying population. The role of the elite, a role whose importance tends to be overlooked in ages and countries in which repetition of shibboleths about "equality" and "democracy" muddy perception, is thus of very great significance in underdeveloped countries. Accordingly, since development cannot be achieved so long as most of the elites are opposed or neutral thereto, its initiation entails the enlisting of enough of the existing elites and/or the creation of new elites who stand to profit from such development.[120]

It has been implied that there is potentially much scope in every society for logical or rational behavior, that is, for the careful selection of alternatives, and that development presupposes the realization of this potential. (i) Within the realm of means to ends rationality manifests itself insofar as it is not suppressed by ignorance of the efficacy of alternative means, or blunted by ideological bias. The scope of the rational may therefore be increased by dissolving sources of ignorance and/or of ideological bias and also by enlarging the magnitude of the universe of choice and decision over which the representative individual believes himself to have some sway—in sum, by substituting the eye of the eagle for that of the worm. (ii) Even within the realm of ends and quasi-ends there is much scope for rationality. There appear to exist very few values or ends the satisfaction of which does not entail the use of scarce means; even worship often absorbs time and other resources that have alternative uses. Yet, whenever alternative use of scarce resources is involved, whether directly or indirectly, some rationality or logicality is necessarily introduced into man's behavior, since then the degree

[120] "No problem is more critical in a modernizing society" than that of "recruiting a functional new elite" whence may come innovators, publicists, and administrators. See Lerner, *The Passing of Traditional Society*, pp. 406-407. See also R. W. Gerard, "Problems in the Institutionalization of Higher Education," *Behavioral Science*, II (1957), 138-139.

of satisfaction realizable of any particular value is subject to the constraint of its being compatible with the satisfaction of competing values.

The elements or values present in the mind are both variously interrelated and differentially sensitive to change. Within a given mind a given value may be complementary to some other value, substitutive for it, repellent to it, or neutral to it. Furthermore, similar patterns of relationships of complementarity, substitutability, repellence, and neutrality are likely to be found in the minds of many individuals who share common cultures or subcultures.[121] Of the values found in any such pattern some will be more accessible to external manipulation or influence, some will be more modifiable and flexible, than will others. It is among the values both accessible to manipulation and quite susceptible of modification that one finds values of strategic concern to those who wish to bring about development-favoring change in underdeveloped countries.

It is possible to identify and sequester values and then classify them in terms of intervalue complementarity, substitutability, repellence, and neutrality. Further analysis may then reveal which of the values or sets of values are most accessible to external manipulation or influence, and which of this selected category are also relatively modifiable. The values found to be both accessible to external influence and relatively modifiable may then be classified into those unfavorable and those favorable to economic development. These values may then be described as of strategic importance for those wishing to orient the values present in the minds of the members of a community more fully to economic development. For whatever weakens accessible and modifiable development-retarding values directly will also in time operate indirectly to weaken various of the development-retarding values which are less accessible and immediately less modifiable; for many of the latter values tend to be complementary to the former. Similarly, whatever serves directly to strengthen accessible and modifiable development-fomenting values also serves to strengthen less accessible and less immediately modi-

[121] E.g., see W. A. Scott, "Empirical Assessment of Values and Ideologies," *American Sociological Review*, XXIV (1959), 299-309, especially 304 ff. See also works cited in note 122 below.

fiable development-fostering values which are complementary to the former.[122]

Which of the contents of the mind answer to the description of strategic as developed in the preceding paragraph? While identification of such values or mental elements lies outside the scope of this paper, an illustration may be found in the values involved in scientific inquiry and objectivity, in what Veblen described as a "passionless matter-of-fact" approach to the study of man and his conditions of life.[123] These values favor technological progress and, as Ayres points out, run counter to the change-opposing "static force of ceremony—status, mores, and legendary belief."[124] It is quite likely also that the diffusion of these values in an underdeveloped society would be accompanied not only by dissipation of what I have called ideology but also by a weakening of many growth-retarding non-rational elements present among the contents of the mind encountered in underdeveloped countries. For, when scientific objectivity, together with the values and instrumental means associated therewith, becomes sufficiently developed and diffused among a people, it apparently becomes self-perpetuating and self-reinforcing. These values may be introduced from abroad as well as developed internally. They may be diffused through educational and related institutions, provided that educational resources are utilized appropriately instead of in the inculcation of casuistical values and of humanistic training beyond a requisite minimum.

Emphasis upon scientific objectivity and related values is not likely, at least in the short run, to foster the development of one type rather than another of politico-economic organization. It would make for rationality in the selection of means and for increase in the care with which the costs of realizing alternative values or objec-

[122] On the clustering of values, etc., see Parsons, *Social System*, chap. v. See also on the difference between the "latent structure of aptitudes and attitudes" of persons ready to modernize and that of those opposed thereto, in Lerner, *The Passing of Traditional Society*, pp. 72-73, 104, 430-446.

[123] See T. Veblen, *The Place of Science in Modern Civilization and Other Essays* (New York, 1919). While the value of science is widely recognized in the underdeveloped world, its application presupposes a suitable conceptualization of "nature." See Northrop, *The Taming of The Nations*, pp. 133-136, 191, and *The Meeting of East and West*, p. 434.

[124] See C. E. Ayres, *The Theory of Economic Progress* (Chapel Hill, 1944), chap. viii; also "The Evolution of the Scientific Point of View," Veblen, *The Place of Science*, pp. 32-35.

tives are assessed. It would also make for recognition of the importance of differential rewards and of appeal to private interests and advantage. But, since differential rewards can be used effectively in a collectivized society, and since many members of the actual or the potential elite in underdeveloped countries deem use of a powerful state-apparatus initially essential to getting economic development underway, it is probable that in many underdeveloped countries the role attempted by the state in the near future will be much greater than it was in the West.[125] In the somewhat less near future, however, given that employment has become comparatively "full," that extreme capital scarcity of the sort characteristic of underdeveloped countries has been alleviated, and that it has become possible to satisfy a wide variety of consumer demands, a considerable decentralization of entrepreneurial decision-making, together with an increasing reliance upon the price system for guidance, is to be expected.[126]

[125] For illustrations of this role see also Hugh G. J. Aitken, ed., *State and Economic Growth* (New York, 1959); S. Kuznets, W. E. Moore, and J. J. Spengler, eds., *Economic Growth: Brazil, India, Japan* (Durham, N. C., 1955).

[126] E.g., see *ibid.*, pp. 378-379. The tendency to decentralization at the center will be accentuated also by the need to decentralize economic authority and permit greater regional autonomy as regions relatively removed from what had been the center of economic gravity become developed.

2

The Social Framework of Economic Development

Wilbert E. Moore

INTRODUCTORY

A standard complaint by many sociologists and anthropologists that economists do not adequately take into account "cultural" or "social" or "institutional" factors is scarcely justified as applied to those economists studying economic growth. With sufficient frequency that it may now be taken as a norm, such economists explicitly recognize that entrepreneurship, capital formation, labor transfers, technological innovation, or rationalization of production and distribution depend upon and interact with a complex social matrix. Both for empirical and theoretical research and for counsel on developmental policies, identification and analysis of the "factors" in economic growth clearly require crossing conventional disciplinary boundaries. This the economists have explicitly recognized.[1] The blunt fact is that they have been asking pointed and often acutely perceptive questions of other social scientists and getting vague, hortatory, or no answers.

The present paper will not provide a set of the answers needed, wrapped in a small, neat package. It will endeavor, however, to indicate the way a sociologist may provide a view of social factors in economic development that is somewhat more systematic than the

[1] See especially James S. Dusenberry, "Some Aspects of the Theory of Economic Development," *Explorations in Entrepreneurial History*, III (1950), 63-102; Everett E. Hagen, "The Process of Economic Development," *Economic Development and Cultural Change*, V (1957), 193-215; Simon Kuznets, "Toward a Theory of Economic Growth," in Robert Lekachman, ed., *National Policy for Economic Welfare at Home and Abroad* (Garden City, 1955).

usual pious and inconsequential insistence on the relevance of culture.

Generalization is both important and hazardous. At a minimum, a discussion of the social framework of economic development should provide a systematic check-list of variables for particular analyses. A somewhat more ambitious aim, which it is hoped the ensuing discussion will partially achieve, is to establish among the relevant variables types of relationships which will be applicable to any particular area by a process of filling in details. The maximum aim of theory is to establish highly general "laws" of economic growth. The hope for this achievement is, it appears, premature, although suggestive attempts have been made and are by no means fruitless.

The hazards of generalization include the sometimes dismaying complexity and diversity of social systems. These difficulties are not to be treated lightly. True believers in cultural relativism (or national differences) resist attempts at generalizations about societies, or even about more limited processes like economic development. This is sometimes called the "Pango Pango Principle," namely, that for every generalization about structural relationships in social systems there is an exception, known best by the objector, in some suitably obscure corner of the world. Yet it is the point of view adopted here that it is possible and appropriate to deal with the major functional areas observable in any continuing society (e.g., biological reproduction, socialization of the young, economic production, maintenance of order) and to analyze the general or typological relations that pertain among the specific structures that fulfil these universal functions.[2]

Generalization also, however, involves a difficulty of an intrinsic sort. Theory construction is a process of abstraction, the counterpart of which is loss of information. No theory will yield a *specific* prediction, or yield a *specific* guide to policy (given an end to be achieved) except by reversing the process and adding information to the general proposition. The excuse for this elementary exercise in logic is simply that the principle is often overlooked by hard-pressed decision-makers when they seek guidance from scientists. Even scholars expert in particular eras and areas tend to resent "glib" generalization that is "too far" removed from the rich reality of social experience.

[2] See Marion J. Levy, Jr., *The Structure of Society* (Princeton, 1952).

The present paper aims, then, to outline a way of analyzing the social framework of economic development and to note at least some generalizations concerning relationships among standard variables. This will be done by identifying four "levels" of analysis of social systems, which, since we are dealing with *systems*, are interdependent but may be conveniently distinguished. These are identified as ideological, institutional, organizational, and motivational. The "ideological" level concerns common orientations, including notably ultimate values and specific collective goals and aspirations. The "institutional" level, namely, normative complexes relating to major functions or aspects of social systems, also relates essentially to the society as a whole. The "organizational" level is concerned with concrete subsystems of society. The "motivational" level is concerned with translating institutional and organizational prescriptions into behavior, although here we are of course not primarily concerned with the individual personality as a system but only with motivated action as the agency of social relationships and institutional order and change.

Ideological Framework[3]

Standard anthropological and sociological analyses of societies, cultures, and lesser social systems place great emphasis on the "integrative" function of "values." The emphasis is not misplaced, if it stops with the functional importance of ultimate explanations and justifications for specific beliefs, rules, and patterns of action. The emphasis is misplaced, however, if such values are regarded as immutable, and therefore as "permanent" sources of differences in social systems or at least as tremendous barriers to the acceptance of any such social novelty as new forms of economic activity. Precisely because of their pervasive, integrative function, values are likely to be slow to change, and to furnish resistance to innovation in subtle ways. Nevertheless, some value changes do occur, and "traditions" may evolve, become adapted to objective changes in social

[3] This section is drawn primarily from Arnold S. Feldman and Wilbert E. Moore, "Social Structure," in Moore and Feldman, eds., *Labor Commitment and Social Change in Developing Areas* (to be published by the Social Science Research Council), chap. iv.

conditions, and even decline.[4] Crude historical experience also offers ample evidence that ideologies are transferable between social systems. Thus belief systems ranging from the strictly religious (such as Christianity or Islam[5]) to the seemingly secular (such as economic development[6]) have shown remarkable powers of expansion among otherwise diverse cultures.

First-Order Requirements

One of the most commonly noted features of industrial societies is their internal diversification. A complex division of economic function is integrated through the impersonal operation of the market or the quasi-impersonal discipline of administrative organizations. Urbanization and other forms of geographical mobility potentially bring together people of highly diverse backgrounds. Income and status differences result in quite variable styles of life. A multitude of associations vie for members, whether to press economic and political interests or simply to represent expressive and recreational affinities.

Behind such diversity there are three principal common orientations: a minimal cognitive consensus, an acquiescence in if not positive acceptance of a normative order without which co-ordination could not emerge from specialization, and a minimal consensus on ultimate values.

The importance of formal education in providing common cognitive orientations will be noted below. Many less formal agencies of socialization operate also—at work, in the market, in urban neighborhoods. Increasingly, also, "mass communication" media are used both for quick dissemination of information and for propaganda and persuasion. The person in transitional situations must learn a multitude of facts and skills, from survival tactics in urban traffic to the arbitrary divisions of life's activities into temporal units.

The normative order will be a central concern in the following section but needs one point of emphasis here. It is in the general nature of rules to be specific, and therefore to arise in particular

[4] See Bert F. Hoselitz, "Tradition and Economic Growth" in this volume.

[5] See Ishtiaq Husain Qureshi, "Islamic Elements in the Political Thought of Pakistan," in this volume.

[6] See Wilbert E. Moore, "Creation of a Common Culture," *Confluence*, IV (1955), 229-238.

action contexts. It does appear, however, that more general normative orientations operate pervasively. Promptness and a rational orientation to decisions are two examples of such generalized norms in industrial systems. The transferability of such norms from one action pattern to another not only aids individual role-playing, but also serves indirectly to maintain the systemic (or integrative) character of highly specialized substructures.

A minimum value concensus is also a theoretical necessity of a viable social order. Not only is the normative order usually referable to common values, but such values may be given specific ideological explication and thus serve as direct incentives to appropriate action.[7] Standards of equity and justice; the allocation of wealth, power, and position; the maintenance of institutional balance—these serve as value premises for particular sets of rules. Additionally, political and religious ideologies may provide goals as well as standards of conduct.

The debate over the importance of Protestantism in the rise of capitalism is now largely academic, yet the general problem of ultimate values is not. The mystical elements in nationalism, the transformation of "scientific socialism" into religious doctrine, the very acceptance of economic development as a goal serve as warnings that common ultimate values cannot be dismissed as inconsequential for policies and patterns of action.

Economic Development as a Goal. The growth and diffusion of the desire for a common minimum level of living is an outstanding feature of the postwar world. In a sense, for perhaps the first time in the history of the modern world a universal goal is gradually evolving. Even in cultures traditionally based on an ideological system that emphasizes other-worldliness, the desire for change in this world is constantly increasing. Indeed, the desire for such change has itself become a *spiritual* force of great importance in those areas of the world.[8]

Although it may be impossible to state in detail the specific content of the goal of economic development, it undoubtedly in-

---

[7] See Joseph J. Spengler, "Theory, Ideology, Non-Economic Values and Politico-Economic Development" in this volume; also Levy, *op. cit.*, pp. 168-197.

[8] Moore, "Creation of a Common Culture," *loc. cit.*, also Feldman and Moore, "Commitment of the Industrial Labor Force," in Moore and Feldman, *op. cit.*, chap. i.

cludes a certain minimum economic standard, particularly in regard to the material conditions of life. The type of change required, then, is to a considerable extent change in socio-economic institutions. Thus economic development can be interpreted both as an end and as a means to that end.

The ideological goal is a necessary but by no means sufficient condition for social transformation. The "means" turn out to be new patterns of daily existence, and thus in conflict with an intricately interrelated social structure. These patterns of behavior and their normative sanctions in turn relate to goals and values other than economic development or material well-being. Since material well-being is not the sole goal of any society, and could not be if it is to survive as a viable system, the value conflict is not trivial or simply based on temporary ignorance or misunderstanding.

Second-Order Requirements

The undoubted costs (in terms of value sacrifices) entailed in economic development may be partially offset not only by new distributive rewards of one sort or another, but by additional collective ideologies.

Nationalism. It is commonly, and probably correctly, assumed that wherever economic development becomes a matter of public policy (and that is nearly everywhere), the state is likely to play an active role, at least wherever critical barriers appear. Although the economic activity of the state in the historic "laissez-faire" economies should not be minimized,[9] there is ample reason to assume that the contemporary state will figure more largely as an agent of growth than was true in the past.[10] Questions of political loyalty and participation therefore assume an importance directly relevant to economic development, in addition to the structural position of the state as the focus of national integration and identity and the ultimate enforcement agency for social codes.

[9] See Joseph J. Spengler, "Laissez-Faire and Intervention: A Potential Source of Historical Error," *Journal of Political Economy*, LVII (1949), 438-441.

[10] See Henry G. Aubrey, "Role of the State in Economic Development," *American Economic Review*, XLI (1951), 266-273; G. Gambia, "The Role of the State in Underdeveloped Areas," *Economic Record*, XXIX (1953), 245-256; Bert F. Hoselitz, "Economic Policy and Economic Development," in Hugh G. J. Aitken, ed., *The State and Economic Growth* (New York, 1950), chap. xii.

The repeated association between deliberate economic development and extreme nationalism is surely not accidental. Nationalism presents an essentially non-rational unifying force that may ease and rationalize the hardships of personal change. This explicitly common ideology increases in importance precisely to the degree that rapid economic transition is likely to undermine various "intermediate" social structures that shared or even captured loyalties in the preindustrial system.[11]

INSTITUTIONAL FRAMEWORK

It is the general function of institutions, as complexes of norms, to relate standard patterns of actions in a society—often encompassed in concrete social organizations—to the general system of functional requirements and values of that society. This statement, although cryptic, has some implications that are substantive as well as conceptual. The set of prescriptions and expectations comprised by the institution of monogamous marriage, for example, appears, correctly, to have primary relevance to family and household composition. By the same token, however, the institution has relevance for the heterosexual relations of adults generally, the socialization of the young, the mode of distribution of goods and services, the modes of assigning general social status, and—in more attenuated ways—maintenance of order and preservation of values. In other words, assignment of an institutional complex to a particular functional area —familial, economic, political, religious—is always in some measure improper. It is precisely one function of institutions that they be *relational,* that is, that they provide the bonds or cement among particular patterns of social action.

These general comments are prompted by the circumstance that

[11] See David E. Apter, *The Gold Coast in Transition* (Princeton, 1955); Apter, "Political Organization and Ideology," in Moore and Feldman, *op. cit.* James C. Coleman, "Nationalism in Tropical Africa," in Lyle W. Shannon, ed., *Underdeveloped Areas* (New York, 1957), 37-52; Manning Nash, "Some Social and Cultural Aspects of Economic Development," *Economic Development and Cultural Change,* VII (1959), 137-150.

Hoselitz, in his paper in this volume, notes that explicit traditionalism is a common reaction to current crises accompanying economic change. See also Mary Matossian, "Ideologies of Delayed Industrialization: Some Tensions and Ambiguities," *Economic Development and Cultural Change,* VI (1958) 217-228

we shall here be sketching the significance of institutions that are in the first instance "economic," before moving to "political," "educational," and other institutions.   In no instance, however, is the designation precise, since we shall be dealing always with *degrees* of relevance for the production and distribution of goods and service.

First-Order Requirements

Traditional economic analysis would have dealt with land, labor, and capital as "factors of production" and later theorists would add "entrepreneurship" or "organization."   This conceptual framework has basic difficulties, as there is really little sensible or useful distinction between land and capital, and entrepreneurship may properly be considered a particular kind of skilled labor.   It seems preferable, therefore, to adopt a somewhat different conceptual scheme. We shall here deal with three interrelated institutional complexes— property, labor, and exchange.   All three seem to define aspects of relations between persons and "things"—their control, transformation, and distribution.   However, all also define social relationship— between owners and non-owners, between persons performing various productive roles, between persons involved in distribution.   No society is or could be lacking in rules governing such relationships, but their form and content differ and these differences are centrally relevant for the possibilities of economic development.

Property.   A property relationship is at the minimum triadic: the person or other social unit, the object or locus of scarce values, and the potential challenger to "rights."   Property relationships may also be very complex, with various social units holding common or diversified rights in the same locus of value, varying rights of disposal, transfer, use, and appropriation of increase.[12]

The important point in the present context is that the property systems of most underdeveloped areas do not favor modern forms of economic enterprise.   This is generally true, for example, of the older property laws and practices in Latin America.   The application in the Spanish colonies of quasi-feudal land-tenure conceptions (often through the specific forms of the *repartimiento* and *encomienda,* which "entrusted" indigenous populations and their labor to land-

[12] See Wilbert E. Moore, "The Emergence of New Property Conceptions in America," *Journal of Legal and Political Sociology,* I (1943), 34-58.

lords) encouraged large estates but not necessarily their efficient operation or easy transfer to more efficient producers. The *hacienda* system and often other forms of plantation agriculture have often been wasteful of both labor and capital (land and its fertility). Perhaps most importantly it established the basis of a socio-economic elite dedicated to traditional economic and social forms.

Modifications of traditional property systems have not necessarily brought them "closer" to the institutional requirements for economic development. Sale and other forms of non-hereditary transfers are generally easier, but titles are not uniformly secure, introducing a risk in capital investments that may discourage modernization of productive technique. "Land reforms," on the other hand, may lead to more intensive utilization but often still with archaic techniques and with overcapitalization of equipment that must be held by each cultivator of a small holding. The Mexican *Ejido*, which was of course undertaken primarily in the interests of social justice rather than economic modernization—in this it was like most land reforms—has not encouraged transferability of property and has probably contributed to hidden unemployment in agriculture.[13] Put in the bluntest possible terms, peasant proprietorship is more likely to impede than to facilitate economic development.

Fears of domination by foreign capital have been linked in many newly developing countries with nationalistic values and concern for social welfare to produce regulation of enterprises (that is, limits on property rights) in forms and degrees that may have discouraged private investment. The particular issues and instances are too numerous and complex to be argued here. The economic sector of a society can never be autonomous and subject only to economic "laws." The question is raised here, however, as to whether particular economic policies have been optimal in their accomplishment of various social objectives, including the objective of economic development.[14]

Any property system consistent with modern forms of produc-

---

[13] See Wilbert E. Moore, *Industrialization and Labor* (Ithaca, 1951), pp. 237-238; Beate R. Salz, *The Human Element in Industrialization*, published as a supplement to *Economic Development and Cultural Change*, Vol. IV, No. 1, (1955), pp. 1-265.

[14] See P. A. Baran, "On the Political Economy of Backwardness," *Manchester School*, XXIII (1952), 66-84.

tion tends to "expropriate" the worker from ownership of most tools of production. The avoidance of this by socialist organization or nationalization of capital is only partial and partly fictitious, since essential controls of capital allocation and disposition remain in the hands of relatively limited members. The economies of scale characteristic of modern economic enterprise can be achieved only by correlative unity of control, however the ancillary rights and benefits may be distributed.

Labor. The norms governing productive work are simply aspects of more general norms that control status and role assignments in a continuing social order. In a non-industrial or, more properly, in a non-market economy the separation of useful activities into "labor" and "other" is likely to be difficult and abstract, except with reference to the production of physical goods.[15] Any society is characterized by considerable specialization of roles, including, in this narrow sense, productive roles. Generally, although not entirely,[16] this specialization in non-industrial societies is determined on grounds of age, sex, kinship, and hereditary social position. Competence is then developed for predetermined positions in the process of socializing the young. Such an institutional structure is likely to function adequately for limited specialization and minimal change. It is scarcely suitable for an economic system that entails extensive specialization and relatively rapid change in occupational structure. The difficulty of institutional adaptation is made more acute by the circumstances that new forms of demand for labor represent a radical shift in social role, and are intrusive in the traditional structure.

The quantitative supply of labor is generally adequate in under-developed areas, and in many instances redundant relative to given employment opportunities. Labor shortages are of two sorts: (1) unskilled and badly paid workers for agricultural monocultures, where employers have difficulty in holding employees if any other opportunities exist; (2) an endemic shortage of skills of all sorts.

Much has been written about the various socio-psychological barriers to labor recruitment and efficient utilization in newly develop-

[15] See Wilbert E. Moore, "The Exportability of the 'Labor Force' Concept," *American Sociological Review*, XVIII (1953), 68-72.
[16] See Stanley H. Udy, Jr., *Organization of Work: A Comparative Analysis of Production among Nonindustrial Peoples* (New Haven: HRARF Press, 1959).

ıng areas.[17] However, the realities of landlessness and other forms of poverty, and the existence of craft skills among predominantly "agricultural" sectors of the productive population combine to make labor transfers feasible.

Among the many institutional difficulties with respect to labor mobility, several may be especially noted. Strong traditional attachments to the land (with ancillary handicraft production) discourage movement to other modes of production without the pressure of poverty. Moreover, where large-scale agriculture is the norm, various covert forms of peonage or debt servitude are by no means unknown. Finally, it is arguable that "advanced" labor legislation in many newly independent countries may possibly ease the transition from the worker's point of view, but not from that of the entrepreneur, since economic support of high labor protection may rest upon higher labor productivity than typically prevails in pioneering enterprises.

The problem of securing enterprisers, managers, and technicians for modern economic production is partly educational—the sheer undersupply of skills. The institutional order in the normative sense is also relevant, however.[18] Traditional forms of division of labor have placed considerable value on public administration and the older professions, less on business administration, risk-taking investments, or various kinds of engineering. It is not clear how acute this institutional barrier to development may be, but there is some suggestion that both managerial innovation and capital formation are hindered by persistent high evaluation of a "leisure class" and the

---

[17] See Moore, *Industrialization and Labor.*

[18] See Yale Brozen, "Entrepreneurship and Technological Change," in Harold F. Williamson and John A. Buttrick, eds., *Economic Development: Principles and Patterns* (New York, 1954), chap. vi; Frederick H. Harbison, "Entrepreneurial Organization as a Factor in Economic Development," *Quarterly Journal of Economics,* LXX (1956), 364-374; Frederick H. Harbison and Charles A. Myers, *Management in the Industrial World* (in press); Bert F. Hoselitz, "Entrepreneurship and Economic Growth," *American Journal of Economics and Sociology,* XII (1952), 97-110.

Feldman and I have commented:

"The importance of managerial skills . . . should not be exaggerated into a doctrine of 'entrepreneurial determinism,' which would imply that the notable barriers to effective labor supply of all types could be erased by the comparatively simple expedient of training managers with appropriate leadership and even manipulative talents. The supply of executives and coordinators depends upon both educational and motivational qualifications. *The same is true of other occupations.*" (Feldman and Moore, "The Market," in Moore and Feldman, *op. cit.,* p. 47).

choice of current luxury consumption over reinvestment and productive expansion.

Exchange. Some minimum form of exchange prevails in any society, for transfer of products from the specialized producer to the generalized consumer. However, the elaboration of exchange relationships *may* be no greater than the degree of productive specialization. Typically, too, exchange relations are closely intertwined with other social bonds in preindustrial societies. Even "markets," which are a feature of many agrarian areas, may involve a complex of social relationships and of barter according to traditional terms of trade rather than consideration of current supply and demands.[19]

Economic development depends upon institutional transformation in the direction of "impersonal" markets, not only for goods but also for labor. These are linked by profits, salaries, and wages, all of which are virtually meaningless in the absence of a commodity market. Wherever transportation facilities and communications permit in Africa, Asia, and Latin America, there is evidence of the gradual or abrupt transformation of traditional trading relations into something approximating the economists' model of a market.[20]

Second-Order Requirements

In addition to those normative complexes that have primary relevance for the production and distribution of goods there are other systems of values and prescriptions for behavior that modify or affect the course of economic development. Although the question of the temporal order of institutional changes is by no means irrelevant,[21] these additional institutional requirements for economic development will be treated here primarily in a static, functional context.

Political Order. Because manufacturing and "primary" production, as distinct from many aspects of trade and commerce, depend heavily on fixed capital installations, political order is a prime req-

[19] See Talcott Parsons and Neil Smelser, *Economy and Society* (Glencoe, 1956); M. R. Solomon, "Structure of the Market in Underdeveloped Economics," *Quarterly Journal of Economics*, LXII (1948), 519-541.
[20] See Richard H. Holton, "Changing Demand and Consumption," in Moore and Feldman, *op. cit.*
[21] See Wilbert E. Moore, "Problems of Timing, Balance, and Priorities in Development Measures," *Economic Development and Cultural Change*, II (1954), 239-248.

uisite for most forms of economic development.[22]   This require-ment is accentuated by the extensive development of a credit struc-ture, often on long-term bases, that characterizes both the capitaliza-tion and the trade of industrial societies. The *area* of political order is, moreover, of some importance, since the "factors of production" for manufacturing must typically be assembled from scattered places, often transcending national boundaries.[23]

The notable political instability in many underdeveloped coun-tries cannot fail, accordingly, to have an adverse effect on many forms of economic development. Mere transfers of power, with or without electoral sanction, may have little consequence, of course, but rapid changes in legislation and administration set up difficult if not impossible conditions for long-term planning and commit-ment of resources.

Science and Technology. Modern economic production rests heav-ily upon the development of science. Initially, it is the systematic knowledge of the non-human environment that is paramount, but large-scale production and distribution and the persistently trouble-some questions of human aspirations also make *social* knowledge rel-evant.[24] The development of exact science and its application to particular problems in the form of various technologies rest upon education systems and research establishments, but these in turn rest upon norms that specify a rational, problem-solving orientation to the natural and social universe.

It is often noted that late-comers in the process of economic development are heirs to the accumulated technology of the older industrial areas, and thus do not need a complete recapitulation of the sequence of the time initially required for that accumulation. It is less often noted that any technology is part of a functional con-text, beginning with such mundane considerations as parts' suppliers and repair facilities, extending to skilled technicians, and finally to the institutional system itself. When we add the important qualifi-cation that many technical developments are "labor-saving," which is not a matter of fundamental economic importance in most under-developed areas, we have seriously modified the easy acceptance of the "acceleration principle" in the diffusion of technology.

[22] Nash, *op. cit. passim.*
[23] See Wilbert E. Moore, *Economy and Society* (Garden City, 1955).
[24] See especially Joseph J. Spengler's paper in this volume.

New Modes of Stratification. The previous discussion of property and labor institutions implied a further institutional requirement for economic development: the establishment and normative sanctioning of new methods of social evaluation and rewards. Economic development entails, for a shorter or longer transitional period, competing *systems* of social stratification. Ethnic origin and family lineage, position in a rural, land-based community, or membership in traditional elites are challenged by the rise of what is elliptically called the "middle class."[25] What actually happens in the early course of industrialization is the appearance and growth of new occupational groups, but also of new class distinctions based on new modes of productive organization.[26] Subsequent developments tend to diversify the bases of differentiation and to blur "class" lines that extend across very numerous occupational groups. All of this, however, implies a basic change in institutional structure, particularly in the direction of "status achievement" as a norm.

Organization and Institutionalization of Change. In most societies in the history of the world, change has been largely unintentional and often simply the response to natural or social crises. It is a special feature of industrial societies that a great deal of social, including economic, change is deliberate. This is closely related to the norms governing science and technology, particularly as the latter are viewed in an appropriately extended sense. Historically it appears that the development of change as a *norm* was slow and characteristic precisely of inventors and entreprenuers. In the contemporary world the primary source of this institutional transformation is likely to be governmental, only gradually extending to more "private" sectors of social systems. The acceptance and active fostering of the "rational spirit" in all aspects of social behavior,[27] with

[25] See Theo R. Crevenna, ed., *Materiales Para el Estudio de la Clase Media en la America Latina* (Washington, D. C.: Departamento de Asuntos Culturales, Union Pan-Americana, 1950-51), 6 vols.

[26] See Arnold S. Feldman, "Men and Machines," *Challenge*, Vol. 8, No. 3 (1958), pp. 62-66; Melvin M. Tumin, "Competing Status Systems," in Moore and Feldman, *op. cit.*, chap. xv.

[27] See Wilbert E. Moore, "Measurement of Organizational and Institutional Implications of Changes in Productive Technology," in International Social Science Council, *Social, Economic, and Technological Change: A Theoretical Approach* (Paris, 1958), pp. 229-259. See also the excellent discussion of the interrelations between ideology and social theory in Spengler's paper in this volume.

its attendant subversion of the power of tradition, appears to be a necessary if often unwelcome correlate of economic growth.[28]

Recapitulation

If one were to attempt a one-word summary of the institutional requirements of economic development, that word would be *mobility*. Property rights, consumer goods, and laborers must be freed from traditional bonds and restraints, from aristocratic traditions, quasi-feudal arrangements, paternalistic and other multi-bonded relations.

In somewhat extensive terms, *part* of the relations in a modern "industrialized" society, and particularly that part relating to the production and distribution of commodities, must be near the pole of universalistic, functionally specific, impersonal, affectively neutral relations.[29] Since no society could long remain cohesive on the basis of such normative patterns alone, there tends to be an especially acute dynamic tension in the institutions of industrialized societies. This is one of the subtler sources of their continuous change, but this has been too little analyzed to allow precise theoretical statement of forms and direction of changes in normative patterns.

ORGANIZATIONAL FRAMEWORK

Institutional complexes are translated into patterns of action partly through concrete subsystems of society. Although forms of rationally constituted productive organization are probably much more common in preindustrial societies than is commonly supposed,[30] they constitute a central and pervasive characteristic of economically advanced societies.

First-Order Requirements

The organizational requirements of modern economic systems are in one sense true by definition. That is, if industrialization is

---

[28] The confrontation between the "rational spirit" and the "power of tradition" presented here is too sharp, as the Hoselitz paper in this volume makes clear. See also Matossian, *op. cit.*

[29] See Talcott Parsons, *The Social System* (Glencoe, 1951), pp. 66-67, 101-112.

[30] See Udy, *op. cit.*

equated with factory production, all that remains is to specify the social characteristics of the latter. However, it is also true that almost any economic development will require rationalization of organization and the creation of concrete systems of action designed for specific and limited functions.

The theoretical statement of organizational requirement rests on less solid ground than appears at a superficial view. Neither in empirical nor analytical terms have the range and adaptability of productive and distributive systems been adequately explored.

Rational Organization of Work. Whether in "primary" production, manufacturing, or commercialized services, the productive efficiency of modern economic systems rests in large measure on specialization and the organized co-ordination of specialized activities. Older economic theory neglected this feature of productive organization by persistent emphasis on co-ordination through market mechanisms or exchange. This neglect persists wherever economic analysis rests upon the supposed decisions of singular "entrepreneurs" rather than the complex decisional processes of administrative organizations.

The fact is that a great deal of the co-ordinative counterpart of specialization in modern economics rests on *authority*. This remains true whether the ultimate source of authority is "public" or "private," whether resting upon "property" or on "function." Within organizations this authority is distributed in terms of spheres of competence, on "scalar" principles of delegation but also in terms of technical knowledge and competence.

The ideal model of the rational administrative organization is well known, but as a theoretical conception rather than on the basis of empirical experience. It is never pure in fact, and probably could not be. Approximations to the model, however, appear on the basis of crude historical experience to have stood the test of productive efficiency.

Such organizations, modified in various ways by particular historical circumstances and adaptation to social systems largely organized on other principles, are now generally to be found in government and public administration in underdeveloped areas.

There are, however, certain noteworthy difficulties even in this area of social life, and the difficulties become more acute as one moves to the predominantly economic sectors of social systems. The principal problems are closely interrelated. (1) There are departures, often major, from the primacy of competence in selection and promotion, and from the primacy of organizational over individual interests.[31] (2) In any event, given various restrictions on intergenerational and career mobility, and the correlative paucity of educational facilities, recruitment tends to be confined to very small segments of the social structure. At the same time the role of foreign administrators and technicians presents its own problems.[32] There is a strong and understandable temptation on the part of national governments to insist on various quotas of nationals in administrative positions, an insistence that may or may not violate the primacy of competence.

Modifications of the formal model of rational administrative organizations are many, especially in the form of adaptations to social systems lacking in "industrial traditions." It should be noted, however, that seemingly short-term transitional measures may be "frozen into" organizations (such as the failure to develop local skilled-labor supplies) with long-term adverse consequences for continuing increases in productivity.

Specific Organizational Forms. The triumph of manufacturing over primary and craft production is not the sole, and perhaps not even an essential, organizational characteristic of economic development. Financial organizations, the development of "social overhead" capital expansion such as communication, transportation, and power facilities, and the organization of trade—any or all of these and others may prove to be the particular strategic factors in programs of deliberate development of the economy.[33]

Second-Order Requirements

Since the economy can never be an autonomous sector of social systems, other types of social organization are also relevant to eco-

[31] See Cyril S. Belshaw, "Adaptation of Personnel Policies," in Moore and Feldman, *op. cit.*, chap. vi; Peter B. Hammond, "Management in Economic Transition," in *ibid.*, chap. vii; Melville J. Herskovits, "The Organization of Work," *ibid.*, chap. viii.
[32] See Mason Wade, "Social Change in French Canada," in this volume.
[33] See United Nations, *Measures for the Economic Development of Under-Developed Countries* (New York, 1951), *passim.*

nomic development. Some of the principal ones are sketched briefly in the following paragraphs.

Residential Location—Urbanization. Historically, the economic transformation of the "advanced" industrial countries was closely related to the rapid growth of cities. It is sometimes argued that modern technology, particularly readily transportable sources of power, decreases the dependence of industry on urban concentration.[34] It remains true, however, that at least the pattern of community organization is transformed along with economic change, and that a change in residential location will be required of substantial portions of the population.

The correlation between industrialization and urbanization is not perfect in any event. Large cities have developed in many countries as "cultural" and governmental centers, as "overgrown villages" of agriculturalists, as residences of absentee landlords, and as centers of trade.[35] Much of the future economic growth will probably be centered in these urban areas, simply because they are there and provide both pools of labor and various public facilities.[36] Continued urbanization, including the growth of new population centers, is to be expected.

Unions and Other Occupational Groups. It is typical of the transfer of large numbers of workers to new employments, often in new locations, that new organizations will develop around common occupational interests or common employee status. (These two principles of "economic" group formation stand in a somewhat dialectic relation in all industrial societies. Emphasis on either principle does not completely suppress the alternative).

Such organizations often, indeed commonly, have strong political

[34] See Henry G. Aubrey, "Small Industry in Economic Development, *Social Research,* XVIII (September, 1951), 269-312.

[35] See Kingsley Davis and Ana Casis, "Urbanization in Latin America," *Milbank Memorial Fund Quarterly,* Vol. XXIV, Nos. 2 and 3 (1946), pp. 186-207.

[36] Of the very extensive literature on urbanization, the following sources are especially valuable: Kingsley Davis and H. H. Golden, "Urbanization and the Development of Pre-Industrial Areas," *Economic Development and Cultural Change,* III (October, 1954), 6-24; Bert F. Hoselitz, "The City, the Factory, and Economic Growth," *American Economic Review,* XLV (1955), 166-184; and "The Role of Cities in the Economic Growth of Underdeveloped Countries," *Journal of Political Economy,* LXI (1953), 195-208; UNESCO, *Social Implications of Industrialization and Urbanization in Africa South of the Sahara* (London, 1956); Philip M. Hauser, ed., *Urbanization in Asia and the Far East* (Calcutta, Research Centre on the Social Implications of Industrialization in Southern Asia, UNESCO, 1957).

orientations as "protest movements," particularly at early stages of industrialization and persistently where democratic political institutions are meagerly developed.[37]   It should be noted that "class polarization" in the new system of stratification introduced by economic development is likely to be greatest at *early* stages of the transition, when managers and workers are typically drawn from quite distinct segments of the pre-existing social system, and the development of multitudinous "intermediate" positions is not far advanced.

The new organizational forms, which are to be expected in any case, will usually be viewed with misgivings or hostility by "entrepreneurs" and often by governmental officials as well. The point of present concern is that such groups rarely represent "economic" interests alone, and may facilitate rather than impede economic transition by providing substitutes for traditional social bonds. In some instances, admittedly rare, labor organizations may act as recruiters of industrial workers and develop programs ranging from education to recreation in factory towns.[38]

New Forms of Voluntary Associations. To speak of voluntary associations as organizational "requirements" of economic development may appear to be an exaggeration. Yet the historic fact is that the expansion of organizations ranging from the political pressure group to the primarily expressive or recreational body has accompanied urban industrialization. Sociological theory suggests that this is more than historical chance. Involvement in highly specific and often casual and temporary economic relations, together with occupational and residential mobility, leaves to the individual both time and disposition to join or organize groups around his various life interests. Except where some form of totalitarian control and integration of groups is attempted, this may still leave an essentially fractionated individual. Moreover, the evidence of formal associational memberships in industrial societies dictates some cautions. "Joiners" are commonly not drawn from socio-economic groups that

[37] See William H. Knowles, "Industrial Conflict and Unions," in Moore and Feldman, *op. cit.*, chap. xvi.
[38] For a description of multifunctional unions (*sindicatos*) in Mexico, see Moore, *Industrialization and Labor*, pp. 239-240, 282-284. Wade's paper in this volume traces the transformation of the French Canadian Catholic workers' syndicates into genuine collective bargaining units.

might be thought to "need" most leisure satisfactions in compensation for dull and frustrating occupations. Yet closer inquiry would probably reveal the functional equivalent of such groups (perhaps without organizational titles and charters) in nearly all segments of urban-industrial society.

New Family Organization. Modern economic systems tend, at least in the long run, to diminish the strength of extended kinship ties. This is in a sense a by-product of residential mobility and occupational mobility within and between generations. This essentially mechanical explanation fails to touch some deeper processes. What appears to be the social separation of adult generations interacts with extremely close bonds in the socialization of children within the family unit. Formal agencies of socialization such as the schools do not essentially minimize the role of the family in attitude formation and internalization of norms. It follows that the family may act as an agency of change as well as a mode of maintaining normative continuity.[39] The small-family system tends more in this direction, but the relationship is not perfect.

Although the family has historically "lost" functions to more specialized agencies in industrial societies, it does not follow that the family is doomed to eventual disappearance. It is precisely the small-family system with its emphasis on emotional security of children *and* adults that is of crucial functional importance in a society otherwise characterized by emotionally neutral and segmental relations.

The family as the agent of legitimate reproduction is also crucial for demographic problems. Demographers and others have repeatedly noted the danger that reduced mortality without reduced fertility will seriously impede the rate, or perhaps even the possibility, of economic growth. Once more the problems are complex, for some members of a population are producers as well as consumers, and even an expansion of consumers may provide an impetus to the development of internal markets. Yet it is also true that a rapidly growing population has a high ratio of dependents to producers, tends to accentuate needs for consumer goods over capital

---

[39] This point is elaborated by Bert F. Hoselitz in his paper in this volume. Hoselitz questions the standard generalizations concerning the dysfunctions of extended kinship for economic modernization. See also his "The Market Matrix," in Moore and Feldman, *op. cit.*, chap. xii.

expansion, and places serious burdens on the possibilities of educational developments.[40]

Although the links between economic development and smaller families are not fully established, it appears clear that they center in part on the institutionalization of mobility, in part an emphasis on familial (as distinct from extended kinship) values themselves.

MOTIVATIONAL FRAMEWORK

Since human motives, or at least those of direct relevance for economic behavior, are largely the product of socialization, they may be viewed as simply the counterpart of institutions and organizations already discussed. The justifications for their separate consideration are several: (1) Even in the most "tightly structured" social system, values, institutions, and specific organizational commitments involve some cross-pressures and permit some latitude for choice and innovation. (2) The socialization process itself will scarcely produce precise duplication and maintenance of traditional behavior and may provide an important key to the direction of change in social systems. (3) Particularly in social systems where novel forms of behavior, such as new productive and distributive systems, are being introduced, the motivational counterparts of the social transition require examination somewhat additional to the motivational inferences that may be drawn from analysis of stable social structures.[41] (4) It is possible that "the content of men's minds" may be altered somewhat independently of changes in structures and institutions.[42]

[40] The literature on "economic demography" is very large. The following should be especially noted: Kingsley Davis, "Population and the Further Spread of Industrial Society," *Proceedings of the American Philosophical Society*, No. 237 (1945), pp. 1-11; Wilbert E. Moore, "Population and Labor Force in Relation to Economic Growth," in Simon Kuznets, Wilbert E. Moore, and Joseph J. Spengler, eds., *Economic Growth: Brazil, India, and Japan* (Durham, N. C., 1955), chap. vii; Joseph J. Spengler, "The Population Obstacle to Economic Betterment," *American Economic Review*, XLI (1951), 343-354, (Supplement); United Nations, *The Determinants and Consequences of Population Trends* (New York, 1954). The United Nations study has a very comprehensive bibliography.

[41] See Melville J. Herskovits, "Motivation and Culture-Pattern in Technical Change," *International Social Science Bulletin*, (1954), 388-400; Wilbert E. Moore, "Labor Attitudes toward Industrialization in Underdeveloped Countries," *American Economic Review*, XLV (1955), 156-165 (Supplement).

[42] This position is taken by Spengler in his paper in this volume.

One important theoretical implication of this way of posing the issues should be noted. Sociologists and psychologists have commonly dealt only with the socialization of children, and have too readily accepted Freudian dogma concerning the exclusive importance of early emotional experience. What we are dealing with is a large measure of *adult* socialization in the behavioral aspects of economic development. That is, prior to the establishment of "industrial traditions" and their presumable perpetuation from generation to generation, we are interested in precisely the departures from traditional norms and canons of behavior, and the process whereby adults —even if typically young adults—become involved in and perhaps emotionally committed to novel social situations.

A further prefatory comment concerns the question of "economic" *versus* "non-economic" motives. This sham battle in social scientific literature has had pathetic consequences, among them total confusion of the issues. There are no more purely economic motives than there are purely economic organizations. There are, however, motives of high relevance to the form and level of production and distribution of goods and services. Wherever a developed monetary-market system permits, it may be convenient to weigh the relative appeal of financial and non-financial incentives. It must be remembered, however, that the efficacy of financial incentives is always relative to whatever, in the given state of the market, money will buy; this may be as non-material as symphonic concerts or the support of missionaries in far places. It must also be remembered that the combination of all incentives bearing on production and consumption will not equal the total range of human motivation, and could not in a continuing social system that depends upon the performance of all manner of actions that do not move through a market system. At early stages of economic development the "economic" *share* of total human motivation is likely to be small, because of the meagerness of goods and services available through market transactions. Within the economic sphere, however, the monetary orientation is likely to be relatively pure, because new non-financial incentives have little or negative standing in the traditional scheme of values. It follows that through time financial and nonfinancial incentives may be increased simultaneously, and this is indeed one of the dynamic laws of economic growth.

First-Order Requirements

Our concern here, then, is with motivational patterns appropriate to change of economic processes, and the commitment of participants to new organizations and institutions.

Marginality, Enterprise, Mobility. Almost by definition, economic innovators or those willing to become involved in new economic processes are marginal to the traditional order.   Hagen[43] has emphasized the role of "subordinated" groups, but the broader term "marginal" seems more appropriate.   Young wives in traditional, Chinese households, men in some African matriarchal societies, the Indian caste untouchables, the younger sons in a system of male primogeniture, merchants "unclassifiable" in feudal Japan, dispossessed landlords subsequent to a land reform, foreign enterprisers, and the indigenous hungry and landless poor everywhere—these are predictably the people who will lead or follow economic innovation.[44] Indeed, it is easier to account for the motivation for change than to account for its occasional or partial success.   For this, however, we have not only the clues provided by more strictly structural analysis, but also the additional clue of political sponsorship.   Hagen has extended his concept of subordination to nationalism, and it does seem clear in the modern world that national political leaders are in many instances economic innovators on partly nationalistic grounds.

A word of caution is in order here.   Particularly within a given country, the circumstance that innovation is perpetrated by marginal groups may precisely inhibit general acceptance.   The real or imagined benefits must sooner or later have a wider appeal if development is to continue.

Education, Skills, Industrial Traditions. The idea of intergenerational or career mobility is in most non-industrial societies alien and revolutionary.   Continuing economic development precisely depends on the motivational acceptance of this idea, and its translation into aspirations for general education and for specific specialized skills. The mere organizational provision of educational facilities is a necessary but not sufficient condition.   Even if general education is made

[43] *Op. cit.;* see also Hagen, "How Economic Growth Begins: A General Theory Applied to Japan," *Public Opinion Quarterly,* XXII (1958), 373-390; Nash, *op. cit.*

[44] Spengler, in his paper in this volume, has noted that exaggerated organic or functional models of society do not permit identification of elements of variability, strain, and dissidence.

compulsory, there is no guarantee that positive orientations to achievement will be thereby assured; on theoretical grounds the contrary would be true. If the formal agencies of education are to function as transformers of *attitudes*, some affective links must be established. That is, teachers or other students, parents, lay or religious leaders to whom the individual looks for models of behavior and belief will link cognitive with affective learning. To restate, schools or other formal training organizations can indoctrinate, can establish new "traditions," only on the basis of already favorable attitudes or on the basis of emotional bonds supplementary to cognitive instruction.

Involvement in the Market Matrix. A part of the motivational framework for economic development depends upon a growing orientation to an exchange economy, and to exchange moreover stripped of part of its archaic social appurtenances. In many "underdeveloped" areas of the world, the consumer has had a fairly fixed level of demand. In these situations, even if the laborer (or, for that matter, manager or merchant) becomes involved in a monetary system, his demand for money has more or less early limits and is perhaps confined to highly specific products. However, by a process of diffusion that has been little studied and little understood, there is substantial evidence of a growing acceptance of enlarged demand schedules when goods and services are actually available in the market.

The problem, indeed, is often not one of insufficiency of aspiration but rather insufficiency of effective demand owing to low wages and inflated prices. Where labor is in excessive supply, low wages make eminently good economic sense for the individual employer, eminently bad sense for the economy as a whole if an expanding internal market is desired. Moreover, there is a kind of vicious circle that links low wages and low productivity. Given any kind of market orientation on the part of workers, uneconomically high wages may be the correct transitional strategy. Thus, minimum wage laws, with governmental subsidy if necessary, may not be as silly as conservative economic doctrine would indicate.

New Status Systems. We return once more to the fact that economic development entails a new system of social placement and differential valuation. Systems of stratification may compete for considerable periods. The point of present relevance is that the change to new economic activities almost inevitably entails a change of most aspects of the "way of life," and the motivational rewards and penalties for the individual will necessarily include his position in the community, the esteem of his "reference groups," and his expectations for himself and his children. Because man does not live in isolation, the appropriate motives will be largely determined relative to immediate social environments, although some degree of heroism or martyrdom may be found. The individualizing of incentives implicit in mobility orientations is thus always likely to be tempered by group orientations and collective aspirations. These may be as particular as the "circle" of family and friends, as general as class or even national orientations.

Second-Order Requirements

As we near the end of this expedition, it seems fair to say that motivational analysis is even more complex than analysis of the organizational and institutional frameworks. One final point may be added, however, because it appears theoretically to have greater strategic importance than it has been accorded in actual policy.

Sense of Participation. Current empirical research on worker satisfaction and productivity consistently indicates the importance of a sense of participation in decisions and policies. True, these studies have been carried out almost exclusively in "advanced" industrial countries, with educated workers and established industrial traditions. It is probably true, however, that the typically authoritarian character of modern economic administration consistently wastes both energy and talents among those at lower administrative levels, and particularly at the bottom. Occupational associations and labor unions provide one partial answer to this situation, whether accepted by policy formulators or not. There is at least theoretical justification (and some seeming empirical evidence from communist countries and scattered areas elsewhere[45]) for suggesting that the

[45] See especially Daniel Lerner, "Introduction" to Special Issue on Attitude Research in Modernizing Areas, *Public Opinion Quarterly*, XXII (1958), 217-222; also Lerner and others, *The Passing of Traditional Society: Modernizing the Middle East* (Glencoe, 1958). The theoretical bases for the expectation of the importance of participation were discussed in Wilbert E. Moore, "Labor Attitudes Toward

sense of participation would also be an important incentive toward economic development in countries where orderly speed is regarded as of some importance. Do we not now know enough of human motivation to suggest that since economic development is literally revolutionary anyway, it may be facilitated by sharing responsibilities and giving up sole reliance on contractual and market incentives, or the yet more dismal use of economic and political duress?

Industrialization in Underdeveloped Countries," *American Economic Review, XLV* (1955), 156-165 (Supplement).

3

Tradition and Economic Growth*

Bert F. Hoselitz

A widely held body of ideas in the study of economic development is founded on the conception that advanced and underdeveloped countries are distinguished mainly in that the former have rationally organized economies, whereas in the latter tradition prevails. This distinction is often traced back to Max Weber and sometimes even to earlier writers in sociology and cultural anthropology.
For example, in a recent essay submitted to an international symposium on the study of social implications of technical change, a
team of eminent British social scientists argued that "technical—(and
associated economic)—progress is a necessary concomitant of the
movement in time from affective behavior to rationality as between ends and as between means" passing in this movement through
the stage of traditional behavior.[1] Though the authors of this text
do not accept this evolutionary scheme which they attribute to Max
Weber, and especially argue against his stipulating a specific spirit
which characterizes a given system of economic organization, they do
accept the distinction between rationality and tradition as marks of
the differentiation between technologically and economically advanced and underdeveloped societies. An extended search through
the pertinent literature would reveal many instances of similar rea-

*I gratefully acknowledge valuable criticisms of an earlier draft of this
paper by Reinhard Bendix, Arnold Feldman, McKim Marriott, Neil Smelser, and
Myron Weiner. I am especially indebted for a long written and extensive oral
criticism to Kathleen Gough Aberle. If I have not accepted all suggestions and
have stubbornly held to some of my previous views, the blame is all my own.
[1] Raymond Firth, F. J. Fisher, D. G. Macrae, "Social Implications of Technological Change as Regards Patterns and Models," in International Social Science
Council, *Social, Economic and Technological Change: A Theoretical Approach*
(Paris, 1958), pp. 289-290.

soning. Tradition is quite generally seen as a factor inimical to economic growth; whoever wants progress must get rid of tradition.

It is strange that a factor whose detrimental impact upon economic growth has been so widely decried should have received so little detailed study. Are all traditions the same in their impact on economic growth? If it is granted that the prevalence of tradition makes for stability or stationariness, can we not find some uses for tradition in a situation of rapid economic development when the threat of widespread social disorganization is ever present? And finally, is it reasonable to stipulate any traditionless society, and may we not even say that at a certain stage of social and economic development the exercise of rationality itself in given fields of social action becomes a tradition?

The following pages will be devoted to a more detailed analysis of tradition and its role in economic and associated social change. An attempt will be made to answer some of the questions posed in the previous paragraph, and if in some instances final answers will not be forthcoming, we may at least succeed in clearing away some of the intellectual underbrush so as to have a clearer path to a final resolution of the analysis of tradition and its relation to social change and economic development.

Since so much of the analysis of traditional as against rational social action stems from Max Weber's distinction, it may not be inappropriate to start with his views of this problem. Though Weber refers in many places to various sorts of specific traditions, he discusses the problem in a general way in two places in his work. The most general treatment is to be found in the early pages of *Wirtschaft und Gesellschaft* and a more specialized distinction is made in his work on the sociology of religion. In the former book he makes the distinction between rational and traditionally oriented social action, referred to earlier. But it is interesting to note in detail what he says about traditional behavior. Though he regards it, in general, as action very close to automatic reactions to habitual stimuli, he adds that traditional action may become self-conscious and that in this case it "may shade over into number two (*Wertrationalität*)."[2] Brief reflection will show that a description of traditional behavior in this sense allows us to interpret it as a class

[2] See Max Weber, *The Theory of Social and Economic Organization*, trans. by A. M. Henderson and Talcott Parsons (New York, 1947), pp. 115-116.

including widely varying forms of behavior, ranging from the purely automatic, often not meaningfully oriented, behavior to a highly self-conscious behavior whose underlying principles are reflected upon and often highly "rationalized." It is difficult not to agree with Talcott Parsons who writes in the Introduction to this work that "in contrast with . . . rational types [of social action] he [Weber] formulates what are essentially two different residual categories."[3] Parsons refers to affectual and traditional action. Since affectual behavior has a biologically or emotionally tinged dimension, Weber's classification of value-related social action reduces then to a clearly defined class, rational action, and a residual class, traditional action, which embraces various forms of behavior.

This conclusion makes it all the more necessary to distinguish the different varieties of social action falling into the class of traditional action. It is in this sphere that Weber's second discussion of traditional action becomes important. In his work on the sociology of religion, Weber states that "traditionalism . . . shall refer to the psychic attitude-set for the habitual workaday and to the belief in the everyday routine as an inviolable norm of conduct."[4] Here two kinds of action are specified. The first comes close to the earlier statement of habitual behavior. The second implies more self-conscious action, i.e., the belief that a certain routinized kind of social action is a behavioral norm. One could add still a third class in which the degree of self-consciousness of a given inherited action pattern is held with even greater force. This has been pointed out by Edward Shils in his distinction between tradition and traditionalism. Shils defines traditionalistically oriented action as a state of affairs in which we find a "self-conscious deliberate affirmation of traditional norms, in full awareness of their traditional nature and alleging that their merit derives from that traditional transmission from a sacred orientation."[5]

The development of traditionalistic patterns of social action will occur only in societies in which there exist survivals of a sacred past

[3] Talcott Parsons in *ibid.*, p. 14.
[4] Max Weber, "The Social Psychology of the World Religions," in H. H. Gerth and C. W. Mills, eds., *From Max Weber, Essays in Sociology* (New York, 1946), p. 296.
[5] See Edward Shils, "Tradition and Liberty: Antinomy and Interdependence," *Ethics*, Vol XLVIII, No. 3 (1958), pp. 160-161.

or in which explicit and conscious revival of religious or political traditions have taken place. In other words, traditionalistic action takes place within a context in which explicit reference is made to the past history and development of a society and to previous states of its existence. Hence societies in which "great traditions" have developed,[6] may arrive at a point at which traditional norms are not only consciously held as true, but in which it is asserted that they derive their validity because of their transmission from a sacred origin. As we shall see later, there may be a considerable difference in the reaction of traditionally oriented social groups and traditionalistically oriented social groups to social and cultural change. If traditional norms are self-consciously held, without necessarily being attached to sacred origins, and without being justified and "rationalized" as deriving their validity from their connection with these sacred origins, they will be more easily subject to alteration and even rejection, than if a set of norms is considered to derive their authority because they are transmitted from a sacred source in the past. In the latter case we deal not any more with a tradition-oriented society in Max Weber's sense but with one in which a rationality of ends is postulated. These ends are defined, it is true, as imperatives imposed by the sacred origin of the tradition. But a system in which traditionally determined ends are consciously held, is still *wertrational* in Weber's sense, for the major requirement of such a system is that it is oriented to a clearly formulated goal, or to a set of values which are clearly formulated and logically related.[7] If in such a system the means to achieve traditionally sanctioned ends are rationally determined we may have a social system which is both *zweck*-and *wertrational* in Weber's sense, even though the ultimate authority for its value structure is derived by traditional transmission from a sacred origin.

These considerations would lead one to reject Weber's classification between rational and traditional systems of action as unsuitable

[6] The concept "great tradition" is due to Robert Redfield. The mechanism by means of which such "great traditions" are elaborated is described in Redfield's book, *Peasant Society and Culture* (Chicago, 1956), chap. iii, and Robert Redfield and Milton B. Singer, "The Cultural Role of Cities," *Economic Development and Cultural Change*, Vol. III, No. 1 (1954), pp. 53-77. See also McKim Marriott, "Little Communities in an Indigenous Civilization," in McKim Marriott, ed., *Village India* (Chicago, 1955), pp. 171-222.

[7] See Parsons in Weber, *Theory of Social and Economic Organization*, p. 16.

to practical application.[8] Yet his having postulated the class of traditional action has been of value in that it led us to a further exploration of this "residual" category. This in turn enables us to elaborate several positive variants of traditional action. The criteria of our classification will be the degree of self-consciousness, the degree of formalistic sophistication, and the degree of normative weight imparted to tradition-oriented action. These criteria are usually not independent, and a greater degree of self-consciousness will normally be associated with a more elaborate formalism, a more strict adherence to norms, and a more highly intellectualized sophistication of behavior.

With these considerations in mind we may then propose four distinct forms of tradition-oriented behavior. Moving from the simplest, most "automatic," to the most complex and value-endowed forms of action we may distinguish between traditionally transmitted (1) habits, (2) usages, (3) norms, and (4) ideologies.

It may aid in understanding the distinctions made in the discussion so far if we place the various forms of traditional action in a table, clearly distinguishing between the three axes along which differentiation has been made. Such a table would have the following appearance:

Habit	Not normative	Not self-conscious	Not formalized
Usage	Normative	Not self-conscious	Not formalized
Norm	Normative	Self-conscious	Not formalized
Ideology	Normative	Self-conscious	Formalized

There is little that needs to be added to this schematic presentation of the four classes of traditional action. It may be useful, perhaps, to stress again two points. (1) The distinction between formalized and non-formalized action relates to the degree of ultimate rationality (*Wertrationalität*) attached to different forms of social behavior. Non-formalized normative self-conscious action is action based on a traditional norm which does not necessarily form part of a systematic complex of purposive action deriving its validation from the past, whereas formalized action is part of such a

---

[8] See also the extended discussion by Parsons, (*ibid.*, pp. 15 ff.) on the shortcomings of Weber's classification of social action with regard to their application to a social system, and also with regard to their exhaustiveness.

complex. The distinction will become clearer in the latter part of this paper when a more detailed discussion of norms and ideologies and their differences is presented. (2) It should be emphasized again, though this may be redundant, that we are concerned in the classification presented in the schema above not with classes of societies, but with classes of socially relevant behavior. All forms of traditional behavior are likely to be encountered in every society, no matter how "rational" or "traditional" it may be. But the mixture of action patterns may differ as between societies or social groups. Moreover, the mixture of action patterns may differ in the same society at different periods of its historical evolution. Hence it is not untrue to say that in Western societies habits, usages, and traditional norms played a greater role in determining social action in the Middle Ages than at present, and that one of the distinctions between different social groups in some underdeveloped countries today is the difference to which in their social behavior they are more or less subject to traditional ideologies.

We shall turn now to the examination of traditionally transmitted habitual behavior. At one extreme, habitual behavior comes close to affectual behavior, though it normally does not involve expenditure of emotional energy. Some forms of habitual behavior are related to biological states, e.g., certain traditionally transmitted body-postures, habituation to certain foods, or times of the day at which meals are taken. But it must be pointed out that these behavioral forms are primarily culturally determined; just as more "meaningful" forms of behavior, they must be learned and are transmitted through the process of socialization to which members of a culture are subjected.[9] But they soon tend to become automatic, and quasi reflex-like, and this automatism aids in their transmission. Habitual behavior may again be divided into two subclasses: those forms of behavior to which meaning is attached and those to which it is not. For example, the particular form of squatting normally has no special meaning attached to it (unless it is an expression in dance, drama, or otherwise endowed with some connotation in the process of communication). On the other hand, gestures used in greeting another person, or habitually employed linguistic expressions have

[9] See Gordon W. Hewes, "World Distribution of Certain Postural Habits," *American Anthropologist*, Vol. LVII, No. 2 (1955), pp. 233.

social meaning, though no special valuation may be attached to them.

Habitual behavior, regardless of whether meaning is attached to it or not, is of importance for economic development not because of its position in the value hierarchy, but rather because it creates a physical and, within limits, social disposition toward certain forms of action which are relevant in a situation in which patterns of production are changed. Two examples will make this clearer. Certain kinds of machines require that the operator stand or be seated on a narrow, high stool while servicing them. It has been reported that some Indian workers, who are accustomed to squat for hours, but tire easily when they have to stand in one place or sit on such a stool, when working with these machines have extremely low efficiency as compared with European workers.[10] If the servicing mechanism of the machines could be shifted, so that the workers could squat, instead of standing, it is likely that the difference in efficiency between the Indian and the European workers would be reversed. It is clear that in this case the "adaptation to the machine" is made more difficult because of traditional forms of body postures prevalent in a culture. There attaches no intrinsic valuation to squatting as against standing, but it will be easily understood that, to the extent to which the need to stand imposes an added physical strain (in addition to operating the machine), the evaluation of the work process and the attitudes of the worker, or, in economic terms, the disutility of labor, will be different from what it would be if the worker could take a pose to which he is accustomed.

Another instance of this kind is suggested by Melville Herskovits' discussion of the interaction between habitual mealtimes of primitives and factory routine. Not only does work in the factory or mine not differentiate between seasons, but whereas the typical

---

[10] Based on oral communication of an Indian official in charge of supervision of small-scale industry. A similar instance is reported by Marcel Mauss ("Les Techniques du Corps," *Journal de Psychologie Normale et Pathologique*, Vol. XXXII, No. 2 [1935], p. 273), concerning differences in the manner of digging between British and French soldiers during the First World War. Mauss reports that "the British troops . . . could not use the French spades, which made it necessary to change 8,000 spades every time a French division relieved a British division, and *vice versa*." If differences in the manipulation of a simple tool, such as a spade, are significant between two cultures so closely related as the French and British, it should not surprise us that the manipulation of Western machines in Oriental cultures meets with considerable physical obstacles.

mealtimes in Africa south of the Sahara are mid-morning and mid-afternoon, factories, offices, and mining enterprises have adopted the European meal cycle of three meals a day.[11]   Thus the introduction of factory work may mean for many workers who are used to a different meal-cycle the choice between hunger or oversatiety at different times of day.   There may be nothing sacred about mealtimes, but, as in the case of adopting different postures and getting used to movements different from those habitually transmitted, the problem of adaptation and change is made more difficult, and hence various forms of resistance and loss of efficiency may develop which are otherwise unrelated to the complex of motivations and incentives as regards the work process by itself.

The number of similar instances could be greatly increased.[12] This is not necessary in this place.   It may suffice to suggest that in recent field studies more attention is paid to these factors and that attempts are made, in numerous modern enterprises in underdeveloped countries, not only to adapt workers to the machines and to work routines, but also to adapt work routines and even the design of machines to workers.

Similar to habitual behavior which has some biological relatedness (e.g., posture, food intake, etc.) is habitual behavior which lacks this context.   One of the first writers to stress the importance of these habitual forms of behavior was William Graham Sumner.[13]   It is not necessary to repeat here Sumner's well-known discussion.   But it may be useful to remind ourselves that *Folkways* has the subtitle: "A Study of the Sociological Importance of Usages, Manners, Customs, Mores and Morals."   In this subtitle Sumner lists forms of habitual or traditionally transmitted action in increasing order of valuation. Usages and manners, and even some customs, have few or no direct and conscious values attached to them.   Mores and morals are those forms of traditional action which are very definitely endowed with

---

[11] Melville Herskovits, "The Problem of Adapting Societies to New Tasks," in B. F. Hoselitz, ed., *The Progress of Underdeveloped Areas* (Chicago, 1952), p. 96.

[12] In addition to the interesting article by Hewes on differences in habitual postures, see also the work of Marcel Mauss, *op. cit.*, pp. 271-293, and of Ray L. Birdwhistell, *Introduction to Kinesics* (Louisville, n.d. [*ca.* 1952]), esp. pp. 3-24. See also O. H. Renner, *The Origin of Food Habits* (London, 1944), esp. chap. xii.

[13] William Graham Sumner, *Folkways* (Boston, 1906).

valuation and which often are held as extremely strict norms of behavior.

We shall discuss first usages somewhat in detail, and turn then to mores. Usages are not very different from habits. Rather than trying to determine the origin of usages—a task which Sumner also gives up as basically insolvable—we shall be concerned with attempting to examine the manner in which they are passed on. In this connection routinization and inertia appear to play the foremost role. In fact, one may almost define usages (in the sense in which this term is employed here) as those forms of traditional behavior which are accepted generation after generation not because they are endowed with any high value, not because they have normative appeal, not because they conform to certain biological needs or biologically connected performances, but because they represent routinized action which is repeated over and over again from sheer inertia. Usages of this kind can be found on all levels of social action. They make up a considerable part of everyday behavior of the mass of people in all cultures, but they are also common features of action of special groups. For example, anyone coming in contact with the governmental bureaucracy in India will encounter many forms of behavior which are not logical in the context of a modern government of an independent state, but are "survivals" from the period when India was a colony administered by foreigners.[14] It is difficult to explain these forms of behavior except by regarding them as routine usages which have been preserved by inertia. This is a feature which seems to be true not only of the bureaucracy, but also of other fields of activity, and not only of India, but also of other countries which have emerged to a status of independence.[15]

Just as there is a wide range in the forms of traditionally transmitted social habits, we find wide variation in usages. Some usages are neutral as concerns their relatedness to values or to social struc-

[14] It need perhaps not be pointed out explicitly that reference is made here not to those behavior patterns which are an outflow of governmental authority attached to the office of a government worker, but rather the routine operations of the governmental bureacracy, e.g., the use of forms and schedules, relationships within the office hierarchy and behavior patterns affecting a large portion of the execution of daily business.

[15] See, for example, the excellent discussion of Clifford Geertz, *The Development of the Javanese Economy: A Socio-Cultural Approach* (Massachusetts Institute of Technology, Center for International Studies, Economic Development Program C/56-1) (Cambridge, Mass., 1956, hectographed).

ture. Other usages have elements of valuation attached to them, i.e., they are usages which are considered as implying the proper thing to do. The distinction between a simple usage and one which carries a moral imperative is that sanctions against the breach of a usage are normally not invoked, whereas they are invariably invoked if traditional norms are disregarded or disobeyed.

An important group of usages is made up of those which are related to certain features of social structure, or which reinforce a given pattern of social action. Though these usages may not be sanctioned in the breach, they often show a high degree of persistence; and conformance with the usage is almost universal, though there seems to exist no compelling normative reason why this should be so.

An example is the continued practice among urban Indians to associate socially almost exclusively with members of their own caste, though in their business relations and their associations during work they meet and interact with many persons belonging to other castes.[16] Another more subtle usage which directly affects the form of economic growth has been described in an earlier article of mine in which I discussed differing traditions in British and French entrepreneurship.[17] A third instance is the transference into a situation of modern industrialism of certain personal dependency relations which are characteristic of the earlier feudal social structure in Japan.[18]

I regard these usages as having great importance. They are among those features which we most frequently observe when we try

[16] A telling description of this is provided in an unpublished study by Miss Aparna Mehta on the composition and social characteristics of the Bombay business community. Though businessmen belonging to one caste will be members of trade associations and other professional organizations whose members belong to many other castes, they will not associate with these other members in contexts other than those provided by business or professional organizations. This self-denial of social intercourse will be especially strong in cases where the question of interdining might arise.

[17] "Entrepreneurship and Capital Formation in France and Britain since 1700," in M. Abramovitz, ed., *Capital Formation and Economic Growth* (Princeton, 1956), pp. 303-304, 310, and "Reply," *ibid.*, pp. 391-392.

[18] See, for example, James G. Abegglen, *The Japanese Factory* (Glencoe, Ill., 1958); Iwao Ishino, "The *Oyabun-Kobun*: A Japanese Ritual Kinship Institution," *American Anthropologist*, Vol. LV, No. 5 (1953, pp. 695-707; John Pelzel, "The Small Industrialist in Japan," *Explorations in Entrepreneurial History*, Vol. VII, No. 2 (1954), pp. 79-93; John W. Bennett, "Economic Aspects of a Boss-Henchman System in the Japanese Forestry Industry," *Economic Development and Cultural Change*, Vol. VII, No. 1 (1958), pp. 13-30.

to identify certain ways of acting which exemplify a "national" tradition. It is a moot question whether they are actually anchored in national character, or whether they may be regarded as the outflow of some "collective consciousness" which embraces not only all contemporary members of a society but also most past and future members. Some traditions of this sort tend to survive far-reaching social changes, and though they appear in different external garb, their inner core remains the same even though the environment within which they are exercised changes greatly.

The most telling example of this is Abegglen's analysis of the Japanese factory. Summing up his discussion, he says that "it might be assumed that, more than any other institutions, the large manufacturing plant would represent in its social organization the extreme accommodation of Japanese systems of organization to the demands of industrial technology . . . . [Yet] if a single conclusion were to be drawn from this study it would be that the development of industrial Japan has taken place with much less change from the kinds of social organization and social relations of preindustrial or nonindustrial Japan than would be expected from the Western model of the growth of an industrial society."[19] It is, of course, possible to point to several "environmental" differences in the Japanese and European cases of industrialization which may be held accountable for the differences in development in the two parts of the world. Whereas in Europe industrialism developed, on the whole, under a relatively favorable ratio between human and nonhuman resources, this ratio was much more unfavorable (from the point of view of labor) in Japan from the very early stages of industrialization. Throughout most of its industrial history Japan has had what is sometimes referred to as a horizontal supply curve of labor. This abundance of labor has of necessity created mechanisms in which job security tended to overshadow all other considerations, and it is easy to understand why, in such situations, it may be of advantage both to the employee and the employer to abrogate criteria of achievement in the assignment of economic roles and to replace them by criteria of ascription. For if for every available job there are several, apparently equally qualified applicants, how is the employer to choose among them? He does what seems

[19] Abegglen, op. cit., pp. 127-129.

most natural, and selects the person who because of his family background, or his place of origin, or some other ascriptive criterion seems the most acceptable. Once a policy of recruitment on the basis of these principles is established, it tends to perpetuate itself, and—as Abegglen points out—tends to affect the entire complex of social relations within industry. But if ascriptive rules of assigning economic roles in a country like Japan make sense on general principle, what is more natural than to expect that they will build upon traditions of social relations which were characteristic of a period in the country's social history when ascription as a norm for recruitment was more or less universal? In other words, in Japan conditions of factor supplies during the process of industrialization were such as to make the persistent operation of traditional usages affecting social structure particularly favorable.

Though the environment in France during the nineteenth century was less favorable for the persistence of traditional usages affecting social structure, either the conservatism of the business community or the long standing of certain usages enhanced their capacity of survival. One of the features that has often been commented upon, when discussing the rate of economic growth in France as compared with other countries of Western Europe, has been the apparent lack of initiative of French industrial entrepreneurs, the persistence of relatively small, tightly controlled enterprises in French industry, and the survival of a good deal of paternalism in employer-employee relationships. To be sure, some of these features could be observed also in other European countries at approximately the same stage of industrial development, but there seems to be general consent that in France these characteristics were more persistent and more pronounced than in Britain, Germany, or Scandinavia.

Yet, at the same time, Frenchmen showed surprising genius in the field of financial enterprise. Even under the old regime, such figures as Jacques Coeur or John Law had few counterparts in other countries of Western Europe. But also in the nineteenth century some far-reaching innovations in financial enterprise were made in France, among which the establishment of investment banks of the type of the Crédit Mobilier is only the most outstanding example. How can this contrast between aggressiveness and innovation-mindedness on the one side be reconciled with timidity and an apparent lack of venturesomeness on the other? I have tried to explain this in my essay, referred to earlier in this paper, and it may perhaps be not inappropriate if I repeat the general conclusions at which I arrived. In examining French entrepreneurship in the nineteenth century and earlier one becomes impressed with the fact that among the variables affecting entrepreneurial activity past entrepreneurial performance and traditions of entrepreneurship occupy an important place. Since in a country with long-standing traditions of entrepreneurship there develop well-understood and deeply ingrained usages, any reorientation of entrepreneurial behavior must overcome not only the external obstacles which may be in the way (e.g., scarcity of capital, or a recalcitrant labor force), but also the intrinsic obstacles imposed by existing traditional usages. Industrial entrepreneurship, as distinct from financial or commercial entrepreneurship, imposed new demands and presented new challenges. But in the past the industrial entrepreneur had traditionally been a follower and the governmental bureaucrat or the financier had been an innovator. Hence it required a push from outside the industrial system in the narrower sense to lead to large-scale innovation. It was the bankers and not the industrialists who performed the role of the visonary entrepreneurs with whom Schumpeter has acquainted us. New forms of organization and even new fields of industrial exploitation were suggested by financiers rather than industrialists, and the latter merely followed the suggestions and the leadership of the former. And to the extent this was possible, industrialists would gladly forego large but uncertain profits in exchange for a tight monopoly and the ease and comfort of a secure income as *rentiers*.

It is granted that in the foregoing paragraph the situation in French industry is overdrawn. Industrialists were not quite so timid and bankers not quite so bold as I made out. But there was a tendency towards timidity and the shelter of monopoly among the industrialists and a tendency towards venturesomeness and innovation among bankers which stands in stark contrast to the attitudes of the industrialists and bankers of the other countries of Western Europe. It is difficult to explain this situation in any other way than by the impact of traditional usages among industrial and financial entrepreneurs in France—at least at our present state of knowledge. But I have no doubt that even when we learn more about the chief personalities involved in French industrialization by careful study of the life histories of the major entrepreneurial figures, we will still find that traditional usages played an important role in the over-all distribution of initiative and leadership exercised in the process of nineteenth-century French economic growth.[20]

We have seen that within the classes of habitual action and of usages there is a wide range of actual behavior patterns. The same is true of traditionally transmitted normative behavior. We shall now turn to a brief examination of it. Though I have borrowed the term "usages" from Sumner, I avoid using two other terms which are much more important in his work: "folkways" and "mores." Since there exists a superficial similarity between traditional norms and Sumner's mores, it is important to show the distinction between the two. Sumner explains mores in the following manner: He says that "the folkways take on a philosophy of right living and a life policy for welfare. Then they become mores." In other words mores are folkways which have an ethical content, which have some valuation attached to them. But mores are distinguished also from institutions and laws, and Sumner explains that "the element of sentiment and faith inheres in the mores. Laws and institutions have a rational and practical character, and are more mechanical and utilitarian. The great difference is that institutions and laws have a positive character, while mores are unformulated and undefined. . . . Acts under the laws and institutions are conscious and voluntary; under the folkways they are always unconscious and involuntary."[21]

This description of mores appears to have only limited operational usefulness. It is, of course, easy to distinguish between rules and regulations which are laid down in the form of written laws as against unwritten customs, but not all "laws" are written and then it becomes more difficult to distinguish them from "mores." Moreover, it would be difficult actually to find any mores of significance under which action is unconscious and involuntary. It may be that the actors are unaware of the origin of the rules under which they act, it may also be that they will act without reflection and respond in a more or less automatic fashion to stimuli arising in a situation defined by the mores, but their action will be neither unconscious nor

---

[20] For details of the role of entrepreneurial behavior in the development of French industry, see Bert F. Hoselitz, *op. cit.*

[21] Sumner, *op. cit.*, pp. 34 and 56.

involuntary. For this reason, I think we must reject Sumner's distinction between simple folkways and mores and turn to the distinction between usages and norms.

A traditionally transmitted norm may then be defined as a rule of self-conscious action against the non-observance of which some external sanction is invoked. A traditional norm may have the form of law or it may not have legal status. It may or may not be tied to an institution, though it usually will be tied to one. And it may be exercised with little reflection, or only after careful and deliberate scrutiny of its consequences. What matters is not the conditions under which an action takes place but whether its performance is traditionally transmitted, whether the actor is conscious of his behavior, and whether its non-observance meets with an external sanction. The sanctions invoked against a breach of traditional norms may vary in severity, and in the conditions under which they are imposed. Most of what is commonly regarded as customary law would fall into the class of traditional norms, and in these cases the sanctions would be the impositions of fines or other punishments defined by the legal system. In other cases sanctions may be the visible disapproval of an act by other members of a society, moral indignation, private feuds, or the imposition of some form of penance by religious or other organizations.

In view of the wide range of sanctions which have been suggested in the preceding paragraph, it may often be difficult to distinguish between a norm against which relatively mild sanctions are imposed and a usage which also meets with disapproval in the breach. For example, we have mentioned earlier the refusal to interdine between members of the Bombay business community belonging to different castes, and though this was designated as a usage, it is obvious that some persons persist in it, because they fear social disapproval by members of their caste if they do not conform to this usage. Usages range all the way from behavior patterns which carry no, or at most slight, sanctions to those implying rather serious social disapproval; and norms also vary with respect to the intensity and seriousness of the sanctions invoked in their breach. This inevitably means that if we were to distinguish between usages and norms merely on the basis of the severity of sanctions leveled against deviant behavior, we would not arrive at a useful operational distinction. The crucial distinguishing mark, therefore, is not the severity of sanctions, but the degree of self-consciousness with which different actions are carried out. It is admitted that often it may be difficult to establish empirically the degree of self-consciousness of a social act. Moreover, the degree of self-consciousness with which particular acts are performed may vary between different social groups in the same culture or between different times in the same society. But it is believed that a really thorough examination of a society can bring to light the degree of self-consciousness with which different persons perform different traditional acts. Moreover, though this need not always be true, the breach of a norm will usually carry heavier and more rapidly imposed sanctions than the breach of a usage.

Of all the aspects of traditionally oriented action, the observance of traditionally transmitted norms is the most important. Of course, neither the norms nor the sanctions are rigid and unchanging. In fact, in reflecting upon the manner in which traditional norms operate in a society we recognize that tradition, just like any other form of social action, is subject to change. Traditions change by becoming adapted to changing conditions, but they do not change by consciously planned action. For transmission of traditional norms is not intentionally sought. As we shall see later, those who actively search for a past in order to elevate it to a standard in accordance with which the present shall be ordered are not enhancing the process of genuine transmission of tradition, but are elevating certain rules, beliefs, and norms of the past to a level of authority which they possess not because of their usefulness for the present, but because of their pastness as such. In this manner tradition becomes an ideology; it becomes traditionalism.

But if the transmission of traditional norms is not sought, it is, on the other hand, not a "neutral" process. Traditionally transmitted norms are not accepted because they exist, but because they fill a need to have rules in a given situation. In other words, the attitude towards traditional norms is affirmative; their reception is due to the fact that they set up rules which appear as plausible and acceptable solutions to behavioral problems of the recipient generation, and which have the added weight of past effectiveness (or believed-in past effectiveness). This is the reason why traditional norms meet normally with well-defined sanctions, and why one can determine the actual strength of a traditional norm by the severity and immediacy of the sanction imposed if the norm is violated. Edward Shils has given an excellent description of this circumstance when he says that

Tradition is not the dead hand of the past but rather the hand of the gardener, which nourishes and elicits tendencies of judgment which would otherwise not be strong enough to emerge on their own. In this respect tradition is an encouragement to incipient individuality rather than its enemy. It is a stimulant to moral judgment and self-discipline rather than an opiate. It establishes contact between the recipient and the sacred values of his life in society.[22]

Looked at in this fashion traditional norms may become a powerful impediment to social and technical change, but may also perform an important stablizing function in a society in which economic development is associated with far-reaching tendencies of social disorganization. It is difficult to appraise which of the two impacts in opposite directions of traditional norms will be stronger. It is not unlikely, however, that the stabilizing impact of traditional norms may in many situations prove to have the more lasting and far-reaching impact on economic growth rather than their retarding effect. The more precise determination of this impact depends upon the over-all ideology of a society, and especially the degree of traditionalism implicit in this ideology. In other words, the particular role which traditional norms are likely to play in a society undergoing rapid economic and technical change depends, at least in part, upon the over-all place which tradition-oriented behavior holds in the society and more specifically upon whether or not traditional values are given importance because they are transmitted from the past rather than because they appear to offer solutions of present problems. Hence if we wish to determine the impact of traditional norms upon economic development, we have to consider the role of traditionalism, its form, direction, and strength.

A definition of traditionalism has already been given earlier in this paper. It will be recalled that the central core of this definition turned around the fact that traditionalism does not merely consist in the acceptance of traditional norms because they appear to aid in the solution of current problems, but rather in the appeal to traditional norms because of their antiquity and the alleged sacredness or ideo-

[22] Edward Shils, *op. cit.*, p. 156.

logical superiority of these norms. Traditionalism thus implies an ideology: it is the exaltation of tradition for the sake of tradition.

It would be an interesting exercise to determine the conditions which favor or impede the growth and development of traditionalism. It is wrong, I think, to regard certain peoples or societies as "inherently" traditionalistic, as is done so often, or to argue that certain religions necessarily foster traditionalistic values and attitudes. This last assertion was sharply rejected by Hajime Nakamura, who provided a number of examples showing the frequent instances in which Oriental religions turned away from concern with traditional non-attachment or resignation from the world.[23] The rise of traditionalism in the history of a society seems to be a more episodic occurrence. There are periods when its tide is high, and others when it has few followers and little appeal, and only flickers weakly. But in order to develop a full-fledged theory of the rise and fall of traditionalism one would require more space than is at my disposal.

But it seems to be possible to identify a situation which is favorable for the development of a widespread and strongly held traditionalistic ideology. This is a period when a society or social group experiences a serious crisis which it is difficult to overcome. It should not be surprising that in a time like this many will look back to the good old days, when things were easy and when difficulties were not insurmountable. It is easy to understand that in a period of crisis or in a situation of actual or felt deprivation the remedies and policies that at an earlier time proved successful will be appealed to again. It is also understandable why in such a period of crisis or deprivation the glorious past will be elevated to a high position in the minds of many and why the ways of the past and the norms of the past will be regarded as the only right and proper ways and norms to follow. Under these circumstances the path is smoothed for the development of strong traditionalist ideologies, and those leaders who make genuine or symbolic uses of past norms will find many followers. Of course if a people has had really glorious episodes in its past, it will be easier to recall these than if such episodes are lacking.

It seems that many developing countries are at present in a crisis the way out of which is only dimly seen. In many of the heavily

[23] Hajime Nakamura, "The Vitality of Religion in Asia," in Congress for Cultural Freedom, *Cultural Freedom in Asia* (Tokyo, 1956), pp. 53-66.

populated countries of Asia the obstacles to economic progress are tremendous. These obstacles are not merely economic, such as scarcity of capital, low levels of income, adverse balances of payments, and inflationary pressures. Much more important are the difficulties due to linguistic and ethnic disunity, the lack of genuine participation by the popular 'masses in national development programs and the maintenance or even increase in differentiation in social status, income, and power. Since, in addition, most of the countries of South Asia have gained their political independence only recently and hence are under the sway of strong nationalist sentiments, the soil for the growth of traditionalist ideologies is extremely fertile.

And we actually observe the development of such ideologies. In India and in many Islamic countries there are not insignificant political movements which espouse a strongly traditionalist ideology. In India, as well as in Muslim countries, the conditions for the development of traditionalism are favorable. There is a glorious past. There are past achievements in art, philosophy, state building, and even science which are universally acknowledged as qualitatively commensurate with the best that has been produced in the economically more advanced Western countries. There is a thinly veiled grievance against the West because of past real or alleged sins of colonialism and imperialism. There is a feeling of inferiority, especially among the more westernized intellectual elite, and one possible remedy to overcome this inferiority complex is to extol the past achievements of the indigenous culture and to allege that there exist solutions which are peculiar to the special genius of the indigenous population. One may accept technology from abroad and one may learn lessons in the fields of economic organization and production management. But in the more intimate field of social relations only indigenous solutions are admissable, and these indigenous solutions are to be patterned in accordance with the values and norms which prevailed in the most glorious periods of the past.

In order to provide evidence of how traditionalistic ideologies affect concrete political movements one would have to undertake a study of party programs and platforms of the more conservative political movements in Asian countries. The task cannot be undertaken in this place, though there is little reason to doubt that substantial material supporting the propositions made in the preceding paragraph could be found in, for example, the publications outlining the political aims and methods of the Indian Jana Sangh, a nationalistic, conservative, political party which has considerable following. As an example I wish to cite a few passages from some speeches of Pandit Prem Nath Dogra, the President of the Jana Sangh movement. In an address at Belgaum in 1955 Dogra said about his party:

Jana Sangh stands for the rebuilding of Bharat [India] on the basis of her age-old ideals and culture so that she might grow to be a great united and modern country without losing her soul and her ancient roots. . . . Jana Sangh has been from its very inception laying stress on this cultural and spiritual aspect of our national life even at the risk of being branded reactionary by the so-called progressives. We are convinced that Bharat cannot play its destined role in the world if it gets cut off from its cultural and spiritual moorings.[24]

In another speech Dogra said:

Among the opposition parties in India . . . Jana Sangh is the only party which, while firmly rooted in the Indian soil has something to offer distinct from the western pattern of life. . . . We are convinced that the Congress policy of destroying the age-old values and social anchors of Hindu life . . . will destroy the time-proved system of social security in this country. The alternative presented by the West is a system in which . . . family ties, sanctity of marriage, the caste and craft guilds have little value. . . . The Bharatiya Jana Sangh on the other hand aims at improvement and adjustment of our age-old socio-economic institutions to the changing times, instead of uprooting them.[25]

Further quotations of similar purport could be supplied from the speeches of other leaders of the Jana Sangh movement, from its programs and election manifestos, and other publications.

The passages cited in the preceding paragraph come from programmatic speeches of a politician and references to the traditional ideology are therefore either couched in such general terms as "India's age-old ideals and culture" or "our ancient roots," or cite such commonly understood manifestations of this ideology as family ties,

[24] Prem Nath Dogra, *Presidential Address delivered on 16th April 1955 at the Dakshananchal Jana Sangh Conference at Belgaum* (n.p., n.d., [circa 1955]), pp. 3, 8. On the Jana Sangh in general, see also Myron Weiner, *Political Parties in India* (Princeton, 1959), pp. 177-198.
[25] Prem Nath Dogra, *Presidential Address, Purvanchal Conference and General Council of Bharatiya Jana Sangh* (Calcutta, 1955), p. 10.

sanctity of marriage, caste, prohibition of cow slaughter, and inviola-
bility of sacred places. The audience of these speeches was composed
largely of simple peasants and workers, many of whom were illiterate
and had no knowledge of the high intellectual achievements of the
old Indian civilization. In order to find evidence of that aspect of
traditionalist ideologies which appeals to the works of philosophers
and poets, we must turn to the books written by intellectuals for intellectuals.

Examples of this literature could be cited also in great number.
The main symptoms are the extolling of ancient Indian wisdom and
the assertion that many of the inventions of the modern West, especially in social arrangements and the recognition of social relations,
are already anticipated in the old scriptures of classical Vedic and
post-Vedic philosophy. The lesson to be drawn from this is, of
course, that if the ancient Indian philosophers had knowledge commensurate with that of modern Western science, their teachings and
their doctrines can be looked for as guides for the problems facing
modern India in its struggle to emerge as a new nation. We can
make reference to only two such works. I have intentionally omitted
treatises on philosophy, since here the standard of evaluation of
achievement is somewhat ambiguous, and have chosen a work on
social theory and one on economics. Both are works by eminent
Indian scholars, one a professor at the University of Bombay and the
other a former university professor and prominent member of several governmental and Congress Committees of Enquiry.

The first of these books examines whether or not a value-free
social science is possible. The author asks the question whether it is

possible to depend upon empirical observations at all in the face of . . .
incessant danger of the invasion of the domain of empiricism by subjectivism? . . . Or is it still possible to extricate the "inner man" in such a
way that he rises above the subjective-situational promptings to a plane
of objective or impartial reasoning wherefrom it is possible for him to
enunciate bias-free ideas, normative socio-political theories and valuable
ethical judgments?

The author states that this problem has occupied the best minds
in Western social science from Marx to Freud, without leading to a
full and generally accepted solution, but that a solution is possible.
He argues that

under proper discipline (such as that of *yoga*) it is possible to make the human intellect free from situational motivations, and although subjectivism as such cannot be rooted out of our intellectual activities they can be purified to the extent of being free from the influence of selfish interests and dishonest motives.   In the philosophical literature of ancient India this possibility has been admitted as is evidenced by the epithets used for the *yogi*, such as *samyami* (self-disciplined), *jitendriya* (conqueror of sense-organs), *sthidadhi* (balanced intellect), *atmavana* (self-possessed) and *nishkama* (non-attached).[26]

What matters in this context is not whether Mukerji is correct in his equating *yoga* with scientific objectivity in the social sciences, but the fact that he writes an entire book of more than two hundred pages in which he attempts to show that a recent problem and its attempted solution in Western social sciences has been essentially anticipated already in ancient Indian philosophy.

The same spirit fills the pages of K. T. Shah's book on ancient Indian economics.   He proposes a set of assertions analogous to those of Mukerji for economic science.   In his Introduction Shah says:

I propose not only to point out how ancient are the roots of this important branch of social science—Economics—in India, but also to explain how surprisingly our ancient authorities are in accord, each from a different angle perhaps, with modern thought on the innumerable and ever more complex problems of the study of man in his every day search for wealth or individual well-being.[27]

Now again, we need not concern ourselves to ask how well Shah accomplishes this task.   Parenthetically it may be said that he succeeds not at all except to point out that certain modern practices of economic policy, e.g., the issuance of debased coin, certain forms of taxation, the protection of property, the mechanisms of the market in the determination of some prices, were also known in ancient India. The value of the book does not consist in showing that the ancient Indian treatises on *varta* or *artha* contain any economic science comparable with modern economics, but rather in describing very fully the economic institutions of ancient India and their interpretation in ancient days.   But although the book has, thus, an independent

[26] Krishna Prasanna Mukerji, *Implications of the Ideology Concept* (Bombay, 1955), pp. ix, x.
[27] K. T. Shah, *Ancient Foundations of Economics in India* (Bombay, 1954), p. 2.

value as a scholarly contribution to the study of economic relations in ancient India, its intended ideological impact, like that of the book by Mukerji, is to show that in this field also, in which Western achievement is claimed to be so superior, the ancient Indian philosophers and political writers anticipated modern thought. And although Mukerji and Shah would probably strongly object to being called adherents of a traditionalist ideology, they are precisely this, for to both of them the value of the Indian achievement consists to a large part in its antiquity, in its being allegedly contained in "scientific treatise of hoary antiquity . . . their annotations, . . . historic or puranic authority, not to mention epics and folklore, drama and literature, or even the intimate source of all authority in India—the Vedas."[28]

It is not maintained that the prevailing ideology in modern India is traditionalistic. In fact, the leading opinion in the government and also among a large part of the public is antitraditionalistic. Gandhism, which has often been designated as traditionalism, is, on the whole, a philosophy which, though based on tradition, constitutes an attempt to find new solutions for Indian social life. The same can be said of such "socialistically" oriented movements as Bhoodan or Sarvodaya.[29] But although at present traditionalism in India is rather on the defensive, there are present all the makings which might, in a prolonged economic and political crisis, bring it to the top. As we have seen, there are already available some of the intellectual props for its ascendancy, supplied by men who would perhaps be shocked if they saw what use could be made of their learned treatises. There are also political movements, which still have little power, but which may succeed in mobilizing the bulk of the conservative elements behind them; and though they may not actually be able to take power, their influence may push the Congress into a position more favorable to a traditionalistic ideology.

The effects which a traditionalistic ideology may have on economic development is perhaps best illustrated by the economic history

[28] *Ibid*, pp. 2-3.

[29] On the relation of Gandhian social teachings to the prospects of economic development in India, see Milton Singer, "Cultural Values in India's Economic Development" *The Annals of the American Academy of Political and Social Science*, CCCV (1956), 84-88. On the role and underlying philosophy of Bhoodan and Sarvodaya, see Margaret W. Fisher and Joan V. Bondurant, *Indian Approaches to a Socialist Society* (Berkeley, California, 1956), pp. 35 ff.

of Greece after it had gained its independence from Turkey in the early nineteenth century. With the establishment of the new state in the 1820's there took place an enthronement of an ideology which regarded the little country inhabited by scarcely a million and a half of miserable peasants as the successor of the states of classical Greece and the Byzantine Empire. Wherever possible the attempt was made to revive the spirit of ancient Greece and Byzantium: in education, in the legal system, and most important of all, in foreign policy. Histories of Greece were written which began with Lycurgus and Solon and ended with the description of the reigns of first a Bavarian and later a Danish princeling on the Greek throne. The codex of Justinian was made the law of the land. Books and articles on science and technology had an almost compulsory introduction in which the scientific and technical achievements of the ancients were praised and their having anticipated more modern solutions was expounded. Instead of concentrating in the educational system on technology, medicine, agriculture, and other practical fields, which were badly needed in a poor and economically underdeveloped country, the highest status was given to studies of classical antiquity or Justinian law.[30]

But of equal importance with the prevalence of traditionalist values in education, law, the family system, and other aspects of internal policy, was the constant pursuit of the "Grand Idea" of re-establishing the Greek state on a territory corresponding to the frontiers of Byzantium at the height of its power. Instead of improving the economy at home, the meager resources the poor nation could save were squandered on costly and unnecessary wars, and the bulk of the loans which Greece was able to raise abroad was similarly invested in projects of national aggrandizement and military glory. This romantic dream of rebuilding the Byzantine Empire drove Greece to participate in costly and embarrassing military adventures in the 1860's, the 1880's, the 1890's, the 1910's, and the 1920's. This predominance of Greek traditionalism had disastrous results. It jeopardized the country's credit abroad, and though some benefits were derived from the acquisition of new territory in 1881 and 1913, the net results of these wars were probably adverse as concerns

[30] See Nicolas G. Svoronos, *Histoire de la Grèce moderne* (Paris, 1953), pp. 64-65.

the Greek economy. Though militarism may, in some instances, exert a positive impact on economic growth by stimulating certain industries and providing incentives for the acquisition of new skills in the army, these effects were lacking in Greece, since almost all the war material had to be imported and any of the advantages of new skills were probably outweighed by the prolonged military service of many of the country's young men. And since policy in the eastern Mediterranean in the nineteenth century was made by the great powers any of the "successes" or failures of Greek foreign or military policy were not so much the outcome of the nation's own choosing, but of the adjustments and compromises of the great European powers relating to the "Eastern Question."

Had it not been for this ideology of extolling the past greatness of Greece for its own sake, the country could have made reasonably fair economic progress between the time it achieved independence from Turkey and the outbreak of the First World War. As a consequence of its supranationalistic traditionalism, Constantinople, rather than Athens, was the economic capital of the Greeks during the nineteenth century.[31] And even as sympathetic a traveler as Arnold J. Toynbee, who spent most of the years 1912 and 1913 in Greece, had the following to say about the country at the time of his visit:

The preoccupation with events beyond the frontiers was not caused by any lack of needs and difficulties within them. The army was the most prominent object of public activity . . . it was almost the only public utility with which the nation could afford to provide itself; the traveller from Great Britain would have been amazed at the miserable state of all reproductive public works; the railways were few and far between . . . their rolling stock scanty . . .; wheel roads . . . such as had been constructed had often never come into use, because they just failed to reach their goal or were still waiting for bridges, so that they were simply falling into decay and allowing the money spent on them to lapse into a dead loss. . . . Thus the Greek nation's present was overshadowed by its future, and its actions paralyzed by its hopes.[32]

[31] *Ibid.*, p. 63. On the perennial difficulties of Greece in securing loans in the international money markets, the unproductive use of the loans themselves, and the repeated defaults, see John A. Levandis, *The Greek Foreign Debt and the Great Powers 1821-1898* (New York, 1944).

[32] Arnold J. Toynbee, *Greek Policy since 1882* (Oxford Pamphlets, No. 39) (Oxford, 1914), pp. 4-6.

I should like to make only one correction in this otherwise very acute evaluation. It was not Greece's future, but its past, which overshadowed its present, and it was not its hopes which paralyzed its actions, but its traditionalist ideology.

The case of Greece is merely an example of the serious impediments which a traditionalistic ideology may exert upon economic development. It is possible that under different circumstances its impact may be less disastrous, but it will always tend to affect economic development adversely because it bends the energies of a society toward the achievement of values and goals which are in the past rather than in the present or in the future.

In the discussion of traditionalism and its relation to economic development we have so far been concerned with the grip which a traditionalistic ideology may exert over a whole society or a whole nation, but this is not necessarily the only social unit which may succumb to a traditionalist ideology. Often it is only a more or less small group within a society or nation which looks to traditionalism as a remedy against threatened or actually felt deprivation. An excellent example of this is provided by certain political and social developments among some South Indian rural Brahmans whose status position has become assailed and whose economic security undermined in the past fifty or more years. This development has been reported as follows:

The Brahman community in a village in Tanjore district, which was closely studied for a prolonged period, presents a classical example of an unsophisticated brand of modern Hindu traditionalism. A large number of these Brahmans surrounded almost every act and posture of daily living with sacred meaning, so that alternatives were seen as immoral. They believed in the eternity of the caste system and the supremacy of Vedic knowledge. They supported the Rashtriya Swayamsevak Sangh and the Hindu Mahasabha.[33] Some investigators took this for an expression of the "high caste Hindu tradition," autonomous and free-floating. But upon delving deeper into the reasons for the development of these attitudes one finds that the belief system of these several Brahmans had fluctuated and been

[33] The Rashtriya Swayamsevak Sangh and the Mahasabha are rightist political movements stressing communalism, Hindu orthodoxy, and reconstitution of a united India. For a description of these movements see Weiner, *op. cit.*, pp. 164-187.

modified from time to time even during this century, that the hard core of "rightist" orthodoxy had gained and lost adherents; and that it was intelligible if it was seen as an adaptive response to changing contemporary and vastly threatening relations with other groups and to the increasing deprivation in the various conditions of daily living. During British rule most of these Brahmans had supported the Congress, because British rule had progressively reduced the advantages of their group. It made them subject to land-tax for the first time; it removed the judicial exemptions of the caste; it challenged, through Christian inspired high schools, their intellectual monopoly. Changed relations with lower caste urban trading groups also robbed them of land. Some village Brahmans became educated and profited from British rule, but these usually left the villages, or if they remained adopted altered ideological sets of beliefs.

After independence the Brahmans faced new threats. There was the egalitarianism of Gandhi, whom—while looking to Nehru and Rajagopalachari as Brahman leaders—they had always detested. There were large-scale plans for land reform and moderate actual reforms inimical to their economic interests. After 1948 there was a strong wave of Communist agitation among their own lower caste servants. The Brahman families thus found themselves all poorer than they had been earlier in the century. Those who stayed in the village tended to be rejects from the higher educational institutions, or could not make the grade in government posts; other groups were encroaching on all their bases of self-esteem. An almost fantastic dream of the restoration of "traditional society" and Brahman supremacy was apparently the only ideology which afforded them security. Obviously also the policies of the rightist religio-communalist political groups were the ones best calculated to allow them to retain what land they still had and to restore their prestige as religious specialists.[34]

But the analysis of traditionalism encounters a greater difficulty than the fact that it may sometimes be found only among a particular group, whereas other groups in the same society, and, indeed, in the same locality, may not be affected by it. The very fact that people easily succumb to appeals to tradition has made the intentional use of

[34] The account in this and the preceding paragraph is based on a private written communication by Kathleen Gough Aberle. I am grateful for her permission to use this material.

parts of traditional ideologies an important weapon in the arsenal of progressive political and economic movements. Take, for example, the concept of the sacredness of cattle in Hindu ideology. Clearly this part of the traditional structure of Hindu values may form a significant part of a traditionalist reactionary ideology and, in fact, does figure as one of the planks in the Jana Sangh program. But this very same value may be used by the government of India in an attempt to induce peasants to take better care of cattle, to improve cattle strains, and to contribute, in this way, to economic development. Similarly in the United States the appeal to traditional values of personal freedom has been used to strengthen civil liberties precisely against those reactionary groups who have sought by various devices to curtail them. In other words, where we observe struggles for national or political emancipation and where we find societies straining their energies to overcome the initial inertia to set in motion programs of economic development, we will find that often, indeed, almost universally, some widely held and generally understood part of a traditional ideology is mustered in support of these efforts. Perhaps there is no better proof for the potential usefulness of traditional norms for genuine development than the very ubiquity of their service in progressive causes of all kinds, economic, political, social, and cultural.

But here we must distinguish sharply between a traditional norm and a traditionalistic ideology. The former is merely a single normative proposition which is presented usually in a new and somewhat modernized garb. The latter is a whole body of interrelated normative propositions which together not merely support a particular belief, but which constitute an entire system of beliefs and values. Let us return to our example of the sacredness of cows and the use made of this value for the improvement of cattle strains, on the one hand, and as a part of the political platform of a communalist political movement on the other. In the first case, the sacredness of cattle is a single part of an entire body of religious doctrines which is selected and in this way made use of in a program of economic development. In the second case, the appeal to the sacredness of cattle is merely one part— and a not too prominent part—of a whole body of ideas which include maintenance of caste, Brahman supremacy, religious orthodoxy, and a host of other ingredients which together form the sacred tradition of Hinduism, and had their peak of validity many centuries ago.

Hence if it may be argued that traditionalism is always adverse to economic development, the same cannot be said of tradition. Of course, if a traditionalist ideology is in permanent or temporary ascendancy, traditional norms will enhance the reactionary tendencies prevailing and will constitute an additional obstacle to economic progress. But if the prevalent ideology is one of "modernization," traditionally transmitted norms may exert a positive influence. They may provide stability in a situation of constant and rapid change. They may tend to carve out areas of social action in which known and well-understood behavior patterns prevail, and they may in this way provide a feeling of security in a situation in which there are strong forces pulling into the direction of disorganization, fear, and anxiety. For example, it may be contended that the process of economic development in Japan was enhanced rather than hindered by the preservation of various traditions in Japanese society, while its economy underwent rapid and deep-going changes. The maintenance of many traditional norms in the integrative subsystem of social action provided a backdrop which allowed the more rapid and profound process of alternation in the adaptive subsystem. Another example of the positive role of traditional norms, this time with respect to the maintenance of political liberty, has been presented by Edward Shils.[35] It may perhaps be useful to add a third example, which will show how the interaction between traditional norms and economic growth may lead to mutually reinforcing trends rather than to irrepressible conflict.

In the discussion of the interrelation between kinship systems and economic development, it is usually pointed out that traditions of the extended family are impeding the development of attitudes of venturesomeness and willingness to bear risks or to introduce innovations which are necessary for an entrepreneurial group to become the spearhead of economic development. It is said that an individual

[35] Shils, *op. cit.* On the concepts of the integrative and adaptive subsystem, see Talcott Parsons and Neil J. Smelser, *Economy and Society* (Glencoe, Ill., 1956), pp. 46-51 and the further references cited there; for the application of these concepts to the study of secular economic growth, see Bert F. Hoselitz, "Economic Policy and Economic Growth," in Hugh G. J. Aitken, ed., *The State and Economic Growth* (New York, 1959), pp. 330 ff.

who must share his profits with other members of the extended family will have fewer incentives to take risks, will tend to rely more on the aid of others than his own initiative and ingenuity, and will be less eager to search out and pursue new opportunities for profit. It is also said that this individual will work less hard than he would if he were a member of a small nuclear family, since any gains from his labor must be shared with others and because others will be expected to share their gains with him. This evaluation of the impact of the extended family on motivations for work and gain is based upon the assumption of a basically individualistic society, such as is said to prevail in the West. If we consider, on the other hand, that the traditional norms under which many persons in underdeveloped countries have come to regard their demands upon, and their duties towards, their extended families, we may perhaps understand that because of the prevalence of traditional norms different from those of the West, membership in an extended family may not be an impediment to the development of entrepreneurship or the willingness to work hard. Traditional norms relating to one's relations with one's kin group make persons in Asian countries interpret their own place vis-a-vis other members of their extended families differently from what would be the way if they held Western traditional norms regarding family relationships. And quite apart from this difference, it may be argued that the extended family may be a factor positively furthering and supporting the development of viable entrepreneurship. For example, in India, regular bank credit is almost impossible to obtain for an artisan who wishes to expand his operations. But he can rely on his family to help him with funds to expand his enterprise; any loans that he can raise usually also come from members of his extended kin group.[36] In other words, in this instance the extended family makes possible the expansion of a small inefficient artisan's shop into a small and sometimes medium sized, more efficient factory. One could cite similar examples of how family farms which were threatened by dismemberment were saved through the contributions from the members of an extended family and how the extended kin group through its capacity to pool resources was instrumental in fostering economic progress or preventing economic

[36] See James J. Berna, "Patterns of Entrepreneurship in South India," *Economic Development and Cultural Change*, VII, No. 3 (1959), pp. 343-362.

decay. It is true that these examples do not allow us to generalize on the relationship between a traditional institution operating under traditionally transmitted norms and economic growth as a whole; but it may be asserted that under certain conditions of economic growth or at certain crucial stages of the economic growth process of a society traditional institutions and traditional norms may be a benefit rather than a detriment to the advancement of a nation's economy.

We have, in this paper, merely opened up some of the problems which arise when we try to examine more closely the relations between traditional action and economic growth. The careful analysis of this interrelation has been sadly neglected, chiefly because many social scientists regarded it as either trivial or as a question with a foregone solution. I believe to have shown that economic development and tradition are not aspects of social action which are necessarily antagonistic. It would, therefore, be of considerable value if the suggestions made in this paper were followed up by further research so that we could arrive at more certain and more valid knowledge of the positive as well as the negative influence which tradition may exert on economic growth.

4

Economic Change and Cultural Dynamics

Melville J. Herskovits

The phenomenon of change, which encompasses all aspects of human social life, is at times more apparent than at others. Yet though the clock of change races or is retarded, it never stops, even where the student must seek out and test for movement if he is to perceive it at all.

This difference in the rate of change is not only apparent when we consider whole cultures, it is also to be discerned when we assess change in the several aspects into which every body of custom may be divided. Economic change can be accelerated, while religious conventions hold tenaciously to earlier usage. Or we can find instances where there is a flowering of concern with the supernatural, resulting in great expansion of religious beliefs and practices, in contrast to a concomitant conservatism in technology. The former condition, which characterizes the cultures of Western Europe and the United States as they have developed since the Industrial Revolution, may be contrasted to the many examples to the contrary that are to be found in the aboriginal societies of Central America and the Belgian Congo. And what is true of economics, or technology, or religion, is also true of social and political institutions, of art and music, of language and education, and of the systems of values that underlie all these and give them meaning and purport.

Whether rapid or retarded, change in any culture is consistent. This is the more noticeable where innovations arise from within a society than when they are introduced as a result of contact with groups having different ways. Even in these latter cases, however, no matter how great the pressures for change, continuities will be discernible.   In every instance, innovations are found to have been projected against the background of pre-existing custom.   If these new elements are incompatible with established beliefs and practices, and the recipients are free to determine acceptance or rejection, they will be rejected out of hand.   Where a people have no freedom of choice, as under conquest or enslavement, innovations that are incompatible will be avoided as much as possible, to be replaced by earlier practices, residually continued, when pressures are released.

In cultural theory, this consistency of change, called cultural drift,[1] must be understood if we are to acquire an adequate perspective on what is variously called economic development, or economic growth, or, in the case of the present volume, socio-economic development.   In two important respects, the concept of drift epitomizes a somewhat different orientation from that customarily employed when problems lying in this field are studied.   In the first place, the frame of reference here is cultural and holistic, rather than particularistic, as where exclusive emphasis is laid on the social and economic aspects of change.   Secondly, in this approach the data are analyzed in terms of the methodology of the behavioral sciences, rather than that of the natural and exact disciplines.

It becomes apparent, in terms of this approach, that methodological considerations of primary importance arise when we introduce the concept of culture into the study of economic change.   And because it becomes necessary to assess some of the differences that appear when the attack on these problems is mounted from the position of the sciences of human behavior rather than from that of the natural sciences, we must consider the perennial question of the nature and significance of the regularities in human experience as against the analysis of the unique historical event.   Here we face the issue as to the most effective theoretical orientation for studying economic change, something that brings in the related question of the nature and utility, for this purpose, of those generalizations about

[1] This concept is developed further in Melville J. Herskovits, *Man and His Work: The Science of Cultural Anthropology* (New York, 1948), pp. 580-588.   It is an extension of the concept advanced by Sapir to explain regularities of change in linguistic habits.   See E. Sapir, *Language: An Introduction to the Study of Speech,* (New York, 1921), pp. 157-182.

human behavior and the institutions of society which we term scientific laws.

II

Let us, at the outset, differentiate the concepts of society and culture. A great many definitions of each have been given; for the latter, a compilation of over one hundred and sixty formulations has demonstrated the nuances of meaning that can be assigned to it.[2] For our purpose, we can most effectively conceptualize society as people, interacting in accordance with patterns of relationship that determine the position of the individual in the group to which he belongs. Culture, on the other hand, is to be thought of as *behavior*, in the psychologist's sense of the term, including idea as well as act. The former conceptualization leads to the analysis of social structures, studied at a given moment in the experience of a people. The latter centers on human beings as essential causal agents, and stresses dynamics as the primary object of study.

It must be made clear that to define culture in behavioral terms does not rule out consideration of social relationships, but rather extends their study by bringing sanction and meaning to the forefront. What the cultural approach provides is a way in which particular social phenomena can be set in the totality of a given traditional stream. It means that when we assess the nature and functioning of social relations within a group we also take into account interactions touching on all phases of the life of a people, provided only that these are not biological, but learned. These phases are what we technically term aspects of culture, and represent the universals of human need and satisfaction that can be inductively derived from comparative study of societies all over the world. Translated into our academic tradition, these universals represent the familiar division of labor into the several disciplines of the academic curriculum—economics, political science, language, literature, technology, sociology, art, religion, music, drama, education, to name but some of them.

[2] A. L. Kroeber and C. Kluckhohn, "Culture, a Critical Review of Concepts and Definition," Peabody Museum of American Archaeology and Ethnology, *Papers*, XLVII, No. 1 (1952), 1-233.

We can approach the study of a given culture from either of the two positions we have indicated, the general or the specialized, depending on the kind of problem that is being studied. Here, however, another consideration enters, one that is especially critical where social and economic change in technologically underdeveloped societies is to be assessed. When an analysis of some particular aspect of our own life is made in terms of the concepts and methods of a specific discipline, we can to a considerable degree hold constant the total setting of the phenomenon we are investigating. We cannot do this, however, when our analysis moves to the comparative level, and we seek to generalize concerning human behavior as a whole or, more restrictedly, seek to understand changes in institutions and responses to these changes in another society, where the patterns of behavior and motivation are quite different from those in our own.

A classical example of how far this need to ascertain total setting in studying a problem in a culture not one's own can take one is to be found in the case of R. S. Rattray's work among the Ashanti of West Africa. Early in the 1920's, Rattray, a colonial officer, was assigned by the Gold Coast government to study the political implications of the sacred Golden Stool, which, it was known, was so important a symbol of Ashanti unity that rumors concerning its disposal had been the cause of the serious riots which followed its rediscovery in 1921. His directive lay essentially in the field of politics; but it was only eight years and three books later that he reached his goal and accomplished his mission. He found that he had to move through the fields of religion, ritual, and social organization before he was ready to write his monumental study of Ashanti law,[3] since only with this background knowledge could he grasp and communicate the political problem he was charged to study.

What Rattray came to realize, and what must always be realized in studying any problem that has cross-cultural reference, is that we are dealing with human beings reacting to situations they continuously project against the body of tradition to which they have been encul-

[3] R. S. Rattray, *Ashanti Law and Constitution* (Oxford, 1929). The other volumes were *Ashanti* (Oxford, 1923), on the religion and social organization of this people, and *Religion and Art in Ashanti* (Oxford, 1927). It is also to be noted that Rattray's work likewise led him to publish his *Akan-Ashanti Folk-Tales* (Oxford, 1930).

turated from the moment of birth. Any approach that ignores this culturally apperceived mass of experience cannot but be inadequate for attaining significant and valid findings.

III

This brings us to a matter of some theoretical importance in the behavioral sciences, a controversy of long standing, customarily phrased in terms of whether the study of man is "science" or "history." It may perhaps be best approached by considering its methodological implications, as these apply to the study of phenomena arising out of the fact that culture is learned, in comparison with those employed in analyzing phenomena of the natural world. From this point of view, the difference between the claims of those who hold to the one or the other position becomes clear. This difference, essentially, has to do with the degree of variability found in any given element in the natural world, compared to the extent to which we find variation in behavioral patterns, whether encountered within a single human society or among mankind as a whole. Phrased in this way, it becomes immediately apparent that the former will be found to be incomparably less variable than the latter; in other words, variation in behavioral norms represents a vastly greater degree of plasticity than any non-behavioral phenomenon. In consequence, the degree of predictability that can be achieved in the natural sciences is far greater than in the sciences of man, particularly since in the natural sciences experimental controls can be applied so much more effectively than in the study of human institutions.

Phrasing this in different terms, we come to a more familiar expression when we state that the phenomena of the natural world show far more regularities than do social phenomena. A well-worn example, which loses none of its point or validity through the retelling, can be taken by referring to the basic unit of social organization, the family. This institution, we know, is not restricted to human societies; on the infrahuman level, it is present not only among mammalian forms, but in the lower orders as well. Yet if we analyze the total pattern of organization that controls mating and reproduction in any infrahuman society, the outstanding difference between it and that which obtains in human aggregates is found to lie in the degree of regularity and of predictability that obtains in the one when compared with the other.

If we take as an example the family among the Hamadryad babboons, so ably studied by Zuckerman, it becomes clear that a description of this institution in any given Hamadryad babboon society will portray a mating-reproductive cycle that can be duplicated in any other.[4] Not so with man. In human societies, the family may consist of one man and one woman, of one man and several women, of one woman and several men; the children may live with both their parents or one of them, or with a collateral relative of father or mother elsewhere; or they may be held by adoption. Extensions of the immediate family, lines of incest, and other institutionalized forms of counting and validating kinship and obligations that arise from relationships of this order introduce still other variables.

Prediction of what may be expected in a previously unknown human society is thus impossible, except in terms of a proposition that the social organization of any particular human group will be consistently structured, and will be followed with equal consistency by the members of that society. By extension, we can thus say that while regularities which invite scientific generalization are present in the ways of human groups, they are not regularities of the same order as those which characterize the phenomena studied by the exact and natural sciences. It follows, therefore, that the sciences of man must develop their own conceptual schemes and methodological tools, rather than ape those of these other disciplines.

Two components are essential to any body of behavioral science theory. The first of these components is psychological. It derives from the nature of the conditioning process in man, which gives human learning the particular cumulative character that arises out of man's unique command of the instrumentality of speech. Because of this, the human being learns—or is conditioned to, or, as we say in technical terms, is enculturated to—the particular modes of behavior that, in their totality, make up the culture of the society into which he is born. The individual thereby comes to grasp the nature of his world, regulate his behavior, derive his motivations, and achieve his values in terms of the modes of perception, sanction, and control of his society.

[4] (Sir) S. Zuckerman, *The Social Life of Monkeys and Apes* (New York, 1922).

All this he learns so thoroughly that, for most of his life, he need not call on conscious thought-processes to guide his behavior. In a far larger measure than is customarily understood, he reacts rather than thinks; and the immediacy of his reactions reflects the emotional loading given the behavior he accepts as right and proper. He takes the material world about him for granted, but in terms that do not necessarily structure that world as it is structured by the conventions of science. Research under way, studying differences in responses to tests of visual illusions on a cross-cultural level, even on preliminary analysis, shows the power of the enculturative experience through the consistent differences present in the patterns of perception of African and American groups.[5]

We are coming to understand that for the individual the ultimate nature of reality must derive from his percepts, which, in turn, are screened by his culture. Insofar as the total group is concerned, the conventionalized realities accepted by the members of a society are consensuses of these individual percepts. What is of the greatest importance is that the resulting structure of thought and action is enculturated so early in life, and so thoroughly, that the responses to the socially sanctioned cues to behavior are subliminal, emerging into consciousness only when subjected to challenge. It is apparent that this is a critical point in any theoretical model that is to guide the scientific analysis of phenomena of cultural change. Since this category embraces the social and economic changes of the type with which the present volume is concerned, its relevance becomes immediately apparent.

The second component in the approach of the behavioral sciences to the study of man is historical. This takes its particular importance for our discussion from the fact that in most researches oriented toward the study of changing relations between social and economic institutions, the circumstances of their growth and adjustment resultant on contact tend to be relegated to a minor position, if not ignored, in favor of assessment of contemporary form and function. In studies of economic development, the bias thus introduced is compounded to the extent that the historical component represented by

[5] This research is being carried out at Northwestern University by Donald T. Campbell, M. Segall (of Columbia University), and myself, on the basis of materials gathered by co-operating anthropologists and psychologists in the field principally, but not exclusively, in Africa.

the nature of antecedent tradition in the receiving culture, and its functioning in the contact situation, are not fully taken into account. Models devised to guide studies of this kind are, moreover, not only ahistorical, but where possible developments are calculated, the bases of analysis tend to be ethnocentric. That is, these models take for granted the universality of psycho-social responses which, when comparatively and historically considered, are found to characterize the pecuniary societies of Europe and America to a degree not found outside these cultures, where they are more often than not entirely lacking.

A word may be said as to the meaning of the term "historical" as employed here. It derives from anthropological usage, and in essence implies recognition of the element of time in human experience. While it can comprehend the use of written documentary data where these exist, this is not essential. Perhaps it is best clarified if we consider it as a sense of historicity. Since the narrower meaning of the word "history" is held so widely, the need has arisen to draw a distinction between "historic" and "nonhistoric" peoples. Writing is aboriginally found in relatively few human societies, those of Europe, the Mediterranean basin and parts of Asia. It never penetrated the vast sweep of the Americas, except perhaps for the glyphs of Mexico and Central America. The peoples of Subsaharan Africa, of the islands of the Pacific, of aboriginal Australia, of the Circumpolar regions never developed writing, and the same is true of innumerable societies of Indonesia, Southwest Asia, and of many parts of India.

While in the restricted sense these people are not historical, anthropological conventions do not confuse written history with the total experience of a people or, more simply, with their past. Recognizing that the life of every group, in this sense, is historically developed, and that an unwritten past, no less than one which can be documented in writing, functions as a reality in the present, anthropologists have devised various techniques to recover as much of this as possible. The archaeological record is used to this end; comparisons of similarities and differences in the practices of peoples who can be assumed to have been in contact yield information; unwritten history—that is, oral tradition—when used with the proper methodological precautions, provides further leads.[6] It has been through the use of such techniques that the grand panorama of human history has been recovered, to tell us the ways in which the observed varieties of human culture existing at a given moment have developed, and thereby to provide a base for the long-term analysis of the dynamics of human civilization.

Because time is an ever-present factor in human experience, its neglect has invited serious distortion in findings of studies that concentrate too strongly on the present. Such neglect also increases the likelihood that conclusions of questionable validity will guide recommendations for programs of action. Of particular relevance to the present discussion is the tendency to dismiss earlier, indigenous technologies, which are the result of a long process of adaptation to the demands of the natural environment, when projects to introduce "improved" agricultural methods are under consideration.[7] Another manifestation of this same bias is seen in the failure to give sufficient weight to pre-existing patterns of economic motivation or marketing procedure where recommendations for aid are made.

A further dimension to be taken into account, particularly in the study of economic growth, is that of ideology. An ideology, from the point of view of cultural theory, may be thought of as comprehending those elements in the system of values of a people that can be abstracted from their attitudes and behavior, or is given overt expression in their myths, tales, and proverbs, and comprises the core concepts which justify and give meaning to their acts. We can thus say that an ideology is the socially sanctioned symbolization of accepted values. Obversely, any social institution may be considered the implementation of a particular segment of the total system of values. Because of the circularity of so much human reasoning, however, these values continuously function to reinforce the institutions that implement them. From the point of view of research, it should be clear that to neglect either the aspect of institution or of value, or to overemphasize either, will throw findings out of cultural perspective and to this extent further affect the validity of conclusions reached or recommendations drawn.

[6] M. J. Herskovits, "Anthropology and Africa: A Wider Perspective," *Africa,* XXIX (1959), 225-238.

[7] See, for example, Pierre de Schlippe, *Shifting Cultivation in Africa* (London, 1956).

IV

The analysis of economic and technical change falls under the heading of acculturation research, since we are here concerned with the results of contact between peoples whose ways of life are marked by a machine technology, a pecuniary economy, and what may be called the scientific approach to the solution of problems, and those who do not have these traditions. The societies which have been recipients of impulses emanating from representatives of the machine cultures encompass a wide range of differences, one that is far greater than that among the Euroamerican donor aggregates, which by comparison are relatively homogeneous. As a result, we have a veritable laboratory situation, where advantage can be taken of the historic controls to be derived from the expansion of European and American influence over the world.

Like all human beings, those who carried the industrialized, pecuniary cultures of Europe and America accepted without question the validity of their own values. They held them to be the best of ways because they had been enculturated to believe them so. Yet there was a significant difference between the acceptance of established values in Euroamerican societies and the vast majority of others which came under the influence of the Western World. The donor groups possessed what can be called an evangelistic drive, in terms of which Euroamerican ways were not only held to be best, but in addition brought into play a principle new in human experience, that it was the duty of those whose ways were best to bring their benefits to others. The evangelical tradition, it must be made clear, went far beyond religious considerations which characterize proselytizing activities of other societies, such as Islam. This evangel was secular as well as religious, and was epitomized by such descriptive phrases as "the white man's burden," and the "civilizing mission," used to express the obligation to bring "civilization" to those who lived in accordance with different and therefore less desirable conventions.

This is not the place to analyze the ramifications in Euroamerican culture of this secular evangel. It represents part of a complex of concepts, such as the idea of progress associated with it, that strikes deeply into the belief and motivational systems of European and

American societies. It underlay moves to spread schooling and bring literacy to subject peoples. It is found in the insistence on the superiority of parliamentary democracy to other governmental forms, and gave the rationale for teaching these forms to the inhabitants of colonial possessions. It was behind the drive to bring the findings of scientific medicine to those who used other curing methods. And it has been manifest in the urge to spread to the rest of the world methods to raise standards of living through extending economic aid as a means of achieving technological growth.

If we analyze the complex question of why Euroamerican conventions were able to carry conviction to peoples whose customs were so different, we must first of all make explicit a factor which is not too often enunciated, but whose relevance becomes apparent as soon as it is identified. The success of this particular episode in the long history of the diffusion of culture, that is, arises from the fact that Europe, and later America, could achieve supremacy because they possessed the technical apparatus needed to attain dominance over the peoples with whom they came into contact. From the early days of the expansion of Europe, when the exploring conquerors enjoyed the advantages of superiority in their weapons, to the present time, when we find the great centers of development and dispersion of technical achievement in Europe and America, a situation has obtained in which claims to superiority could be backed by power deriving from demonstrable superiority in the only aspect of culture where superiority is demonstrable, that of technology.

The implications of this latter point, richly documented by the vast body of data accumulated in the comparative study of culture, must be explored further. This is particularly true as concerns our findings that though technological superiority can be objectively demonstrated, other aspects of a technologically superior culture cannot be accorded a concomitant qualitative differential. In the areas of social organization, or art, or religion, or political structure, that is, it has been found quite impossible to set up objective criteria of effectiveness or excellence that will hold under cross-cultural analysis. Here the question of standards that are erected as a basis of judgment, and of the ends that are achieved, make subjective factors so prominent that comparative evaluation having any degree of scientific validity is not possible.

All such evaluations, we find, are culture-bound, and conclusions drawn from them can therefore be meaningful only when accompanied by explicit statements of underlying assumptions. Even on the level of technology, moreover, questions of better or worse cannot be resolved unless we disregard all but purely technical considerations. Attempts to evaluate with similar objectivity the end toward which a particular instrumentality is to be directed encounter insurmountable obstacles. Thus, insofar as capacity to move earth is concerned, the effectiveness of a bulldozer as against a shovel or a hoe cannot be debated. It is only when questions arise as to the amount of earth that is to be moved, or of moving it to a particular place, or moving it too fast, or for whatever other purpose—to say nothing of deeper philosophical questions regarding ultimate ends—that the value of the bulldozer can be argued.

Technological superiority, in the early days of European expansion, meant military superiority, with a disparity of power so great that large aggregates of peoples with less effective military technologies could be conquered, and held under foreign control over long periods by relatively small numbers of invaders. This superiority came to be ascribed to all those who belonged to the dominant peoples, including traders, missionaries, and teachers. Though such persons did not themselves administer the subject peoples, they were able to do their work without interference because of the protection that was actually or implicitly at their disposal in the event of resistance. Hence what these non-military elements stood for also took on, almost as though by contagion, the degree of superiority that is demonstrable when the effectiveness of a gun is compared to that of a spear, or of a bulldozer to a shovel or hoe. The secular evangel, which in these latter days has come to include economic and technological development as one of its most important doctrines has thus also come to be regarded by peoples of the most diverse cultures as valid and in many cases to be valued.

We must also take into account the extent to which the influence of this total complex of ethnocentric attitudes and approaches affected the degree of objectivity of those who are concerned with questions of economic and technological change. Acceptance of the values of Euroamerican culture, and commitment to procedures developed as a result of intensive study and analysis of the economies of Europe and America have deeply influenced the findings of researches in this area.   In cross-cultural perspective, we see that this is why the force of the traditional values of the indigenous peoples in situations of contact have been underestimated, and the institutions on which innovations have impinged neglected.   The inevitability of what is being introduced has tended to be taken for granted, so that the responses of the population in a territory for which development is being planned have not figured.

The degree to which the concept of "human nature," so important in the thinking of the classical economists, enters here must not be overlooked.   It is obvious that today it functions on the unconscious level of thought about economic planning since, like the idea of economic man, it has been largely given over in its original form.   Yet to read the discussions of such a conference as that in which the question of the rise of a middle class in underdeveloped areas was discussed[8] cannot but raise serious questions as to the degree to which unsuspected, culture-bound assumptions of the inevitability of response arising out of the "nature" of man figure in approaches to the analysis of problems of economically and technologically underdeveloped countries.   It is clear, for instance, that this particular discussion lay under the shadow of European social and economic history.   Queries that might be raised as to whether the growth of a middle class in the areas discussed by the conference must be anticipated as inevitable did not arise.   Nor was there speculation as to whether it is desirable or undesirable to have a middle class in all territories where Euroamerican technology is introduced into a non-machine civilization.

If we grant the power of established values to shape reactions of peoples undergoing contact, recognize the depth in time over which these values have existed and allow for their continuing strength, we cannot but achieve a more realistic approach to the problem posed by the juxtaposition of tradition, value, and socio-economic modernization than where any of those factors is overlooked.   This phrasing, moreover, in placing such factors within the framework of cultural theory, makes it possible to attain a greater degree of objectivity than the hidden ethnocentrisms of a more restricted position permit, be-

[8] International Institute of Differing Civilizations, *The Development of a Middle Class in Tropical and Sub-Tropical Countries,* report of the 21st session held in London, September, 1955 (Brussels, 1956).

cause of the emphasis cultural theory lays on the historical approach that requires the student to take into account all relevant elements in the cultures of both societies in contact.   In these terms our particular problem may be set as follows: to determine how ideology, which by definition comprises the non-economic—that is, the non-rational—elements in the antecedent culture of a people, bears on the introduction of an economic system based on a technology that is an expression of the scientific tradition.

V

We may now consider in more specific terms how the student of economic growth can profit from the cross-cultural approach by taking certain aspects of the reactions to culture-contact observable in Africa as examples.   In these instances, we can discern how insight and understanding are enlarged by taking into account pre-established patterns of belief, value, and behavior in the transfer of Euroamerican economic and technological conventions to African societies.   We can at the same time see the gain that accrues from adding this dimension to the conventional analytic approach, which stresses innovation and tends to ignore the cultural background into which cultural theory teaches us innovations must be absorbed if they are to function in their new setting.

Attitudes toward time afford a good beginning.   Instances lying in this field are particularly cogent in terms of the present discussion because of the differences typically manifested in these attitudes among industrialized and non-industrialized peoples, in Africa as elsewhere.   This becomes clear when we consider the depth to which temporal regularities are imbedded in the ideology of industrialization which arises out of the fact that for industrial processes to be effective, it is essential that time be measured accurately and schedules adhered to with rigor.   This has its semantic reflection, since in an industrial society such as our own, time is something we "make" or "save" or otherwise cherish.   Hall has given us numerous illustrations, from all over the world, that demonstrate how unique this is.[9]   His illustrations make it clear to what extent cultural shock

[9] Edward T. Hall, *The Silent Language* (New York, 1959).   See especially chaps. i and ix.

may be heightened, on both sides of the acculturative experience, by varied orientations toward the meaning of and regard for time where there is contact between Euroamericans and non-industrialized peoples.

The difference between industrial and non-industrial societies has been phrased as a difference between groups who use "clock" time and those who live by "natural" or astrological time. It has also been expressed as the difference between time conceived as falling into carefully measured units, often of very small dimensions— seconds, minutes, and hours, as well as days, weeks, and years—and of seasonal time, where the limits of the units are blurred and imprecise, as they follow the uneven round dictated, for example, by the responses of agricultural peoples to the time of planting, cultivating, reaping and then the period when one awaits the turn of the year to begin the cycle again. The tendency to exactitude in measuring time may thus be regarded as an integral part of the technological complex. It derives its importance from the fact that the activities laid down in accordance with it, whether these be mechanical or behavioral, have made it essential that there be specific schedules maintained in all phases of life—a meeting with a friend, a church service, as well as a production line—if the daily round is to move smoothly.

From one point of view, then, technological change is to be thought of as a process of adjustment between two time systems, one exact and demanding, the other imprecise and relaxed. Hence it would seem logical to assume that a primary requirement in bringing about economic and technological change, or "development" in the current sense of the word, would be to effect an adjustment on the part of the peoples who have a less demanding time-system to one under which they must become continuously more aware of the passage of time, and revise their habits accordingly. How far-reaching a process this is can be realized, perhaps, only by those who have watched it at first hand. For it entails change in motivation, in goals, and in values that becomes the more radical when living in accordance with new patterns of conceiving and utilizing time is concomitant with adjustment to many other innovations.

All this may be further complicated by the presence of ideological elements that are political, or moral, or otherwise irrelevant to the particular kind of change we are concerned with here. Thus, for example, an attitude toward time held by a non-self-governing people can symbolize a newly won independence. Shortly after the Sudan gained its freedom, one Sudanese, on being reproached by another for being later than usual in keeping an appointment, protested, "Do you take me for an Englishman?" There are few field-workers among indigenous African peoples, enculturated to the Euroamerican time complex, who have not fumed as they waited for an informant or an interpreter to come at an agreed time. One soon learns to expect a ceremony not to begin at the hour named. More often than not, there will be a wait of long duration until everything has been made ready, or on occasion, the rite will be well under way at the time appointed for its commencement. Eventually the rite does begin, but experience teaches that it is best to come prepared to sit pleasantly chatting until this happens, profiting from whatever opportunities there may be to observe preliminaries. The student in the field also learns that his devotion to accuracy in timing is as incomprehensible to the people with whom he is working, and as irritating, as their disregard of his conventions are to him.

The indigenous tradition, and the attitudes and behavior it engenders, are not difficult to understand and work with once the setting out of which it arises is grasped. The curious thing is that despite its primary importance in shaping adjustment to technical and economic change, specific mention of it rarely enters into the literature. Yet it is not difficult to comprehend that the period a field can wait to be worked is much more flexible than is the case with a machine that depends on a steady flow of raw materials, which it must utilize at a fixed rate, on a fixed schedule. More than this, in a pecuniary economy which is based on a productive process where the concept of overhead is important, a plant that does not function according to plan, or an idle machine, means a diminution of return on investment.

One way in which the problem of adapting a non-industrial people to the demands of accurate timing of the individual process has been met in certain parts of Africa is by employing the compound system. Thus, in the Union of South Africa, steady application to work-schedules in the gold-mines has been insured by housing the workers at the mines. Here they remain for the entire period of their contracts, under close supervision, being allowed off the compounds at long intervals, and then only for a short time. They are therefore always at hand when a shift is called.

Under this system workers are recruited for periods of a year or two. They are brought to the mines from the districts of the Union set aside for Africans, called reserves, or from neighboring Portuguese and British territories, where they leave their families. A variant of this system, aiming at developing a labor supply that will be acculturated to the regularities of time and effort demanded by industrial production and at the same time attack some of the social problems that have arisen where workers are separated from their families under the South African system, is to be found in the copper belt of Northern Rhodesia and the Katanga mines in the Belgian Congo. Here workers bring their families to the mines and are settled there on a more or less permanent basis. The children who come with them or are born at the mines receive schooling where their fathers work. Moreover, in this setting they gain not only a measure of literacy, but learn to accept as normal the industrial round.

Whatever the degree to which this policy has over the years achieved its ends, the basic psycho-cultural considerations that the application of the theoretical principles outlined in our discussion rarely enter into analyses of its results. The employers of labor who worked out the system happened on it through pragmatic trial-and-error, hit-or-miss attempts to solve their problem of obtaining a labor supply whose proper response to demands for regularity of effort, and whose respect for industrial time, would be assured. The cases where certain of these approaches did not succeed—as, for example, the rejection of the South African system in the Belgian Congo—have, significantly enough, been ignored by students. Efforts seem rather to have been directed toward the study of ways and means by which, over the years, changes have successfully been brought about in the attitudes, motivations and values of the African workers that have made them more and more amenable to the demands of the disciplines essential to industrialization.

In terms of a scientific approach, the study of alternative means and results would seem to be called for. Since the human factor here is vital in studying acculturative adjustment, it would also seem advantageous that the problem be attacked on the cross-cultural level in terms of individual adaptation as well as in its institutional dimensions. In regions where the compound system was not used, we may ask, what were the procedures and stimuli that entered into achieving adjustment to the rhythm of industrial labor? To what extent, in this process, have the concepts of time that were current in the pre-industrial situation persisted, and how are these retentions reflected in the attitudes and performance of the African workers? Even more critical in this context would be the study of the cases where attempts to change earlier patterns had failed. Lacking such studies, the validity of any hypothesis, including the one advanced here, that adjustment to the requirements of an industrial effort entails concomitant adjustment to a new conception of the nature and importance of time, remains but an interesting suggestion. It is essential that the total range of alternatives be taken fully into account, since otherwise what may have begun as a question is likely to end as a stereotype.

It should be made clear that advancing a hypothesis such as this does not imply a simplistic approach to the problem. It requires no great acquaintance with situations of cultural contact to realize that the total acculturative process is very complex, the result of the play of many factors. It is essential to grasp the principle that the student is not necessarily committed to a deterministic position when he isolates one of these factors for analysis. The results of such contacts reach into all aspects of life; certainly this has been amply shown to be true as concerns the impact of Euroamerican culture on the indigenous socio-cultural systems of African peoples. The point being made here is that one of the fundamental and far-reaching adjustments in the process that have arisen out of the differing conceptions of time held in indigenous non-industrial groupings and in the impinging industrialized societies has gone unrecognized by those whose concern is to understand and direct economic development and technological change.

VI

Let us consider another phase of contemporary Africa in terms of the theoretical frame of reference that has been discussed above.

This has to do with the relationship between land tenure, patterns governing the ownership of property, and kinship structure, on the one hand, and economic development, on the other.

The importance of the land to Africans can scarcely be over-estimated. In aboriginal convention, land is everywhere held through the sanction of some supernatural force. In some regions this force is an earth god, in others the ancestors, in still others both of these. The present-day place of the land is reflected in the fact that Africa is, and as far as we can tell will in the foreseeable future be, primarily a continent where agriculture dominates the economy. This is apparent from the statistics of exports, since despite its mineral wealth, fibers, nuts, berries, cereals, and fruits constitute a high proportion of its contribution to world markets. If to this is added the value of the food-stuffs grown for internal consumption, agricultural production becomes by far the largest sector of the total economic effort.

Typically, land is held in common. This takes its most characteristic form in family, clan, or local group ownership, title being vested in a king or family elder or local ruler. Tenure, for an individual member of a group, is valid only while use is actually made of ground that is occupied. Though control over and ownership of the products of labor is recognized, the obligation to make available what a man has grown to other members of his group who may be in need is everywhere present. In terms of this communal spirit, it can be said that no one goes hungry except when a crop failure or seasonal fluctuation in supply[10] causes all to hunger. Moreover, in the socially stratified societies of the continent, high rank requires that resources of a ruler be used for the benefit of the community. A king or chief may exact imposts on agricultural yield, or may levy a tax on trade, or may have a pre-emptive right to certain portions of the animals killed by members of his group, but the principle of *noblesse oblige* holds strongly, and he must be ready to extend generous aid and hospitality to those who come to him.[11]

[10] As, for example, is found among the Bemba of Northern Rhodesia. Cf. Audrey I. Richards, *Land, Labour and Diet in Northern Rhodesia: An Economic Study of the Bemba Tribe* (London, 1939).

[11] Cf. R. S. Rattray, *Ashanti Law and Constitution*, pp. 107-119; M. J. Herskovits, *Dahomey, an Ancient West African Kingdom* (New York, 1938), I, 107-134; F. S. Nadel, *A Black Byzantium* (London, 1942), *passim*; John Roscoe, *The*

The application of Euroamerican conventions of private ownership of land to African societies necessitates even more far-reaching
social adjustments than when non-industrial peoples have to adapt
to the requirements of work in the industrial plant. This is not only
because land is so essential to the functioning of African economies,
but also because the powerful sanctions that govern the ownership
of land and its use interpose substantial obstacles to change. Here
another principle in the theory of cultural dynamics can be employed to advantage. This is the principle that, under acculturation,
substitutive innovations require a greater degree of psychological reorientation than when innovations are additive. It follows that re-
sistances to innovation tend to be greater in the former case than in
the latter. In the instances we are considering here, industrialization is an additive innovation, like literacy or, in some parts of the
continent, money. Agricultural reform, and changes in patterns of
land tenure, however, are substitutive, and must be adjusted to pre-
established patterns of response and behavior. Land-use, that is, has
traditions associated with it that are deeply set in the aboriginal
culture, while industrialization, which is something quite new, does
not have to encounter comparable cultural imperatives and affective
associations. The fact that the land is so important for the contemporary economy of Africa, plus the less well recognized factor
of the substitutive character of innovations where land-tenure and
land-use are involved, is why so much attention has had to be given
problems centering about these aspects of African life, with strong
measures frequently being necessary to assure compliance with
changes that have been recommended.

Schemes for the reallocation of land which rest on the principle
of individual ownership are numerous in the eastern and southern
parts of the continent. The rationale of these schemes has perhaps
best been expounded in the *Report* of the Royal Commission of
1953-1955,[12] which investigated, among other things, the question
of the most effective use of the land in British East Africa. The
problem is clearly posed:

Baganda (London, 1911), chap. viii; H. A. Stayt, *The Bavenda* (London, 1931),
pp. 105, 217 ff.
[12] *East Africa Royal Commission, 1953-1955 Report* (Cmd. 9475), 1955. (Here-
inafter cited as *Report.*)

In whatever direction he turns, the African, whether he wishes to become a peasant farmer, a businessman, a wage-earner in the towns or a modern tenant on the land, is hampered by the requirements of his tribal society with its obligations and restraints. As a farmer, in many areas, he cannot buy or lease land or obtain a fully defensible title thereto. In consequence, he cannot easily specialize in particular forms of agricultural production for export or home markets. . . . The fact that the African who has land cannot readily sell it deters him from improving it, as in any case he is not certain that the increased value which he has imported to it by his efforts or by his abstinence will accrue to himself or to his heirs.[13]

Later discussion carries further the reasoning that marks this approach to the problem. Thus we read: "In East Africa peasant agriculture is by and large not directed toward securing the greatest money-incomes, nor is it conducted with the aim or knowledge of how to achieve a net surplus after all the costs involved in production have been accurately taken into account."[14] Flexibility is urged in executing recommendations for land reform, to the end that "a rigid pattern of production which would inhibit changes which may later be found to be economically advantageous" can be avoided. The "acid test" that schemes for agricultural improvement or resettlement must meet in that these should yield "an increased net income to the producers, and to the economy as a whole, commensurate with the resources expenced thereon."[15]

If we analyze this reasoning in terms of the realities of cultural change, and as revealed by application of the theory of cultural dynamics, it becomes apparent that despite the logic of its development out of the premises on which it is based, these premises have little ethnological validity. In this, the *Report* does not differ greatly from other studies of economic growth, particularly those that arise out of requests for technical aid or loans, made by official agencies. Like them, it concerns itself almost entirely with economic considerations, ignoring the fact that the most fundamental problems of change with which it deals are essentially non-economic. This lack of realism in approaching the totality of the cultural scene is compounded by the fact that the economic principles that guide the study

[13] *Report*, chap. v, p. 51, par. 9.
[14] *Ibid.*, chap. xxii, p. 291, par. 2.
[15] *Ibid.*, chap. xxii, p. 293, par. 8.

are strikingly culture-bound, in that they represent economic orientations of Europe and America and, as has been indicated, ignore the
economic patterns of the indigenous peoples who are to change their
ways.

Characteristically, as in the example used above, the remedies
that are proposed cluster about assumptions that land-tenure and the
use of land must be "rationalized" in accordance with the principle
that only through private ownership can individual initiative be
developed, and the best interests of the native peoples be served.
Yet in Southern Rhodesia and the Union of South Africa, it has
been necessary on occasion to employ force when implementing
policies of land reallocation, particularly where these are parts of
resettlement projects and mean displacement of Africans from land
traditionally owned and used by them.   Or, in the case of Ruanda,
rejection of projects directed toward improving agricultural methods
was so strong that it had to be countered by the imposition of penalties by agricultural officers for non-compliance, since attempts to
institute changes of this sort by the use of persuasion tended to meet
with polite but firm scepticism.

The approach to technical and economic change through the application of the theory of cultural dynamics reveals similar problems in still other aspects of the changing economies of African
peoples. Aboriginally, the economics of Africa, as elsewhere, were
geared to requirements of the total social systems of which they
formed a part. Because of this, the communal principle went much
beyond considerations of land tenure, and acted to strengthen the
ties between members of groupings based on kinship or, to a lesser
degree, on age or common interest. The aboriginal systems can thus
be thought of as providing an economic infrastructure on which a
network of rights and obligations could be reared, to bind the individual more closely to the group of which he is a member than could
ever be achieved in societies whose economic systems are based on
private ownership and individual initiative. The question that arises
here, then, has to do with the adjustments that have to be made when
an individual's wealth, traditionally at the disposal of members of his
kinship or age group, has been acquired and can most advantageously
be employed in accordance with the usages of the impinging economic system.

The resolution of this problem by Africans who have become acculturated to the ways of a free enterprise economy understandably entails many difficulties when they must also function as members of their native societies. The African who, by his own efforts and in accordance with principles that have brought Europeans success, has accumulated an economic surplus which he has used to set up as a small shop-keeper in his village affords a case in point. The rewards of his enterprise and his effort, and hence his ability to continue to function in terms of the new system, cannot but be seriously diminished by the play of antecedent patterns which accord kin the right to take what they need from his stock.

A similar dilemma is faced by Africans who are members of the professions. Their obligations to their relatives, in the broad African sense of the term as applied to an extended kinship unit, require them to call on their resources to discharge the traditionally sanctioned demands that may be laid on them. This burden becomes the more onerous when such men, who for the most part live in urban centers, must care for kin-folk who have adapted themselves to city life less successfully than they. Still another difficulty that arises from this lack of congruence between the norms of the cultures that are in contact is to be found in the retention of these older obligations into the acculturated political scene. The inevitable result of the application of the rules governing obligations toward kinsmen to the new order is nepotism. This, however, means the negation of what, in Euroamerican conception, are the advantages to be derived from selecting civil servants impartially, on the basis of competence and merit alone.

These examples afford only a few of the many instances that could be given of the adjustments that come in the train of contact between cultures having institutions with differing ideological components, representing different means-and-end equations, and organized along different lines. New demands, and new responses to these demands, invade every phase of the culture undergoing change, as the members of a society move into an order of things different from that which prevailed in their pre-contact world. New kinds of motivation toward labor, different wants and means of satisfying them, previously unknown methods of exchange must all be, and are being, faced.[16]

This is to say that however complicated the adjustments and however difficult the problems they create, changes are occurring, even though they may not be proceeding according to plan, or in line with the models that shaped the original impulse. Acculturation, like any other phenomenon of cultural dynamics, is not reversible. Once begun, it develops in terms of the new directions taken by its drift, toward a logical working out of the historical impulses it has experienced. This is why efforts to achieve the return of a people to a "native" state cannot succeed. The difficulties encountered in the Union of South Africa stem in large measure from the unrealistic nature of the doctrine of separate development, called *apartheid*, which envisages returning the Africans to their precontact economic, political, and social modes of life. It goes contrary to all we know about the results of cultural contact; it attempts to turn back the clock of history. Change under cultural contact may be freely entered into, or may result from the application of force; it may be slow or rapid; it may be extensive or limited. But some change always results from contact, which has been one of the prime movers in the development of human civilization.

The key word in our formulation is "interaction"; the antecedent elements in the recipient culture mold what they are given, or take, from the donor. This is to be observed in the spread of Euroamerican culture over the world. Despite the evangelistic nature of this diffusion, the assumption of a superiority that could be validated by the control of power and the exercise of this power, the new institutions have not been taken over in their entirety, but have been reshaped so as to bring them into line with pre-existing custom. By the same token, it is well to remember that the behavior of those who belong to the donor group, when operating in this situa-

[16] For various facets of this problem, see Wilbert E. Moore, *Industrialization and Labor* (New York, 1951); Walter Elkan, "Migrant Labor in Africa: An Economist's Approach," *American Economic Review*, XLIX (1959), 188-197; M. J. Herskovits, "The Problem of Adapting Societies to New Tasks," in B. Hoselitz, ed., *The Progress of Underdeveloped Areas* (Chicago, 1952), pp. 89-112; Herskovits, "Motivation and Culture-Pattern in Technological Change," *International Social Science Bulletin*, VI (1954), 388-400; Herskovits, "African Economic Development in Cross-Cultural Perspective," *American Economic Review*, XLVI (1956), 452-461.

tion, is not what it would be in its own setting. To take an instance lying on a simple level of economic activity, it is apparent that European companies trading in Africa must adapt their methods to the African conventions of buying and selling or they will not be successful, whatever the usages of the home office.

It is thus apparent that our understanding of the processes underlying economic change profits by broadening our frame of reference to include the theories and methods of cultural dynamics. Approaches which attempt to take over the methodology of the natural sciences, and employ techniques and concepts developed for the study of phenomena having a far more restricted range of variation than those entering into the category of learned behavior, must be extensively revised if applied to this latter class of data. The use of models which, in the natural world, would be universally applicable, is restricted in the study of human behavior because of the ease of transmissibility and change of learned action and thought patterns. Because in most of the world economic development is an acculturative phenomenon, any theory that guides its study must take account of the theory of cultural dynamics; the methods used to test conclusions must include those of the cross-cultural approach. A fundamental proposition that must never be lost sight of is that institutions rest on sanctions and that these sanctions, in turn, dictate the behavior that is the essence of our study. From this it follows that the problem of economic development, like all problems of cultural change, is essentially one of discovering, assessing, and predicting responses of men and women to innovations that go beyond the bounds of antecedent convention.

5

The Relevance of Political Science to the Study of Underdeveloped Areas

Ralph Braibanti

I

Developments of the last decade in methodology and substance of political science are crucially relevant to analytical schemes of political development which might rise out of the intellectual and institutional ethos which presently characterizes the discipline. Unlike economics, from which the vigorous segment of growth economics has emerged, no such identifiable subdiscipline now exists in political science. There is no evidence indicating the emergence of such an entity; hence it is probable that any contribution which political science may make to political development analysis will occur in the two established fields of comparative politics and public administration. It is not inappropriate to inquire if either of these sectors can bring to bear on the problem of political modernization a specifically relevant unbroken intellectual tradition or a corpus of hypotheses and theories comparable to those of economics.

The contrast between developments of the two disciplines is best suggested by a brief survey of economics.[1] The subdiscipline[2] of

---

[1] The literature on the methodology of economics is voluminous and it would serve no useful purpose to cite here more than a few relevant works. A general survey can be found in Rutledge Vining, *Economics in the United States of America* (UNESCO, Paris, 1956). A description of research and teaching organization can be found in Horace Taylor, "The Teaching of Economics in the United States," *The University Teaching of the Social Sciences* (UNESCO, Paris, 1954), pp. 235-261. A survey of the economist's "analytical universe" which also deals with differences among the social sciences can be found in J. J. Spengler, "Generalists Versus Specialists in Social Science: An Economist's View," *The American Political Science Review*, XLIV (1950), 358-379, esp. 362-364. Two fundamental studies are J. N. Keynes, *The Scope and Method of Political Economy* (London, 1891) and Milton

growth economics, created from and enriched by other specialties within economics, notably economic theory and history, emerged early as an entity and reached a condition of relative methodological autonomy and substantive refinement in the early years following the Second World War. This appears to have been made possible by such factors as a long period of preoccupation dating at least from Adam Smith with one focal concept, capitalism, and with a fairly well-defined field of ancillary foci, such as entrepreneurship.[3] The early ascendency of logical positivism in economics and the consequent facilitation of the construction of theoretical models was well knit into the fabric of economic methodology before model building assumed even limited significance in political science. The Marxist model was a powerful stimulus to economic thought,[4] as were other schema such as Schumpeter's *Theory of Economic Development* which was published in Germany as early as 1911.[5] An immense corpus of literature was stimulated by the construction of such systems. Few methodological forces are more accelerative of progress in theory formation than the model, an edifice both immodest and

---

Friedman, "The Methodology of Positive Economics," in his *Essays in Positive Economics* (Chicago, 1953). See also Lionel Robbins, *An Essay on the Nature and Significance of Economic Science* (2d ed.; London, 1935). Cf. Arthur Smithies, "Economic Welfare and Policy," in Brookings Institution, *Economics and Public Policy* (Washington, 1955), pp. 1-23. See also Henry Sidgwick, *The Principles of Political Economy* (London, 1887), pp. 1-45.

[2] This term is used here not with the implication that growth economics has been administratively structured within American university departments on a par with such established segments as theory, money and banking, and public finance. Its designation as a subdiscipline appears justified on the grounds (1) that a corpus of literature, journals, and textbooks exists, (2) that a significant number of economists devote their full research energies to growth economics, (3) that full courses are organized, and (4) impressive theory has been constructed. See *The University Teaching of the Social Sciences*, pp. 1-35 for a description of academic structure in economics. Subsequent citations within this essay, insofar as they deal exclusively with growth economics, suggest its vigor as a subdiscipline in the sense described above.

[3] Bauer suggests that the "great upsurge of interest" in development economics "represents essentially a resumption of the interest of the classical economists rather than a complete break with tradition." P. T. Bauer, *Economic Analysis and Policy in Underdeveloped Countries* (Durham, N. C., 1957), p. 3. Historical theories of the rise of capitalism are summarized in Benjamin Higgins, *Economic Development* (New York, 1959), pp. 217-238 and in Gerald F. Meier and Robert E. Baldwin, *Economic Development: Theory, History and Policy* (New York, 1957), pp. 19-142.

[4] Joseph Schumpeter, *History of Economic Analysis* (New York, 1954), p. 513.

[5] Joseph Schumpeter, *The Theory of Economic Development* (Cambridge, Mass., 1934) and *Business Cycles* (New York, 1939). See also Richard V. Clemence and Francis S. Doody, *The Schumpeterian System* (Cambridge, Mass., 1950).

bold, which invites alternatively its destruction, renovation, or preservation.   Development economics has also profited from an ironic empathy for sociology—ironic because despite its genesis as a moral science, classical economics identified itself with the view of the universe as being populated by men unmoved by any except an economic motivation.   This empathy may derive in part from the prior existence of economics as an academic discipline within which there were incorporated rudiments of the newer social sciences of politics and sociology before their detachment as administrative if not methodological autonomies.   Sumner's *Folkways*, published in 1907, Tawney's *Religion and the Rise of Capitalism*, published two decades later, and Weber's *The Protestant Ethic and the Spirit of Capitalism*, a preliminary version of which first appeared in German as early as 1906[6] merged sociological and economic thought, and, in the case of the latter two works, focused attention on the very institutions of central concern in economic development.   Attention to aspects of geography and demography further extended the interest range of economics to relevant factors within the empirical universe of concern to economic analysts.   This favorable predisposition provided a versatile intellectual apparatus with which development problems could be probed.   There resulted not only a literature based on classical, Marxist, neo-classical, Schumpeterian, Marshallian, Keynesian and post-Keynesian analysis, but also the significant formulation of new concepts of development such as those of Harrod and Domar.[7]   Another consequence is the disposition apparent in the current work of growth economists to seek out and assess non-economic factors.   Indeed such disposition probably results from the inability of economic growth theory to develop further without the assistance of analytical techniques and information developed by sociology, anthropology, and political science.   Economics has pro-

[6] William Graham Sumner, *Folkways* (Boston, 1907); R. H. Tawney, *Religion and the Rise of Capitalism* (London, 1924); Max Weber, *The Protestant Ethic and the Spirit of Capitalism* (New York, 1930). On the latter see H. H. Gerth and C. Wright Mills, eds., *From Max Weber: Essays in Sociology* (New York, 958), p. 450, n. 1.
[7] See Higgins, *op. cit.*, pp. 144-217; Meier and Baldwin, *op. cit.*, pp. 100-143; J. J. Spengler, "Theories of Socio-Economic Growth" in National Bureau of Economic Research, *Problems in the Study of Economic Growth* (New York, 1949), pp. 47-114; R. F. Harrod, *Towards a Dynamic Economics* (London, 1948); Evsey Domar, *Essays in the Theory of Economic Growth* (Oxford, 1957).

vided the stimulus, pushing the other social sciences,[8] and in some instances impatiently crossing disciplinary lines to find answers to development problems itself.   A relatively high degree of interdisciplinary fomentation is reflected in such enterprises as the University of Chicago's Research Center in Economic Development and Cultural Change, in its journal of the same name published since 1951, and in research done at the Massachusetts Institute of Technology's Center for International Studies.[9]   Finally, the position of economics is strengthened by operational institutions which also assess data, prepare case studies, systematize experience, and test hypotheses; typical are the International Bank for Reconstruction and Development[10] and the International Monetary Fund.   Given these factors of tradition and methodology and especially the foci of capitalism and entrepreneurship, it is not at all surprising that Moore can justifiably claim that growth economists have explicitly given recognition to the interplay of non-economic factors in development problems.[11]

II

Examination of the state of academic political science reveals a different condition of preparedness for the study of underdeveloped areas.[12]   It appears appropriate here to set forth the nexus between

[8] Instances can be found in Peter T. Bauer and Basil S. Yamey, *The Economics of Underdeveloped Countries* (Chicago, 1957), pp. 163-190; W. Arthur Lewis, *The Theory of Economic Growth* (London, 1955), pp. 376-420; Bert F. Hoselitz, *Sociological Aspects of Economic Growth* (Glencoe, 1960); J. J. Spengler, "Public Bureaucracy, Resource Structure, and Economic Development: A Note," *Kyklos*, XI (1958), 459-489 and "Economic Development: Political Pre-Conditions; Political Consequences," *Journal of Politics*, XXII (1960), 387-416.

[9] The work of the Social Science Research Council's Committee on Economic Growth is also significant, but its interdisciplinary quality derives from the aims and organization of the Council itself rather than exclusively from factors internal to academic economics.   The work of the Committee is reviewed by Simon Kuznets in "Notes on the Study of Economic Growth," Social Science Research Council *Items*, XIII (1959), 13-17.

[10] See, for example, the list of IBRD mission reports and other case studies of development in Meier and Baldwin, *op. cit.*, pp. 554-559.

[11] See Wilbert E. Moore's paper in this volume.   See also Meier and Baldwin, *op. cit.*, p. 355; Higgins, *op. cit.*, p. 294; Norman S. Buchanan and Howard S. Ellis, *Approaches to Economic Development* (New York, 1955), p. 406.

[12] The ensuing discussion is meant to have relevance only to underdeveloped states of Asia, although some of the generalizations may be fortuitously applicable to Africa or other underdeveloped areas.

political and economic development. It is assumed that, from the point of view of the underdeveloped state, economic development is a desideratum of higher priority than that of political democracy. This assumption is based on the empirical evidence of the movement away from political democracy in Thailand, Burma, Pakistan, Vietnam, and Indonesia, and conceptually on the inherent function of the state to provide for the livelihood of its members. It is likely that (with the possible exception of India) political democracy will be achieved at a speed unequally articulated to that of economic development and under conditions of tutelage or modified oligarchic controls. The rationale for such controls is usually said to be that they will diminish at a pace approximating the rate of economic growth and the maturation of an effective popular will.

The demands of economic development can be met only by an oligarchic bureaucracy, whose effectiveness as a viable administrative system is limited by the necessity of fulfilling the prescription of dispersed power implicit in popular sovereignty. In such fulfilment the administrative state must give way to the political. Each imputes to itself superior virtue, but in the early development of most states, what virtue there is seems to reside in the bureaucracy. Economic development must be achieved in the matrix of constructing an equilibrium of bureaucratic power and popular control. This must be done even though development requirements are inherently antagonistic to the political results of the very equilibrium which will eventuate. The achievement in disequilibrium of a condition of development which the logic of popular sovereignty demands be achieved in an unattainable equilibrium is the crucial problem in political development.

The valid concern of political science in analysis of political conditions of economic development may be stated as embracing six principal issues. The preparedness of political science to deal with these six issues varies with each. The first three, which have been accorded least attention, are discussed here; the fourth issue, which involves the integration of the first three in a process of cultural transformation, is dealt with in Section III; the two final issues are analyzed in Section IV. Since all underdeveloped states in Asia have passed the period of developing structures of government adapted from Western experience, it may be said that the first four issues are of less immediate utility than the others. Yet they are of more than antiquarian value, for as attention to the fifth and sixth problems increases, there will be quickened recognition of the other four as means of constructing a causal relationship among all six issues. The first three of these relevant concerns of political science are set forth below:

A. *The character of exogenous political ideas and consequent structures which have found a place in the political modernization of the underdeveloped state*

The exogenous elements which are derived almost entirely from settled Western constitutional systems have been subject to scrutiny and rumination for a century, and, in some cases, longer. Political science has developed several issues with an intensity comparable to the economist's longstanding concern with capitalism. Among them are: classic issues of the nature of justice, the conflicting requirements of order and liberty, the tempering of the general will by an elitist will of presumptive superior wisdom, representative lawmaking, the judicial process, civil-military relations, federalism, and administrative rule-making. If the empiricism and precision of scientific method have been absent, this absence was due as much to the incapacity of the phenomena to be quantified as it was to the inherent resilience of the discipline to logical positivism. The lacuna in the discipline is the absence of systematic attention to the question of transfer of these ideas to Asian nations beyond the emotive assumptions which underlay notions of manifest destiny, Christian arrogance, and Anglo-saxon administrative superiority. Nor has political science refined the requirements of constitutional democracy into a hard core of imperatives and a surrounding tissue of acculturated phenomena, the latter being characteristic of western systems, but not universally imperative.[13] Although the experience of the western world is impressive

---

[13] The difficulties in separating imperatives from more trivial phenomena become evident as soon as an effort is made. T. V. Smith, for example, suggested that supremacy of the civilian over the military, separation of church and state, and judicial supremacy, were particularly exportable elements of American democracy. (See T. V. Smith, "American Democracy: Expendable and Exportable," *The Virginia Quarterly Review,* Spring, 1947, pp. 161-178). Yet what Smith regards as imperative others may view as acculturated. The concept of military power is discussed elsewhere in this paper. See p. 173 ff., below. As to Smith's second element it should be noted that it was belief in the universal value of Amer-

when we consider the combined colonial enterprises of Britain, France, the Netherlands, and the United States, systematic analysis separating uniquely acculturated phenomena from universal imperatives has not been a result. The recording of British experience in India perhaps more nearly approached this than any other colonial experience. It was hammered out on the anvil of pragmatism tempered by the heat of Indian nationalism and British humanitarianism. The great issues of dyarchy, the Anglicist-Orientalist controversy, the Platonic guardianship implicit in the Indian Civil Service, the land revenue system, the development of a representative legislature— these were some of the problems the resolution of which separated to some extent the acculturated from the imperative. But until Indian independence this experience had not found its way into American scholarship generally, least of all into political science.[14]

B. *The process by which exogenous values and structures have been transmitted to the receiving society*

The mode or process by which Western constitutionalism was introduced and by which, in colonial areas, power was transferred to the newly independent state has received minimal attention. The experience of the United States in the Philippines and Guam, in Japan and Korea for seven years, and in the Ryukyus for fifteen years is moderately extensive, but circumstances of military occupation and other factors mitigated against the recording of such ex-

---

ican separation of church and state which led to the disestablishment of Shinto, but in a milieu in which there is overwhelmingly one religion, its value is less certain. Finally, judicial review of acts of Congress (as against state legislation) was not, in the opinion of Holmes, indispensable. (Oliver Wendell Holmes, Jr., *Collected Legal Papers*, New York, 1920, pp. 295-296). Cf. Smith's three essentials with those described in Paul H. Appleby, *Big Democracy* (New York, 1949), pp. 36 ff.

[14] Reports of the British, if studied sequentially and with due regard to historical context, reveal a commendable effort to assess the Indian milieu and to introduce certain imperatives of constitutional ideas. The separation is pragmatic rather than intellectually contrived and is implicit rather than explicit in the respect that what was left untouched by the British and hence unmentioned is the tissue of acculturated phenomena. See, for example, *Report of the Public Service Commission 1886-87*, Cmd. 5327 (8 vols.; London, 1887); *Report of the Royal Commission Upon Decentralization in India*, Cmd. 4360 (10 vols.; London, 1909); *Report on Indian Constitutional Reforms*, Cmd. 9109 (London, 1918); *Report of the Indian Statutory Commission*, Cmd. 3568 (London, 1930).

perience in anything more than a fragmentary manner. Problems of colonial administration or of dependent areas have not commanded much attention in political science.[15] For analytical purposes the mode of transfer of ideas and power may be divided into two subcategories. The first relates to the capacity of the administrative mechanism to provide for cultural adaptation in a sophisticated way. The requirement of mechanism is important both in power transfer and in ideological impact. The second subcategory may be labeled as a transformation in which the intellectual content of the ideas, the system of ordering and refining concepts and data are important. These phenomena are in reality commingled, but their abstraction may be of some consequence in assessing the permanence of the new ideas and hence in predicting the direction of political development. Examples drawn from Japanese and Chinese experience and from more recent experience on the Indo-Pakistan subcontinent illustrate these two categories. The two periods of Japanese history during which there was sustained, rapid infusion of Western constitutionalism were the Meiji period (1868-1912)[16] and the Allied occupa-

[15] An exception is Rupert Emerson, *From Empire to Nation; the Rise to Self-Assertion of Asian and African Peoples.* (Cambridge, 1960). A description of a major segment of the literature on occupation can be found in Philip H. Taylor and Ralph Braibanti, *The Administration of Occupied Areas: A Study Guide* (Syracuse, 1949). See also the essays in Carl J. Friedrich and associates, *American Experiences in Military Government in World War II* (New York, 1948); the January, 1950, issue of the *Annals of the American Academy of Political and Social Science* (Vol. CCLXVII) entitled "Military Government," edited by Sidney Connor and Carl J. Friedrich. The official account of the occupation of Japan is unreliable and appears to be designed for public-relations purposes. See Report of the Government Section, Supreme Commander for the Allied Powers, *Political Reorientation of Japan, September 1945-September 1948* (Tokyo, 1949). Nor are the semi-official memoirs more rigorous. See Courtney C. Whitney, *MacArthur: His Rendezvous with History* (New York, 1956); Charles A. Willoughby and John Chamberlain, *MacArthur, 1941-51* (New York, 1954). A useful reference work is Baron E. J. Lewe van Aduard, *Japan from Surrender to Peace* (New York, 1954). A valuable analytical study is Kazuo Kawai, *Japan's American Interlude* (Chicago, 1960). On the Philippines, see J. R. Hayden, *The Philippines: A Study in National Development* (New York, 1942). On the Ryukyus see Ralph Braibanti, "The Ryukyu Islands: Pawn of the Pacific," *American Political Science Review*, XLVIII (1954), 972-998.

[16] For general surveys of the Meiji period, see Hugh Borton, *Japan's Modern Century* (New York, 1955), pp. 69-260; Nobutaka Ike, *The Beginnings of Political Democracy in Japan* (Baltimore, 1950); E. Herbert Norman, *Japan's Emergence as a Modern State* (New York, 1940). The most relevant work on Japan is that of George B. Sansom, *The Western World and Japan* (New York, 1950). In this work Sansom applies his immense erudition to the interaction of Japanese and European cultures during the Meiji period.

tion (1945-1952). Both phenomena were marked by a high degree of systematized and rationally processed transfer of ideas and institutions. During Meiji the orderliness of the process was generated largely by internal sources and selectively controlled by an oligarchy steeped in tradition and possessed of adequate political power. During the American period, the transfer of ideas was again fairly systematic even though under conditions of American rather than Japanese control.[17] Japan's two experiences contrast with China's introduction of Western constitutionalism beginning in 1911.[18] China's adaptation was effected intellectually largely through the mediating role of one person, Sun Yat-sen, who, however effective a revolutionary leader he may have been, evolved a theoretical framework, *San Min Chu I*, which was remarkable for its naiveté as ordered political theory.[19] There was, to be sure, a brief period during which Sun and Liang Ch'i-ch'ao attempted a synthesis of Chinese thought and Western (in this instance, socialist) thought, but the triumph of Sun did not result in the transmission of a refined, sophisticated amalgam. It is possible that there may be a causal relationship between the order emerging from Meiji and the disorder from *San Min Chu I* on the one hand and the degree of rationality and refinement activating the two processes of transfer on the other. The intervention of many variables makes it impossible to isolate this factor, but it should not for this reason be dismissed as inconsequential. Another example, drawn from recent Japanese experience, may illustrate further. After the restoration of sovereignty to Japan in 1952, it was natural to view with concern the

[17] An interpretation of the process of the occupation may be found in Ralph Braibanti, "The Role of Administration in the Occupation of Japan," *Annals of the American Academy of Political and Social Science*, CCLXVII (1950), 154-164.

[18] See Toynbee's statement that "the Japanese Westernizers were more alert, prompt, and efficient than the Chinese." Arnold J. Toynbee, *A Study of History*, Somervell abridgement (London, 1957) II, 182.

[19] Sun Yat-sen's lectures constituting *San Min Chu I* may be found in Leonard Hsü, *Sun Yat-sen, His Political and Social Ideals* (Los Angeles, 1933). A point of view contrasting with that of the present writer may be found in Paul M. A. Linebarger, *The Political Doctrines of Sun Yat-sen* (Baltimore, 1955). For an account of part of the intellectual development of Sun Yat-sen in Japan, see Robert A. Scalapino and Harold Schiffrin, "Early Socialist Currents in the Chinese Revolutionary Movement: Sun Yat-sen Versus Lian Ch'i-ch'ao," *Journal of Asian Studies*, XVIII (1959), 321-342.

continuance of the 1946 Constitution and to assess the effect of the mode by which this constitution emerged. Whether or not it was foisted upon the nation and did not fit the milieu seemed relevant to any evaluation of its permanence. Subsequent research revealed that there was a suggestion of coercion in its "acceptance" by Japan,[20] but the constitution continues in force; thus indicating the strength of other factors. The analysis of process is important because process often rigidifies into tradition, and tradition is used to deter rational change. An example may be drawn from the development of the public bureaucracy, particularly of the higher civil service in Pakistan. No essential change in the training, organization, or ethos of the public bureaucracy in Pakistan has been made since 1947.[21] This stasis is often explained on the ground that the bureaucracy evolved pragmatically to fit the Indian milieu and that an optimum ecological relationship had already been attained. If this process were truly rational, this would be a weighty argument. But the transfer of a concept of Platonic guardianship to India was not as inviolable, because sacred, when it occurred as it now appears to have been. The evolution of the bureaucracy from the establishment of Fort William College in Calcutta in 1800 by Wellesley to the report of the Lee Commission in 1924 was essentially a series of pragmatic responses to the challenges of indigenous demands for Indianization of the services. Indianization occurred along with restructuring and reclassification so that the locus of power continued to rest with the British. The result was a complicated, irrational structure which, under circumstances of independence, has little reason for existing in its present form. Its legitimation may be found in its pragmatic unfolding, but the irrational, political quality of that unfolding is revealed only by careful study of the challenge-response process.

It is important here to distinguish between the process of infusion or transfer and the study of history in the more conventional sense.

[20] See Robert E. Ward, "The Origins of the Japanese Constitution," *The American Political Science Review*, L (1956), 980-1009; Theodore McNelly, "American Influence and Japan's No-War Constitution," *Political Science Quarterly*, LXVII (1952), 176-195.
[21] Elaboration of this example can be found in Ralph Braibanti, "The Civil Service of Pakistan: A Theoretical Analysis," *The South Atlantic Quarterly*, LVIII (1959), 258-304.

History must necessarily be concerned with the reconstruction of data of the past, but that itself often conduces to predispositions antagonistic to the development of analytical judgment requisite in reconstructing the human event as against the isolated fact. When such analytical judgment is absent, historicism is the product. When it is present, combined with disciplined and responsible imagination, as in archeological research at its best, the transformation process is more likely to be analyzed.

Although the major transfer of ideas and power has already occurred, the steady transmission of ideas and techniques continues. The complex network of technical assistance programs to underdeveloped areas now constitutes the principal instrument for such change. Little systematic attention has been given in political science to the theory and organization of technical assistance or to the impact of such programs on the political systems of the recipient country.[22]

[22] Although documentary and secondary literature on underdeveloped areas usually includes some analysis of technical assistance, few major works by a political scientist on this subject have yet appeared. A notable exception is Walter R. Sharp, *International Technical Assistance: Programs and Organization* (Chicago, 1952). Shorter studies are beginning to appear: David Wurfel, "Foreign Aid and Social Reform in Political Development: A Philippine Case Study," *The American Political Science Review*, LIII (1959), 456-483; Hugh Tinker, "The Human Factor in Foreign Aid," *Pacific Affairs*, XXXII (1959), 288-298; and the essay by John D. Montgomery in this volume. Some significant work directly in or bordering on political analysis has been done by other social scientists, e.g., Bert Hoselitz, *The Progress of Underdeveloped Areas* (Chicago, 1952); Morris Opler, *Social Aspects of Technical Assistance in Operation* (The Hague, 1954); see also a sociologist's effort to measure the political capacity of underdeveloped areas in Lyle W. Shannon, *Underdeveloped Areas* (New York, 1957), pp. 456-478, and a sociological view of political development, S. N. Eisenstadt, "Sociological Aspects of Political Development in Underdeveloped Countries," *Economic Development and Cultural Change*, V (1957), 289-307. Such studies as Richard W. Lindholm, *Vietnam: The First Five Years* (East Lansing, 1959), which is a survey of assistance in one Asian country, are uncommon in political science literature. Contributions by political scientists to *Economic Development and Cultural Change* are rare. It should be noted, however, that some contributions by public administration specialists have been made in the *Public Administration Review*. See, for example, Roscoe C. Martin, "Technical Assistance: The Problem of Implementation," *Public Administration Review*, XII (1952), 258-267; William B. Storm and Frank P. Sherwood, "Technical Assistance in Public Administration: The Domestic Role," *ibid.*, XIV (1954), 32-40; John W. Lederle and Ferrel Heady, "Institute of Public Administration, University of the Philippines," *ibid.*, XV (1955), 8-17; John P. Ferris, "Some Lessons in the U.S.-India Foreign Aid Program," *ibid.*, XV (1955), 89-96; Albert Lepawsky, "Technical Assistance; A Challenge to Public Administration," *ibid.*, XVI (1956), 22-23.

C. *The nature and degree of impedance or facilitation which endogenous ideological or other cultural factors present to the infusion of Western constitutionalism*

The third issue involves an examination of the relation of the religious, social, and political traditions of the non-Western states to the new forms of constitutionalism which they have adapted. Part of this issue is the examination of an important strand of Western political thought which assumes that ideals of the Judaeo-Christian heritage are a necessary prerequisite for a functioning democratic system.[23] The implication is that Buddhist, Confucian, Taoist, Islamic, and Hindu cultures of the new Asian states are either inadequate to sustain such a system or that they possess latent similarities to the Western tradition which have not yet been identified and analyzed. Little has been done by Western political theorists to explore these traditions. There exists for students of political theory an opportunity to examine the validity of the assumption that a Judaeo-Christian basis is essential for a modern Western political system. Significant interpretative work on Asian social and philosophical systems has been done, but by sinologists, Islamicists, and social scientists other than political scientists.[24] The political thought

[23] See Ernest S. Griffith, John Plamenatz, and J. Roland Pennock, "Cultural Prerequisites to a Successfully Functioning Democracy: A Symposium," *The American Political Science Review*, XI (1956), 101-137. In this symposium only Griffith explicitly supports the view that "the Christian and Hebrew faiths constitute a powerful matrix, a common denominator of those attitudes most essential to a flourishing democracy" (p. 103). See also A. D. Lindsay, *The Modern Democratic State* (London, 1943), pp. 255 ff. See also Jacques Maritain, *Man and the State* (Chicago, 1951); Walter Rauschenbusch, *Christianizing the Social Order* (New York, 1912); John Hallowell, *The Moral Foundations of Democracy* (Chicago, 1954).

[24] These developments, largely under anthropological auspices, merit careful attention by political scientists, even though they do not deal directly with the "democratic content" in the cultures considered. With Ford Foundation help, the Committee on Far Eastern Studies in 1951 launched a series of interdisciplinary research efforts designed to study the traditional cultures of Asia. The resulting publications constitute a series known as "Comparative Studies of Cultures and Civilization." For a description of the total effort, see the Foreword by Robert Redfield and Milton Singer to the first volume in the series, Arthur F. Wright, ed., *Studies in Chinese Thought*, Memoir No. 75 of the American Anthropological Association, published in Vol. LV, No. 5, Part 2 of *The American Anthropologist* (Dec., 1953), 1-317. Other studies in the series are: G. E. von Grunebaum, ed., *Studies in Islamic Cultural History*, Memoir No. 76 of the American Anthropological Association, published in *The American Anthropologist*, Vol. LVI, No. 2, Part 2 (April, 1954); Harry Hoijer, ed., *Language and Culture* (Chicago, 1954); G. E. von Grunebaum, *Islam: Essays in the Nature and Growth of A Cultural Tradition*, Memoir No. 81

of Asia has never been an integral part of political theory training; significant analyses which have penetrated the political science graduate curriculum have been remarkably few.[25] The reason is not to be found in linguistic difficulties or cultural dissimilarities, great as they are, for little exposition of Plato and Aristotle in American political science is based on knowledge of Greek or on erudition in Greek civilization. Such immersion is probably not essential since

---

of the American Anthropological Association, published in *The American Anthropologist*, Vol. LVII, No. 2, Part 2 (April, 1955); Robert Redfield, *The Little Community: Viewpoints for the Study of the Human Whole* (Chicago, 1955); McKim Marriott, ed., *Village India* (Chicago, 1955); G. E. von Grunebaum, ed., *Unity and Variety in Muslim Civilization* (Chicago, 1955); John K. Fairbank, ed., *Chinese Thought and Institutions* (Chicago, 1957).

For discussion of Islam and political systems, see Province of the Punjab, *Report of the Court of Inquiry constituted under Punjab Act II of 1954 to enquire into the Punjab Disturbances of 1953* (Lahore: Government Printing Office, 1953). The report, commonly called the *Munir Report*, includes (pp. 200-235) an analysis of Islam and the state. The "modern secularist" view of the *Report* is sharply criticized in a publication of the orthodox Jamaat-e-Islami. See Khurshid Ahmad, trans. and ed., *An Analysis of the Munir Report* (Karachi, 1956). The orthodox view is best expressed in Syed Abud Ala Maudoodi, *Islamic Law and Constitution* (Karachi, 1955). Another example of the secularist and modernist positions may be found in the Report on the Commission on Marriage and Family Laws published in the *Gazette of Pakistan, Extraordinary*, June 20, 1956, pp. 1197-1232. The dissent by Maulana Ihtisham-ul-Haq, presenting the orthodox view, is found in *ibid.*, Aug. 30, 1956, pp. 1560-1604. See also Ervin Birnbaum, *Some Theoretical and Practical Aspects of the Islamic State of Pakistan* (Karachi, 1956); Leonard Binder, "Problems of Islamic Political Thought in the Light of Recent Developments in Pakistan," *Journal of Politics*, XX (1958), 655-675 and the two chapters by I. H. Qureshi in this volume.

In Chinese thought other efforts have been made. See H. G. Creel's relatively popular treatment, "Confucianism and Western Democracy," chap. xv in his *Confucius, The Man and the Myth* (New York, 1949), pp. 254-279; and Arthur F. Wright, *Buddhism in Chinese History* (Stanford, 1959). Needham's attempt to analyze the existence of a spirit of scientific inquiry in Chinese thought, particularly in his first volume, is illustrative of examining the content of non-Western thought to determine the existence of specific allegedly western ideas. See Joseph Needham, *Science and Civilization in China* (Cambridge), Vol. I (1954), Vol. II (1956), Vol. III (1959). Northrop's work remains one of the principal stimuli to further exploration. F. S. C. Northrop, *The Meeting of East and West* (New York, 1946), *The Taming of the Nations* (New York, 1952). Note the reference to Northrop in the Redfield-Singer foreword to Arthur F. Wright, ed., *Studies in Chinese Thought*, p. v.

[25] Perhaps the earliest standard work in political theory which treated Asian thought (in this instance, Confucianism) on a par with Western political theorists was Paul Janet, *Histoire de la science politique dans ses rapports avec la morale* (3me. ed.; Paris, 1887). The only well-known text in the United States was Elbert D. Thomas, *Chinese Political Thought* (New York, 1927). There is analysis of Chinese and Indian international thought in Frank J. Russell, *Theories of International Relations* (New York, 1936), pp. 16-51. See also D. Mackenzie Brown, *The White Umbrella* (Berkeley, 1953).

the culture of Greece is part of the unarticulated assumptions of Western thought. The failure to deal with Asian political thought is simply one manifestation of the failure of the Western intellectual tradition to deal with the civilizations of Asia on terms appropriate to its ancientness and its profundity. The underdeveloped states of Asia present the further challenge that requisite structure and attitudes may emerge from sources more secular than either Western or Asian religious traditions.[26] A beginning has been made in political science in the exploration of the prerequisites of Western constitutionalism. The principal deterrent is the highly interdisciplinary quality which examination of social structure demands. The institutions which merit attention in underdeveloped states are often structures which combine in themselves familial, economic, political, legal, social, and traditional functions.[27] They remain in largely an unatomized state, deriving their generative strength from the "cake of custom" rather than from positive law, and from values of intuitional consensus rather than from overtly rational behavior. As subjects for analysis their appeal is mainly to the sociologist and anthropologist, rather than to the Western political scientist. The examination of such structures would require a mode of analysis more sociological than political in the conventional sense.

III

A crude effort to abstract some of the factors relevant to political development and place them in an appropriate relationship in a dynamic process is made in Figure 1. This abstraction and the

[26] For cogent discussion of the importance of structure and attitudes generally, see Seymour Lipset in "Some Social Requisites of Democracy: Economic Development and Political Legitimacy," *The American Political Science Review*, LIII (1959), 69-106, which tends to support "Aristotle's hypothesis concerning the relationship of political forms to social structure . . ." (p. 103).

[27] Illustrative of such institutions are the *tonarigumi* and *buraku-kai* of Japan, and the *panchayats* of India and Pakistan. On the former, see Ralph Braibanti, "Neighborhood Associations in Japan and their Democratic Potentialities," *Far Eastern Quarterly*, VII (1948), 136-164; Robert E. Ward, "The Socio-Political Role of the Buraku (Hamlet) in Japan," *The American Political Science Review*, XLV (1951), 1036-1038. On the latter, see H. D. Malaviya, *Village Panchayats in India* (New Delhi, 1956); Hugh Tinker, "Authority and Community in Village India," *Pacific Affairs*, XXXII (1959), 354-376.

explanation which follows below attempt to group together the political science interests developed in Section II as (A) exogenous ideas and structure, (B) process of transmission, and (C) facilitation and impedance of internal factors. The placing together of A, B, and C into an analytical scheme assists in attaining a fourth political science objective which (following the sequence of items in Section II), might be labeled (D) *the prediction of ideological and structural variants of the political order which evolve from the dynamics of transformation.*

In striving for predictability of variants, two subsidiary objectives are (1) prediction of direction of political change when exogenous ideas have been acted on by forces of impedance and facilitation, and (2) assessment of the degree of permanence of the new political institutions. A first step in achieving such predictability is the abstraction of categories of factors bearing on the transfer of institutions and ideas. Beyond this, little can be done at this stage, for the complexity of the process transcends the analytical apparatus of political science and requires a complex interdisciplinary social science analysis. Part of the explanation of Figure 1, especially for factors whose development is assessed in terms of political science tradition and experience, is found in the preceding discussion of factors A, B, and C of Section II. The ensuing explanation of Figure 1 supplements that discussion by directing attention to the relatedness of the issues. Though Figure 1 as a schematic diagram may be of some utility in conveying the complex of interrelationships and in emphasizing that the transfer of ideas is essentially a dynamic process, it does little else. The next step of refinement of the model and assessment of the relative weights of factors as they appear in particular clusters must await the collation of more data. For purposes of the present paper, Figure 1 is presented as a primitive effort at abstraction, with most of the grossness thus implied.

A fundamental assumption underlying this abstraction is that the relationship of institutions to societal norms is reciprocal. While this is not a novel conclusion, it appears wise to reassert its importance because of attention which has been given by Northrop to a contrary point of view. Northrop's hypothesis of world order rests on his interpretation of Ehrlich's principles, which, he avers, support the view that "positive law is only effective when it corresponds

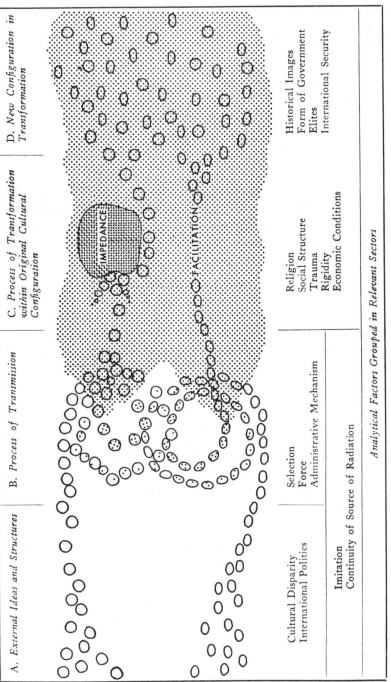

A. External Ideas and Structures	B. Process of Transmission	C. Process of Transformation within Original Cultural Configuration	D. New Configuration in Transformation
Cultural Disparity International Politics	Selection Force Administrative Mechanism	Religion Social Structure Trauma Rigidity Economic Conditions	Historical Images Form of Government Elites International Security
Imitation Continuity of Source of Radiation			

Analytical Factors Grouped in Relevant Sectors

FIG. 1. Schematic Diagram Showing Process of Transformation of External Ideas and Structures upon Contact with Internal Forces of Facilitation and Impedance.

to the underlying living law of the society to which it refers. Law is effective in any society when the norms which it introduces correspond to the underlying normative inner order habits of the living law of the people to whom it is applied."[28] The implication of this doctrine for social change is that the "inner law" of society and subsocieties must be ascertained, and institutions compatible with such "inner law" may then emerge or be created. This appears to be too simple a unidirectional view of a highly complex matrix of transformation in which institutions and norms act and react upon each other. This reciprocal relationship is suggested by the encounter of Western constitutionalism with Asian societies, in which it is clear that political structures more or less resembling Western counterparts have been developed. Equivalence both in structure and governmental process is noted especially in India, Japan, and the Philippines. Such institutional change did not arise as a thrust from the culture but rather was imposed upon it. In the complex matrix which Toynbee describes as "culture radiation and reception" the relationship between institutions and societal norms is undoubtedly reciprocal. The Northrop-Ehrlich unidirectional view is not shared by the psychologist West, or by the jurisprudent Hall,[29] the implications of whose studies corroborate the existence of a reciprocal relationship. Under certain conditions in which an imposed foreign institution may manufacture its own consensual base and thrive, it is as though the order, once imposed, lifts the ideology to it. Indeed the imposition of foreign institutions with the expectation that they will modify attitudes and ideology is the rationale behind the concept of military occupations of the Second World War. Moreover, institutions invariably bring with them sets of ideas, as history amply demonstrates. Sansom has shown that when the Japanese took over T'ang Chinese administrative institutions they were forced to admit into their intellectual system "some of the concepts to which the borrowed institutions gave expression."[30] The implications of a complex set of reciprocal actions within a transforming process are

[28] F. S. C. Northrop, *The Taming of the Nations* (New York, 1952), pp. 5-6; Eugen Ehrlich, *Fundamental Principles of the Sociology of Law*, trans. Walter L. Moll (Cambridge, 1936).

[29] Ranyard West, *Conscience and Society* (London, 1942), pp. 203-212; Carleton Kemp Allen, *Law in the Making* (6th ed.; London, 1958), pp. 30-35.

[30] George Sansom, *A History of Japan to 1334* (Stanford, 1958), p. 70.

significant for political science and particularly for political theory in that the institutions of constitutionalism may generate in society the very values upon which they were based. Or the confrontation of the endogenous value system with the new institutions may elicit from the endogenous system submerged or depressed values equivalent to those which generated the new institutions in their original milieu. In this highly dynamic transformation process, the speed and frequency of the reciprocal actions occurring within it are unknown. But an appreciation of the process seems to preclude ready acceptance of the dictum that Western values must necessarily precede the construction of effective Western institutions.

Figure 1 shows four major divisions and three groups of analytical factors placed in three of the divisions. The list of factors is not exhaustive, and the assignment of particular factors to specific divisions is, in many instances, an expository device, for in reality they cannot be thus confined.

External Ideas and Structures

At least three conditions which govern the selection of transmitted elements of culture and which regulate the intensity and quality of their transmission can be identified. There may, for example, be a disparity in the development of the two societies under impact, or a disparity between equivalent components of the societies. The total configuration of the receiving culture may be like a dry sponge, quickly absorbing from another culture. Thus Japan in the eighth century readily absorbed Buddhism, calligraphy, and the administrative system of T'ang China. On the other hand, those components of Japanese society which were highly developed, such as a concept of an elite of birth, and a spoken language and syntax,[31] were either resistant to or modified their Chinese equivalents. Japan accepted the Chinese institution of a professional group of government officials but the strength of aristocratic feeling in Japan trans-

---

[31] A clear and dramatic instance of the integration of foreign and indigenous institutions is the adaptation of Chinese writing to Japanese spoken language and syntax. The emergence of the two Japanese syllabaries, *hiragana* and *katakana*, and their use (*a*) to bring together Chinese logographs in Japanese syntactical form, and (*b*) to render the logographs into Japanese phonetics constitutes a remarkable instance of integration. See G. B. Sansom, *A Historical Grammar of Japanese* (Oxford, 1928), pp. 1-69.

formed the bureaucracy from one based on natural *aristoi* to an *aristoi* of noble birth. Similarly the Chinese theory of sovereignty which allowed for change in rulers when the celestial mandate was lost, was influenced by strong concepts of hereditary rule, and was transformed in Japan into a celestial mandate with no right of over-throwing the ruler. In modern Pakistan certain economic structures were quickly developed, but the bureaucracy, which was as highly developed as any in the West, resisted change. It is characteristic of most developing Asian states that they have highly developed literary, aesthetic, and religious components but poorly developed economic and political components. Economic and political institu-tions may appear to be readily absorbed, but the ideas accompanying them may be resisted or transformed. The effectiveness of change in any component is limited by the uneven degree of facilitation or impedance presented by other components. The component ele-ments of any culture are closely woven in a fabric; but the fabric appears even more tightly woven in those Asian societies which can be described as archaic.[32] Disparities of culture may be in juxtaposi-tion, e.g., the receiving culture may be more highly developed than the transmitting culture, as was the case in the Mongol and Manchu conquests of Han China. In these instances military prowess, ruth-lessness, and aggressive leadership appeared to be transitory phe-nomena the utility of which disappeared as the necessity to conquer a highly advanced society ceased to exist.

Another factor may be the capacity of the external ideas and struc-tures to induce imitation. Allen,[33] relying on Tarde[34] and Maine,[35] describes the power of extralogical forces of imitation which not in-frequently result in the spread of institutions as in a "craze." Allen asserts that once the process of imitation is begun it goes "far be-

[32] The use of the term "archaic" is taken from Robert Waelder, "A Hypothesis About the Nature of An Archaic Society," *World Politics*, XXI (1959), 92-103. Waelder's psychoanalytic analysis focusing on "amoral familism," does not, however, embrace the characteristic of cohesion described here.

[33] Allen, *op. cit.*, pp. 96 ff.

[34] Gabriel Tarde, *The Laws of Imitation* (trans. Elsie Crews Parsons from the 2d French edition; New York, 1903).

[35] Henry Sumner Maine, *Dissertations on Early Law and Custom* (New York, 1883). On the pre-eminence of Maine's studies of primitive legal institutions de-spite half a century of modern anthropological research, see Robert Redfield, "Maine's *Ancient Law* in the Light of Primitive Societies," *The Western Political Quarterly*, III (1950), 574-590.

yond the stimuli of expediency and utility alone, and gathers momentum of its own motion." The "influence of the mimetic faculty has not been confined to casual or trivial social phenomena: it has also affected fundamental institutions." He cites Maine's defense of the power of imitation: "If anybody is inclined to think that the process of copying models by entire societies is extinct, he should look at the way in which the British Constitution which was once regarded by men more civilized than the English as an eccentric political oddity, has spread over nearly all Europe in less than seventy years."[36] A re-examination of the role of extralogical imitation may be valuable in this kind of analysis. Maine may have overlooked the latent compulsion behind the spread of the British constitution in areas subject to British domination, but there are numerous instances of the ready acceptance of new institutions where there is no apparent or covert compulsion nor any relatedness as part of a cluster of other institutions adopted. Such imitation may be related to the prestige of certain institutions which symbolize the attainment of ideals regnant in society. It would be rewarding, for example, to account for the rapid spread of judicial review[37] even in systems which have adopted the British cabinet system. There may be rationalization of its adoption in each instance,[38] but it is possible that the rationalization may have followed the fact. It is possible also that the prestige of foreign institutions may suffer rapid decline and even rejection. The increased popularity of the presidential form of government over the parliamentary form in Pakistan and in other new states may be due as much to the relative change in the status of Britain and the United States as world powers, as to the allegedly superior capacity of the presidential form to cope with the urgencies inherent in governing an underdeveloped state. Conditions of international politics affect both the prestige of external ideas and structures and the effectiveness of their transmission. Strategic requirements of the radiating society may lead to a policy of aggressive

[36] Allen, *op. cit.*, p. 106 quoting from Maine, *op. cit.*, p. 284.

[37] An account of the extent of this institution is given in David Deener, "Judicial Review in Modern Constitutional Systems," *American Political Science Review,* XLVI (1952), 1079-1100.

[38] See, for example, Sri Ram Sharma, "The Supreme Court of India," *Public Law,* Summer, 1958, pp. 119-134.

economic aid accompanied by explicit as well as implicit conditions. Thus the status of the radiating societies in world politics may also affect both the quality of imitation and the more rational reception of ideas and structures.

Process of Transmission

The spirals in "B" sector of Figure 1 touch the original cultural configuration which extends into that sector. This is meant to portray a field of interaction in which ideas and structures introduced externally have contact with internal factors before they invade fully the indigenous society. The indigenous society responds to its external universe in varying degrees of passivity or dynamism. The greater the initiative and dynamism of the indigenous society, the more the nature of the ultimate amalgam will depend on the genius and selectivity of those who act as agents for that society, and the less it will depend on the transmission activated by the radiating society. It is possible that coloration (or indigenization) acquired by the external ideas in this transmission may affect the reception and permanence of the external ideas once they are introduced. Examples of the Meiji reformers and Sun Yat-sen have already been given. Another example might be the long period of border interaction of Manchu and Han Chinese which ended in Manchu domination and assimilation by the Han.[39]

The transmission process is especially crucial in the modern phenomenon of technical assistance, although it has not been subject to the political science scrutiny which it deserves. In this process there must be identified an administrative mechanism which will allow for a spiraling indigenization of external ideas and structures. If the externals are unilaterally introduced by force, their reception and permanence may be different from what they would have been if prior indigenization had been possible. In this process there inheres the strategic advantage of creating an indigenous vested interest which can later champion selected change against other indigenous opposition and which can later regulate the implementation of the change and hence control the direction of its variance. Beyond this strategic consideration is the more important intellectual indig-

[39] A description of this can be found in Franz Michael, *The Origin of Manchu Rule in China* (Baltimore, 1942).

enization which is possible. This involves a selection of those aspects
of the intruding culture which are deemed to be imperative as well
as selection of indigenous ideas which are deemed equally imperative. In this preliminary synthesis, participants on both sides must
have an intellectual grasp of the distinctions between imperatives and
acculturated phenomena. The "programming" of missions of the
United States International Cooperation Administration is really an
effort to mold this sort of synthesis, although official reports may
not thus have described the process. Ideally, a grasp of the imperatives on both sides should be within the intellectual control of one
person or a very small group of persons, for such limitation is resistant to political contrivance and conducive to a higher degree of
rationality. Since the ideal is almost impossible to achieve, the outside survey mission is used with great frequency. Survey missions
are typically technically expert, but only rarely comprehending of a
cultural milieu in which they are called upon to advise, and even less
rarely are they likely to have separated in their own minds the imperatives from the acculturated phenomena of their own (the radiating) culture. In the abstract, ideal technical assistance programming involves the interplay of (1) the over-all mission point of
view as represented by the director, who is presumably aware of indigenous political sensitivities and aspirations; (2) the technical
expertness of the mission staff member (such as chief of public administration, chief of police administration), who is also presumed
to be aware of the indigenous technical point of view. Both of these
influences are usually thought to be empathetic to the indigenous
needs. (3) The external survey mission team, recruited temporarily
from the radiating culture, whose members are presumed to have
had multinational experience, and who can, because of their exter-
nality, bring to bear a detachment and universality which balance the
parochialism and empathy of the mission itself; (4) the indigenous
technical expert, who is presumed to have translated his generalized
professional needs into a particularized program; (5) the indigenous
policy-maker who presumably integrates the segmented technical
need with the larger political program. Only rarely are these roles
played with the neat separateness implied by the abstraction. There
is usually a bewildering overlapping if not confusion of roles compounded by the highly charged political setting in which the roles

are played. The technical staff expert on the American side may not be confidently expert, with the result that he may be antagonistic rather than empathetic to indigenous needs. His indigenous counterpart may be so intensely Western-oriented that he may ignore the cultural and political realities of his own nation. His proposal may be an extravaganza restrained by quixotic rather than rational response of the American staff member. The survey team may thus be placed in a position in which it serves as a protagonist of the indigenous point of view and its detachment and rationality may be correspondingly reduced.

In the transmission process technical assistance programmers are often confronted with formidable and unreasonable resistance from representatives of the receiving society. But the far greater problem is that of overwhelming the indigenous point of view by the prestige and wealth of the radiating society and the zeal and enthusiasm of its representatives. No doubt there is an extralogical element of imitation and prestige involved in this phenomenon. It has not been uncommon in past instances of culture contact for the most externally oriented of the receiving society's representatives to manifest extreme distaste for their own institutions and to depreciate them or, mesmerized by the new, to neglect significant values of the old.

The transmission process is complicated further in technical assistance relations between sovereign states by the presence of several independent assistance programs such as those under the Colombo Plan, the United Nations, and private philanthropies such as the Rockefeller, Ford, and Asia foundations. The private philanthropies are necessarily less bureaucratically rigid in their operations and perhaps somewhat more responsive to whims which may not necessarily be integrated into an over-all country program. When relations between foundation representatives and government technical assistance programs are less than cordial, there may be subtle competition for various programs, with the indigenous government playing one against the other.

What is needed most and what is frequently lacking is an institutionalization of the process of transmission wherein there can occur adequate defense of indigenous imperatives and sophisticated separation of imperatives and acculturated phenomena in the radiating society. From the point of view of political science research, careful analyses of this process are needed before a meaningful correlation between process, on the one hand, and impedance or facilitation on the other can be established.

There may be importance in continuing to invigorate transplanted ideas and structures by contact with their cultural source. This factor is relevant both to the transmitting process and the process of transformation (Sector C in Figure 1). The issues which require examination are: (1) whether such invigoration occurs, and if so, by what means, and (2) whether such invigoration changes the process of transformation by delaying indigenization or by preserving the identity of the external ideas and structures. It may be suggested that where transfer of ideas occurs largely through the medium of conquest and occupation or colonialism, the continued identity of officials with the wellsprings of their own culture is an important element in maintaining the pristine vigor of externally introduced institutions. It is for this reason that foreign officials have typically kept aloof from the indigenous milieu in which they have controlling roles; failure to do so has usually resulted in cultural assimilation.

In the cultural impact of sovereign states, the adjustment of an externally derived juridical system to customary or religious law enhances continuity of the source of radiation. If this adjustment were merely supersession of indigenous law applicable to all spheres of human life and activity by a Western legal system, competition among co-existent systems would be minimized and such continuity would be less than crucial. But total supersessions of one system by another have seldom occurred, although in Turkey and Japan the transition to Western systems was less gradual and subtle than elsewhere.[40]

In almost every Asian state in which Western jurisprudence has been adopted, the totality of legal activity has separated into spheres of validity in which different legal systems operate concurrently and, to some extent independently but competitively. In cases such as China and certain Middle Eastern countries, a relatively simple dichotomy of customary law and western law may exist.[41]

[40] Research on the interaction of legal systems by the Committee on Comparative Law of the International Association of Legal Science should be noted. See a report of its symposium held in Istanbul in 1955, "Reception of Foreign Law in Turkey," *International Social Science Bulletin,* IX (1957), 7-81; and K. Lipstein, "The Reception of Western Law in India," *ibid.,* IX (1957), 85-95.
[41] On China, see Roscoe Pound, "Comparative Law and History as Bases for

In other instances, four or even five spheres may exist with highly complex and subtle patterns of interaction.   In Malaya, customary (*adat*) law co-exists with Hindu, Muslim, Chinese, and Western legal systems; in Indonesia, *adat*, Chinese, Muslim, and Western systems are found.[42] Thus customary or religious law expressed by the Hindu *pandit*, or the Muslim *mufti, panchayat,* tribal council, or family council are operative within groups or in matters (such as family law) most untouched by Western values.   Concurrently, Western law is operative in its own sphere of validity, which may be spatial, substantive, or both.   While there may be conflict, the very existence of different spheres enables an externally derived system to operate within changing contours of effectiveness.   Each juridical sphere has a permeative dynamism which affects the contours and size of the other spheres.   It would be wrong to assume that the interaction is always characterized by enlargement of the externally derived system and shrinkage of the indigenous systems.   In Indonesia, for example, it was deliberate colonial policy to expand *adat* law and to keep it from being overcome by Western law.[43]   Even in India where British law profoundly influenced indigenous law,[44] English judges serving in local (*muffassal*) courts were influenced by Hindu law to some degree.[45]   In China before communist domination, the

Chinese Law," *Harvard Law Review,* LXI (1948), 749-762; and Meredith P. Gilpatrick, "The Status of Law and Lawmaking Procedure Under the Kuomintang, 1925-1946," *Far Eastern Quarterly,* X (1950), 38-56. On Middle Eastern countries, see J. N. D. Anderson, *Islamic Law in the Modern World* (New York, 1959), esp. pp. 99-100; Herbert J. Liebesny, "Religious Law and Westernization in the Moslem Near East," *The American Journal of Comparative Law,* II (1953), 492-504, and "Impact of Western Law in the Countries of the Near East," *The George Washington Law Review,* XXII (1953), 127-141.

[42] See B. Ter Haar, *Adat Law in Indonesia* (New York, 1958). On Malaya, see J. N. Matson, "The Conflict of Legal Systems in the Federation of Malaya and Singapore," *The International and Comparative Law Quarterly,* VI (1957), 243-262; and P. P. Buss-Tjen, "Malay Law," *The American Journal of Comparative Law,* VIII (1959), 29-43. The pattern of interaction appears to be even more complex in Africa. See J. N. D. Anderson, *Islamic Law in Africa* (London, 1954), and J. N. Matson, "Conflict of Laws in the Gold Coast," *The Modern Law Review,* XVI (1953), 469-481.

[43] B. Ter Haar, *op. cit.,* p. 13.

[44] Harrop A. Freeman, "An Introduction to Hindu Jurisprudence," *The American Journal of Comparative Law,* VIII (1959), 29-43.

[45] Alan Gledhill, "The Influence of Common Law and Equity on Hindu Law since 1800," *The International and Comparative Law Quarterly,* III (1954), 576-603.

interaction of the two spheres was such that one observer could say that "the hope of Goodnow and Willoughby's generation that China could be swung into the path of Anglo-American legal tradition is now rapidly fading."[46] Nevertheless, a synthesis of spheres of legal systems appears to be characteristic of the modernizing of most Asian states. The application of the doctrine of *stare decisis*, the almost exclusive reliance upon Western judicial precedent, the sense of identification of jurists with a body of law transcending national and cultural limits, are all factors which draw directly from the source of radiation. Customary law is deeply imbedded and has tough resilience. Until Western legal values have so rearranged the fabric of indigenous societies that the weave matches the pattern of the law, the externally derived system cannot be secure in either its dynamism or its dominance. It must draw heavily from its radiating source and in so doing its permeative quality is improved and its prospect of permanence heightened.

As with law, the continuity of source of radiation is strengthened by the professions and education. The remarkable attachment of elites educated in the British system to the values of that system is a familiar phenomenon.[47] It is at least of equal importance that through licensing and certification requirements (for chartered accountants, physicians, architects, lawyers, etc.) and university examining procedures a strong link with the source of radiation continues. It is strengthened further by large numbers of Asian students who study in England. The weight of influence is slowly shifting to the United States and will move more quickly in that direction when a generation of American-trained professionals reach positions of influence and authority on certification boards and university faculties. In government also a wholly new pattern of intellectual and professional allegiance is being forged as larger numbers of executives are trained in the United States in programs of the International Cooperation Administration. In public administration 1,085 officials from South Asia and the Far East were trained from 1952 through

[46] Meredith P. Gilpatrick, *loc. cit.*, p. 39.
[47] On British education in the subcontinent, see Edward Shils, "The Culture of the Indian Intellectual," *The Sewanee Review*, LXVII (1959), 231-261, 401-421; Hugh Tinker, "People and Government in Southern Asia," *Transactions of the Royal Historical Society* 5th series, IX (1959), 141-167; Sir Ivor Jennings, *Problems of the New Commonwealth* (Durham, N. C., 1958), pp. 72-92.

1960.[48] In some countries, notably Vietnam, Pakistan, Taiwan, and Japan, the movement away from the colonial tradition (French or British) to United States influence, even though vigorously denied by Anglophiles and nationalists, is not only perceptible but even dramatic in its effects.

Process of Transformation

Facilitation or impedance of external ideas and structures is influenced by a large set of factors whose identification and correlation with factors inherent in the external universe and in transmission remains one of the crucial problems of social science. Assessment of such factors may help in determining the degree of permanence and direction which change will take.

In an earlier period of scholarship in socio-economic development it was not uncommon to assume that religion, tradition, and social structure were almost unassailable bulwarks against social change. Hoselitz has suggested, however, that tradition may even serve as a vehicle facilitating change.[49] The earlier assumption was usually based on scanty empirical evidence, the erroneous transfer of experience from one setting to another or from conditions of gradual change to those of accelerated economic growth. In the subcontinent, for example, the assumption that caste would be an immense hindrance to industrialization was not supported by later empirical evidence which suggests that while caste does not disappear under industrialized conditions, neither does it hinder industrialization.[50]

The influence of religion and social structure can be assessed in terms of their rigidity or historical depth. Some phenomena of re-

[48] Data supplied by Public Administration Division, International Cooperation Administration, in letter to present writer, dated July 5, 1960. This figure does not include those trained under earlier programs from 1948 to 1952 or under leadership programs of the Department of State or United States Information Service.

[49] See Bert F. Hoselitz' paper in this volume.

[50] See Morris David Morris, "Caste and the Evolution of the Industrial Workforce in India," *Proceedings of the American Philosophical Society*, CIV (1960), 124-133, and "The Recruitment of an Industrial Labor Force in India, with British and American Comparisons," *Comparative Studies in Society and History*, II (1960), 305-328, esp. 325. See also Richard D. Lambert, "Factory Workers and the Nonfactory Population in Poona," *Journal of Asian Studies*, XVIII (1958), 21-42; and Arthur Niehoff, "Caste and Industrial Organization in North India," *Administrative Science Quarterly*, III (1959), 494-509.

ligion and social structure appear to give way more easily; it is as though there exist several layers of factors—soft at the edge of the configuration and hardest at the core. Classification of relevant phenomena within a society in terms of degree of rigidity may be related to the previously described categories of imperatives and acculturated phenomena for the former may owe their classification primarily to their rigidity. Rigidity may be due to several factors such as utility, support of a vested interest, identification with a web of social and economic factors or historical validity. It is at this point of analysis that historical study plays a crucial role, for it is history which most effectively reveals how deeply imbedded an institution may be. Historical analysis must reach back through successive mutations at least until a given mutation appears to have no operative significance. An example may be drawn from the occupation of Japan. Assume that the decision to extend suffrage to women was based on an assessment of the resistance or facilitation which this change might encounter. Historical analysis extended three centuries might have resulted in a negative prognosis but if extended to the twelfth century and beyond, the revelation of a different tradition might have encouraged the success the change contemplated.[51] Such historical analysis, while difficult because of the relatively undeveloped state of scholarship on Asia, is essential as a means of extracting the intrinsic significance of an institution and of revealing submerged bases for facilitating or impeding change. Careful historical study, utilizing some qualities of social science analysis, may also separate the mythical utility and effectiveness of institutions from the reality. An illustration drawn from the subcontinent is the role of the *panchayat*, commonly assumed to be an idyllic council of five village elders to whom can be entrusted development problems with little or no risk of political turmoil or corruption.[52] Thorner, characterizing this view as Rousseauan, asserts that "the fundamental error in the idealized version of village life is that it underestimates the extent, the depth, and the antiquity of the disparities characteristic of all spheres of Indian rural

[51] On the social causes of the subordination of women from Fujiwara to Muromachi, see Sir George Sansom, *Japan, A Short Cultural History* (New York, 1943), p. 362.
[52] See citations in note 27 above, and Daniel Thorner, "The Village Panchayat as a Vehicle of Change," *Economic Development and Cultural Change*, II (1953), 209-215.

society." The historical dimension of rigidity is of even more subtle and complex utility as an analytical tool since its value, far from being fixed, varies in relation to other factors. An instance from Indian and Pakistani experience will illustrate. Consideration of the history of the different responses of Hindu and Muslim to British educational values and of the independence movement might lead to the conclusion that Pakistani rejection of British influence would be more complete than Indian rejection after independence. But the reverse has been true, at least, in government reform. Pakistan relied on the British tradition far more than did India as is evidenced by retention of British officials as Establishments Secretary and as Director of the Civil Service academy for nearly a decade of its existence and by the sending of its higher civil service probationers to England until 1960. India, on the other hand, severed these institutional bonds immediately in 1947. The expectation derived from earlier history was obviously modified by a set of more contemporary influences. Among them might be mentioned: (1) the greater self-confidence of the Indian intellectual and administrative system, sustained by the Brahminical tradition and continuity of administration; (2) the success of the Appleby mission and the establishment of the Indian Institute of Public Administration, which identified reform more with the United States than with Britain; (3) the discontinuity, instability, insecurity, and lack of confidence in Pakistan which encouraged an irrational adherence to the British system, which became an entrenched symbol of order. This example suggests that predispositions revealed by historical analysis are not final determinants of the future course of events but serve as an essential basing point modified by more contemporary events.[53]

Other factors within the cultural configuration affect ideas and structures externally introduced. It is possible that social trauma or stress in the society may facilitate the acceptance of the new. This was suggested by Leighton's study of the Japanese Relocation Center at Poston, which was essentially a study of a society under stress.[54]

[53] For a penetrating analysis of the role of history in culture change, see Bronislaw Malinowski, *The Dynamics of Culture Change* (New Haven, 1954), pp. 27-40. See especially his *caveat* that a "legitimate historical explanation is only possible when we can trace the development of an institution and establish continuity in function as well as in form" (p. 154).

[54] Alexander Leighton, *The Governing of Men* (Princeton, 1946), p. 302.

Leighton's hypothesis merits further careful investigation to determine if some types of social stress may produce in some institutions unusual resilience to change and in others facilitation of change. There may also be a correlation between degrees of completeness of social breakdown and success of new institutions. Finally, economic conditions and problems of international security as viewed from within the nation affect the success of induced change.

The further identification of factors relevant to the process of transformation remains an outstanding social science problem to which political science must make a contribution. In Column C of Figure 1 the circles shown being deflected from a barrier of impedance are meant to suggest that where there is impedance, a variation of the induced change may result and it may assume a different form and even a different function in the adjusting society. Political science can, with profit, utilize a functional rather than an institutional approach in analysis of change. The functional approach[55] postulates that human activities can be classified into categories, that these activities are universal in all cultures but are not necessarily carried on by institutions which are alike in the compared cultures. Hence a variant may assume different form but perform the same function. Much effort may be wasted unless this is probed, for the political scientists with an institutional bent may be misled into assuming the disappearance of functions which have merely assumed different institutional form.

New Cultural Configuration

Little is known in political science of the nature of new institutions which emerge after transformation. Analytical apparatus must be borrowed almost entirely from the highly developed work of anthropologists dealing with culture change. Malinowski's study of culture change in Africa with its accompanying analytical scheme ("synoptic chart") is of particular value.[56] He reviews three theories of culture change which he labels (1) "contact situation as an integral whole," (2) "diffusion," and (3) "mixture of elements" and suggests the inadequacy of all three in the light of empirical evidence

[55] For pertinent definitions relevant to his theory of culture change, and partly relevant to this discussion, see Bronislaw Malinowski, *op. cit.*, pp. 41-51, esp. 44, 45.

[56] *Ibid.*, pp. 14-26.

in Africa. The "integral whole" notion regards the factors of the intruding culture on a parity with those of the receiving culture. Of this, Malinowski states, "Above all, it obscures and distorts the only correct conception of culture change in such areas: the fact that it is the result of an impact of a higher, active culture upon a simpler, more passive one. The typical phenomena of change, the adoption or rejection, the transformation of certain institutions and the growth of new ones, are ruled out by the concept of a well-integrated community or culture."[57] He objects to the assumption of passivity in the notion of diffusion, and places emphasis on the aggressive and dynamic quality of the transmitting culture, which he characterizes as embodying definite forces and pressures.[58] In an uncommonly perceptive critique of the notion that change is essentially a "mixture of partially fused elements which can only be understood in terms of the parent cultures," Malinowski asserts that this notion underestimates the dynamism and complexity of the process of change and that it is unprofitable to "treat the process as a mechanical mixture where the main problem consists in sorting out and invoicing back elements." The culture which emerges is the result of a process, he argues, which embraces "three orders of reality: the impact of the higher culture; the substance of native life on which it is directed; and the phenomenon of autonomous change resulting from the reaction between the two cultures."[59] The three orders of Malinowski correspond to columns A, C, and D of Figure 1. He does not isolate a group of factors relevant to a transmission process which in the scheme here presented in Figure 1 is treated as an autonomous process. It may be that in describing a colonial situation rather than a relationship between sovereign entities, the transmission process was not as rational as would now be the case in technical assistance. Nevertheless, it may be assumed that he regarded what is here labeled as the process of transmission as important since he viewed European entrepreneurs, administrators, and other residents in Africa as the main agents of change. Further, a major part of his analysis embraces the concept of "common factor" or "common measure" by which he meant an identity of European and African interests, which

[57] *Ibid.*, p. 15.
[58] *Ibid*, p. 19.
[59] *Ibid.*, pp. 26, 52.

would result in an ecologically rational and harmonious policy and development.[60]

Of particular merit to political science is the necessity to view the ultimate institutions which emerge (column D) as constantly changing and as a result of a complicated process moving in the direction of columns A through D. In political science, as in anthropology, it would be far more rewarding to utilize a functional rather than an institutional approach, because the former assumes that there are certain systems of activities which are carried on in all societies and it seeks to universalize and categorize such activities, which vary both spatially and temporally. The institution performing a given function may be quite different in the new cultural configuration (Column D) from what it was before or during contact with external ideas. In this respect the efforts on the part of Lasswell, and more recently, Almond, to isolate common functions of political systems[61] are significant steps in political science analysis of political change in underdeveloped areas.

IV

There remain two issues which would profit from political science analysis. The fifth issue may be stated in this way:

E. The variants which emerge in the changed cultural configuration must be assessed in terms of their adequacy to satisfy the expectations of modern constitutional government, e.g., to maintain the viability of the state, to provide economic well being, to provide a framework of order, and to accommodate to the general will.

Not only will analysis be facilitated by the functionalism alluded to in Part III of this essay, but a revaluation of certain institutions must be made. Limitations of space permit mention of only two of these: civil public bureaucracy, and military bureaucracy. The civil bureaucracy in most Asian states owes its origin conceptually either to the Confucian concept of the mandarinate or to the British

[60] *Ibid.*, pp. 64-83.
[61] Gabriel A. Almond and James S. Coleman, *The Politics of the Developing Areas* (Princeton, 1960), pp. 3-64.

development of the Indian Civil Service. In both traditions there is an assumption of superior virtue residing in the bureaucracy rather than in the public mass. This is chiefly the result of the fact that in large measure the civil public bureaucracy has also been the intellectual group[62] of the nation. Conditions of tension between the intellectuals and the powers which Shils so well describes[63] have been absent in many Asian underdeveloped states in which the intellectuals were and are the powers. As an intellectual *corps d'élite* the bureaucracy regards itself as the guardian and transmitter of the polity of the state and imputes subversion, if not disaster, to any enlargement of the influence of the public mass or its representatives, the politicians. The power of the bureaucracy is further strengthened by an underlying optimistic and naïve reliance on a concentrically radiating permeative virtue which emanates from the locus of power and which infuses and consequently rectifies society. Its distinctly separate identity is enhanced when there is a bifurcated society (as in India, Pakistan, Ceylon, and Malaya) in which the bureaucracy is secular-minded, Western-oriented, and English-speaking and the public mass is religion-directed, tradition-oriented, and vernacular-speaking. Cultural bifurcation between rulers and ruled is to be expected in a colonial situation in which an oligarchy of one value system rules the masses of a wholly different culture. Too great a chasm between masses and rulers in a system predicated on popular sovereignty will result in one of the following: (1) permeation of each value system by the values of the other system and consequent hazing of distinction; (2) increasing tension between the two systems; (3) dominance of one system over the other. It is likely that when the last alternative occurs bureaucracy will be strengthened further by its role as interpreter of a new polity and creator of its own consensus.

[62] Shils's definition merits quotation: "In every society however there are some persons with an unusual sensitivity to the sacred, an uncommon reflectiveness about the nature of their universe, and the rules which govern their society. There is in every society a minority of persons who, more than the ordinary run of their fellow-men, are enquiring, and desirous of being in frequent communion with symbols which are more general than the immediate concrete situations of everyday life, and remote in their reference in both time and space." Edward Shils, "The Intellectuals and the Powers: Some Perspectives for Comparative Analysis," *Comparative Studies in Society and History*, I (1958), p. 5.

[63] *Ibid.*, pp. 5-22, and Edward Shils, "The Concentration and Dispersion of Charisma: Their Bearing on Economic Policy in Underdeveloped Countries," *World Politics*, XI (1958), 1-20.

In the interim, which may be measured in decades, the orthodox Western notion of consensus as a prerequisite for democracy must be revaluated[64] and the educative role of an elitist bureaucracy reassessed. It is not likely that the bureaucracy will lose much of its charismatic quality as a result of more representative recruitment policies, for the scanty evidence available for Pakistan and India suggests a continuation of rather than a departure from social patterns of recruitment.[65]

The ethos of the bureaucracy and the training conducing to it are of considerable importance. The value-judgment sector of bureaucratic decision-making expands when pertinent data cannot be reduced to incontrovertible or, at least, to empirically oriented factors. In heterogeneous societies in which mass values are different from those of a ruling elite, the bureaucratic disposition may be at variance with that of the public mass; and, since developing states rarely have the restraints on bureaucracy manifest in experienced constitutional systems, the impalpability of bureaucratic discretion increases. Hence, attention must be paid to the predispositions which mold the values held by the men who make the decisions. It might, perhaps, be reasonable to assume that the training of bureaucrats in the United States is of minimal importance because the training is amorphous and is later vitiated by identification of the bureaucrats' "personal expedience" with his agency's "principled interests." But in the bureaucracies of underdeveloped states, bureaucratic values, including "principled interests," derived from many sources, are cast in a rigid and enduring mold either by an exclusive training program, which may be the descendant of Haileybury College, or of the examination cells of the Confucian tradition. In early stages of political development, there is little inclination of a bureaucratic agency to identify itself substantively with the clientele it serves. The ethos is more philosophical, perhaps almost mystical, and principled interests are to a greater degree the totality of individual values derived from

---

[64] For an illuminating analysis of an empirical effort to determine if consensus is a necessary condition for the existence of democracy, see James W. Prothro and Charles M. Grigg, "Fundamental Principles of Democracy: Bases of Agreement and Disagreement," *Journal of Politics*, XXII (1960), 276-295.

[65] Even in the United States and Britain, according to Gusfield, there is apparently less equalitarian effect in bureaucratic recruitment than is commonly assumed. See Joseph R. Gusfield, "Equalitarianism and Bureaucratic Recruitment," *Administrative Science Quarterly*, II (1958), 521-541.

society at large and from institutional training. The sources, quality, dynamism and persistence of such values can best be ascertained by analysis of the whole culture and of the training systems which add to that culture a charisma or an exclusivity.

In the absence of a vigorous and respectable tradition of politics, a civil bureaucracy sustained by traditional factors is likely to remain the most important element of government. Western political-science analysis must accommodate itself to the notion that the public bureaucracy in early political development will not play the role of the politically neutral agent responsive to popularly determined policy. What must be studied is the phenomenon of an elitist bureaucracy initiating change, not always with maximum regard for the aspirations of the public mass, regarding itself as the embodiment of Platonic guardianship, creating its own consensual base. The further problem for political science is to determine how this bureaucratic power can be contained, how it can be made to serve without arrogance, and how it can with good grace relinquish its power and transform its function when a mature, viable political system begins to operate as the source of polity.

There is a strong tradition of analysis of bureaucracy in American political science deriving from Weber and stimulated by Friedrich, Cole, and others. Moreover, there is fortunate interdisciplinary exchange (perhaps deriving from the fact that Weber was a sociologist) and considerable contemporary work in sociology, notably by Eisenstadt and Bendix.[66]

The role of the military bureaucracy also needs revaluation by political science. A civil bureaucracy whose traditions are not strong enough to sustain it in the midst of political disorder, or whose pre-

[66] The literature on bureaucracy is too voluminous to mention in detail. A few pioneering or recent works may be usefully cited. See especially *Administrative Science Quarterly*, III (1960), the entire issue of which is devoted to comparative public administration. Two of the articles conveniently classify and analyze the pertinent literature: Alfred Diamant, "The Relevance of Comparative Politics to the Study of Comparative Administration" (pp. 87-113), and Ferrel Heady, "Recent Literature on Comparative Public Administration" (pp. 134-155). See also S. N. Eisenstadt, "Internal Contradictions in Bureaucratic Polities," *Comparative Studies in Society and History*, I (1958), 58-76; "Political Struggle in Bureaucratic Societies," *World Politics*, IX (1956), 15-36; Reinhard Bendix, "Bureaucracy: The Problem and Its Setting," *American Sociological Review*, XII (1947), 493-507; Ferrel Heady, "Bureaucratic Theory and Comparative Administration," *Administrative Science Quarterly*, III (1959), 509-525; Robert V. Presthus, "Social Bases of Bureaucratic Organization," *Social Forces*, XXXVIII (1959), 103-109.

dispositions are so overwhelmingly literary-generalist or legal, may not be as effective as a military bureaucracy in the early stages of political development. One of the prime requisites of bureaucracy in underdeveloped areas is an appreciation of empiricism. Domination of the bureaucracy by the predisposition of the classical generalist is likely to be detrimental to the attainment of efficiency and integrity and to the acceleration of economic growth. Administrative and economic order depend on the accurate reproduction of reality, the isolation of predictable factors, the assessment of their impact on reality, and consequent rational planning and forecasting, all of which are predicated on an empirical methodology. Of all sectors of the public bureaucracy the military, by virtue of its mission, can be expected to discard more quickly both the intuitive disposition of the masses and related literary-generalist tradition of the civil bureaucracy. Although it is preoccupied with the requirements of order and stability, its concern for precision in situation analysis disposes it favorably toward empiricism. It is possible that a military bureaucracy, manifesting sufficient patience with the complexities of long-range planning, can create an environment more favorable for economic development than a civil government can. It is not inconceivable that alleged attitudinal dangers of the military and corresponding virtues of the civil are the result of an uneven pace in the absorption of empiricism and political values by different sectors of a society.

In some instances, notably Indonesia, where a civil bureaucratic tradition is weaker than on the subcontinent, military bureaucracy embodies nationalist and revolutionary ideals and manifests a zeal, sense of sacrifice, and devotion to duty greater than any other element in society.[67] Since national integration is one of the serious problems confronting many underdeveloped states, the role of the military as agents of nationalism cannot be overlooked. One of the elements calling for further study in analyzing the role of the military bureaucracy is the possibility that forms of military authority may have

[67] For a persuasive argument that the officer corps in Southeast Asia are the only hope for maintaining stability in the face of the communist threat and should therefore be encouraged and supported by the United States, see Guy J. Pauker, "Southeast Asia as a Problem Area in the Next Decade," *World Politics*, XI (1959), 325-346.

[68] On nationalism, see Rupert Emerson, "Nationalism and Political Development," *Journal of Politics*, XXII (1960), 3-28.

shifted from "domination" to "manipulation" and that the military bureaucracy tends to display more and more characteristics of the civil bureaucracy. This thesis, as developed by the sociologist Janowitz,[69] must be seriously considered by political science in any comparative analysis of the role of civil and military bureaucracies in developing states. Janowitz argues that technological change has increased the military establishment's interdependence with civilian society and that the shift in military mission from preparation for violence to deterrence of violence has involved military elites more and more in political and diplomatic warfare. Moreover, "the classical view of the military standing in opposition to technological innovation is inapplicable as the present cycle of the arms race converts the armed forces into centers of support and concern for the development of new weapons systems."[70] Innovation is facilitated further by "the continual need for retraining personnel from operational to managerial positions and from older to newer techniques [which] has led to a more rational spreading of higher education throughout the career of the military officer rather than the concentrated dosage typical of the civilian in graduate or professional school."[71] Further analysis should determine if Janowitz' observations are applicable to the military establishments of developing states as well as to that of the United States. If such change is occurring at a significant pace, it is possible that even after an initial period of achieving economic order, the military bureaucracy may have been so transformed that it may continue to rule within a democratic structure. In any event the rise of military bureaucracy as a vehicle for establishing economic and administrative order creates a major dual problem for political science: the dilemma of transforming the military into a civilianized entity and relinquishing complete power to the sovereign public mass and their political representatives.

One final observation on bureaucracy may be made. It is theoretically possible that either civil or military bureaucracy may be so modified that it will develop a representativeness and responsiveness to the public mass nearly as effective as those of a popularly elected legislature. Through elaboration of the administrative hear-

[69] Morris Janowitz, "Changing Patterns of Organizational Authority: The Military Establishment," *Administrative Science Quarterly*, III (1959), 473-493.
[70] *Ibid.*, p. 479.
[71] *Idem.*

ing process this has, to some extent, developed in the United States. It will probably never equal the system of legislative dominance as a means of controlling power, but it may be possible to soften or almost eliminate the oligarchic arbitrariness characterizing administrative rule in the past.   And since it may be presumed to be more rational than the legislative process, a bureaucracy in which democratic patterns have been extended and fortified may not be the worst fate which might befall a developing nation.[72]

The sixth and last proposition which is deemed to be of concern to political science may be stated thus:

F. *From the experiences of separate states in different stages of development and in different cultures, hypotheses of a political process of presumptive universal validity may be verified and laws of politics may emerge.*

As stated in the opening of this essay significant developments in the two established subdisciplines of public administration and comparative government have taken place.   These activities have been almost entirely directed to this sixth proposition.

The formulation of models[73] and of hypotheses presumed to have transnational validity has begun although in no sense has it reached the same stage of development as in economics.   There has been a recent tendency to avoid the grand conceptualization of Pareto and Weber and to direct research to what has been called " 'middle range' theory which attempts to abstract from the whole social context some limited but, hopefully, meaningful segment for analysis."[74]   Stimulated by the Committee on Comparative Politics of the Social Science Research Council, much significant research has been done in the last

---

[72] For a suggestion that bureaucracy is not an inevitable disease of technology or bigness but might have further democratic potentialities, see Alvin W. Gouldner, *Patterns of Industrial Bureaucracy* (Glencoe, 1954), and "Metaphysical Pathos and the Theory of Bureaucracy," *American Political Science Review*, XLIX (1955), 496-507.

[73] See, for example, Fred Riggs, "Agraria and Industria—Toward a Typology of Comparative Administration," in W. J. Siffin, ed., *Toward the Comparative Study of Public Administration* (Bloomington, 1957), pp. 23-110.   For an excellent definition of models and analysis of their use in politics, see Colin Leys, "Models, Theories, and the Theory of Political Parties," *Political Studies*, VII (1959), 127-146, esp. 129-132.

[74] Robert V. Presthus, "Behavior and Bureaucracy in Many Cultures," *Public Administration Review*, XIX (1959), 25-36, at 26.

decade, both substantively and in the formulation of systems and models.[75] The criticism which once could justifiably be directed against a general failure of political scientists to appreciate the cultural configuration as it relates to politics[76] can no longer be made as the cultural factor, especially in non-Western research situations, is more and more considered.[77] With respect to Asian societies, several research strategies have been suggested.[78]

In the public administration, the concept of a science of administration, transcending cultural and national boundaries, has been given impetus by publication of the *Administrative Science Quarterly,* started at Cornell University in 1956.[79]

Developments in both comparative government and public administration have in common the objective of discovering universal laws. The first major result of the work of the Social Science Research Council's Committee on Comparative Politics has been the volume *The Politics of the Developing Areas.*[80] The methodology is clearly set forth in an introductory chapter by Gabriel Almond. The political systems of Southeast Asia, South Asia, Sub-Saharan Africa, the Near East, and Latin America are then analyzed with reference to the conceptual apparatus given in the introduction.

This work is especially valuable because the drive toward scientific generalization has not eclipsed entirely a consideration of the total culture configuration of each area. The Almond-Coleman hypotheses

[75] A brief review of this activity can be found in the introduction to a substantive comparative study, Taylor Cole, "Three Constitutional Courts," *The American Political Science Review,* LIII (1959), 963-985, at 963-965. See also Gunnar Heckscher, *The Study of Comparative Government and Politics* (London, 1957); Sigmund Neumann, "Comparative Politics: A Half-Century Appraisal," *Journal of Politics,* XIX (1957), 369-390.

[76] See especially criticism of a 1952 report of the Social Science Research Council's Interuniversity Research Seminar on Comparative Politics, "Research in Comparative Politics," *The American Political Science Review,* XLVII (1953), 641-675, esp. 666-669.

[77] An example is Richard W. Gable, "Culture and Administration in Iran," *The Middle East Journal,* XIII (1959), 407-421.

[78] See, for example, Lucian W. Pye, "The Non-Western Political Process," *Journal of Politics,* XX (1958), 468-486; and George Mc. T. Kahin, Guy J. Pauker, and Lucian W. Pye, "Comparative Politics of Non-Western Countries," *American Political Science Review,* XLIX (1955), 1024-1027.

[79] The first article to appear in the new journal by its principal organizer, Edward H. Litchfield, "Notes on A General Theory of Administration," *Administrative Science Quarterly,* I (1956), 3-29, is a cogent statement of a science of administration.

[80] Cited above, n. 61.

of a political process common to many cultures must ultimately deal with relationship of non-political cultural factors. Scientific comparability and cultural analysis are interdependent steps to the attainment of scientific generalization. In the present essay it is suggested that these steps occur in a logical methodological sequence as follows: (1) The effort to hypothecate phenomena of the political process common to all (or almost all) systems. The characteristics of political systems arrived at by the Social Science Research Council Study group, and elaborated in Almond's introduction, constitute this necessary first step. Almond groups these into two categories: input and output functions. In the former, he places political socialization and recruitment, interest articulation, interest aggregation, political communication; in the latter he places rule-making, rule application, rule adjudication. (2) There must then follow empirical validation of the incidence of each of these political functions. This step is now being taken by several field studies sponsored by the Social Science Research Council. In preliminary fashion, this validation has also been made by the remaining chapters of the Almond volume. (3) From the first two steps will result a pattern of similarity or dissimilarity among various systems. (4) The results of the first three steps are tabulative rather than explicatory. The next inevitable question to be asked is why these phenomena occur or do not occur in the pattern revealed. This question can be answered only by minute examination of the causative factors making for occurrence or non-occurrence in each system. (5) The pattern of occurrence must then be integrated with the pattern of causation, and from this integration principles of universal validity may be drawn. Ultimate comparability, then, will be not of external political functions alone, but of causality and function.

Steps 1, 2, and 3 do not involve extensive knowledge of the culture in which the political functions have been determined. The two final steps require a highly versatile knowledge of the cultural context if a pattern of causality is to be worked out. The apparatus for such cultural analysis in American social science has been largely the result of an emphasis on an interdisciplinary area approach. If, as Almond states, the prediction of trends in political development in accordance with his methodology "implies the obsolescence of the present day divisions of the study of politics into American, European, Asiatic, Middle Eastern, African, and Latin American 'area studies',"[81] then some other means of providing an analytic competence to deal with the total fabric of culture must be found, if a meaningful relationship between causality and function is to result. This requirement assumes somewhat different dimensions for public administration and politics. It is sometimes assumed that emerging bureaucracies in underdeveloped states are less intricately imbedded in the matrix of culture, since the bureaucracy is often more secular-minded and Western-oriented than the public mass. Moreover, the technical aspects of administration are more clearly divorced from parochial cultural attributes and are transnational. Further, since the bureaucracy is often not directly responsive to the public mass, it derives its generative strength and perhaps even ethos, to a greater degree from universalistic values divorced from indigenous culture. From this it might be argued that the more universal and rational administration becomes, the less the importance of analyzing indigenous cultural attributes in arriving at a pattern of causality. Yet even if the cultural and political autonomy of the bureaucracy developed in this way, it could not be totally uninfluenced by its own culture. Hence cultural analysis would continue to be important, not so much for determining the cultural origins of bureaucratic functions, but for determining causation in the modifications of those functions to which even a quasi-autonomous bureaucracy is subject. In the broader problem of political functions generally, the detachment from cultural context may not be as pronounced and the need for examination of that context may therefore be somewhat greater.

Summary

Only in the subdisciplines of comparative government and public administration has substantial progress been made in analyzing the process of political development. Even in these fields, the stage of testing many hypotheses has not yet been reached. Of the six problems posed for political science research, only the sixth, namely the effort to arrive at universal laws of politics, has yielded substantial understanding of political development.

[81] Gabriel A. Almond and James S. Coleman, eds., *op. cit.*, p. 64.

The process of transmission of ideas and structures and their reception and transformation has not been adequately dealt with in
political science despite the importance of that process in technical
assistance. The problem of political development is so intertwined
with that of culture change that it may not be possible for political
science ultimately to predict the direction of political change or to
arrive at a theory of causality of universal political functions either
without substantially greater interdisciplinary activity, or without in-
corporating within its own methodology elements of anthropological
and sociological method.

6

The Background of Some Trends in Islamic Political Thought

Ishtiaq Husain Qureshi

All thought, to possess any social validity, must be related to the society which it seeks to serve. In studying the various trends in Islamic political thinking, therefore, it is necessary to find out the social ideals which were prevalent at different times and to examine the structure of society itself in the world of Islam. These are complex subjects in themselves and cannot be dealt with adequately within the limits of a single chapter. For our purposes, however, such a detailed examination is not necessary; it will suffice to mention broad tendencies to illustrate their impact upon Muslim social and political thinking and to understand its aims, achievements, and shortcomings.

Leaving aside the Muslim belief that all revealed truth was Islam and that it began with the first spiritual wisdom vouchsafed to humanity, we shall deal with the subject since the beginning of the mission of the Prophet Muhammad, because it is the body of his teaching which is identified with Islam in common parlance.[1] Muhammad was born in a tribal society which was in a state of perpetual anarchy, developing the virtues and faults which such conditions foster.[2] Qualities of courage, bravery, and leadership were highly valued and therefore assiduously cultivated; pride, bravado, and bluster were perhaps the necessary foils for these virtues.

[1] The events referred to in this paper are generally known to students of Islamic history. A convenient book to consult for those who are not familiar with Islamic history is Syed Ameer Ali, *A Short History of the Saracens* (London, 1921).

[2] For a description of Arab tribal society, see Ilse Lichtenstadter, *Islam and the Modern Age* (New York, 1958), pp. 33-46; also Ilse Lichtenstadter, "From Particularism to Unity," *Islamic Culture* (Hyderabad), XXIII (1949), 251-280.

Through his teachings the Prophet was able to ennoble the Arab character and create in Arab society an integration which it had lacked before.[3] The legacy of a tribal past was not easy to obliterate. A large proportion of the Arabs continued to take some of the features of tribal society for granted, because even in the context of a new religion and a different philosophy of life, the structure of society retained many characteristics of its previous pattern.[4] Islam has perhaps been more successful in affecting patterns of social organization than many other philosophies, but it could not work outside the framework of history. Though tribal patterns continued in operation after the conversion of the Arabs, the fundamental philosophy of Islam in the matter of social organization was, nevertheless, diametrically opposed to tribalism. It did not succeed in obliterating tribalism from the world of Islam; indeed it could not do so without corresponding changes in the economic life of the converted peoples; but it did create the psychological and spiritual background in which the transition from tribal structures could be easier. The basic elements of this philosophy were, in order of their importance, the doctrine of the brotherhood of all believers, the emphasis upon piety and personal qualities as the source of greatness and nearness to God, and the playing down of birth as a factor in entitling any individual to distinction or eminence. Differences of race and color were characterized as being merely incidental and of little importance, useful only in recognizing different groups of humanity.[5] In spite of all this so great was the weight of previous tradition that the earlier Arabs found it a little difficult to absorb into their system the new converts from non-Arab peoples. The best they could think of was to affiliate them to their own tribes.[6] The Arabism of the

[3] J. Wellhousen, "Muhammads Geneindeorgrung von Medina," *Skizzen und Vorarbeiten* (Berlin), IV (1889), 74; also, Qur'ān, iii, 103.

[4] This is demonstrated by the existence of tribes and tribal feeling even today in Saudi Arabia. Indeed, in the greater part of the country the government still functions through the agency of tribal sheikhs.

[5] There are numerous references in the Qur'ān to the unity of mankind; the text above is almost a translation. Another one often quoted says, "All men are like a single nation." Qur'ān, ii, 213. Also, *idem*, iv, 1. The statement in the text is based on Qur'ān, xxx, 21, 22 and xlix, 13, of which it is almost a paraphrase.

[6] This was the system of "clients" (Arabic, *mawali*) by which a non-Arab tribe was affiliated with an Arabic one. Zake Ali, *Islam in the World* (Lahore, 1938), p. 81; Carl Brockelmann, *History of the Islamic Peoples* (New York, 1939) p. 78; Gustave E. Von Grunebaum, *Unity and Variety in Islam* (Chicago, 1955), Part II.

Umayyads was resented not only by the non-Arab Muslims, but also by the learned among the Muslim Arabs, who found it intolerable that the non-Arab converts should be asked to pay the *jiziyah*. The Islamic teachings regarding the equality of all Muslims ultimately triumphed and legal and political discrimination against the non-Arabs were removed.[7] This is the classical example of the assertion of the doctrine of Islamic brotherhood in the early history of Islam, but there were other, more subtle, manners in which the structure of society and political thinking alike were affected by the doctrines of Islam. Here it is sufficient to discuss the political aspect alone. For this we shall have to go to the very beginnings.

When the Prophet Muhammad went to Medina from Mecca, since the leaders of the latter city had made it impossible for him to carry on his mission, he found himself at the head of a small community of believers. For them he was not only the source of religious inspiration, but also their leader in mundane matters. This endowed him with political power as well. This power was exercised for furthering the welfare of the community and the promotion of the interests of Islam as a faith and as a way of life. Muḥammad did not establish a church or a priesthood; as the recipient of the divine revelation he was the source of guidance for his people, but this position of his was unique in the community. When the prophet died, it was realized that the prophethood had come to an end and that there was no question of his being succeeded by anyone else for the performance of the prophetic duties which had been vouchsafed to him alone at that time for the guidance of humanity. There was still the task of keeping those teachings alive and of interpreting them for the benefit of the believers.[8] This responsibility was now shared by the entire community of believers and every individual was responsible to the extent of his ability.[9] Thus those who devoted their entire lives to the study of religious sciences had the duty of explaining to other believers their duties and of adding to their own as well as to the community's understanding of the truth of

[7] Brockelmann, *op. cit.*, p. 92. This happened under the Umayyad caliph, 'Umar ibn 'Abd-u'l-'Azīz.

[8] For the role played by the ulema in this matter, see Erwin I. J. Rosenthal, *Political Thought in Medieval Islam* (Cambridge, 1958), p. 22. Their role is described in Qur'ān, iii, 70.

[9] Qur'ān, ii, 141, 286.

Islam; in this sense the learned in the religious sciences have been compared to the prophets of Israel.[10] The basic notion behind this comparison is that while the people of Israel were guided by a succession of prophets and a continuation of the divine inspiration, the Muslims had now to look to their own resources of intellects to interpret for themselves what had been revealed so that it could be applied to their lives. Thus there was no room for a priest-hood, though there was the need of learning. The learned, how-ever, were not given any authority; they could express their opinions but these opinions as such had no binding force. They had to receive acceptance to become part of the beliefs of the people; even then they occupied only a secondary position in the formulation of Islamic theology and law.[11] It will be necessary to elaborate this point further at the appropriate stage; but it should be mentioned here that Islam did not set up an organized instrument for the interpre-tation of its teachings or for their elaboration; the question of the acceptance of any elaboration or interpretation put forward by indi-viduals is a different matter, and will be discussed later.

The Muslim community never discarded the theory behind its organization as it came to be understood in the lifetime of the Prophet.[12] It was a community organized for the purpose of being able to live its life in accordance with the teachings of Islam. This was fundamental; everything else was subsidiary. Thus it was a community of believers existing for what is fundamentally a religious end; there have been other communities in history which have been organized for religious purposes; however, the Muslims are different from many other religious communities in two important respects; Islam has no priesthood and hence no church and Islam believes that religion cannot be separated from the rest of life.[31] Thus the Mus-lims, in the ideal Islamic environment, would be a community of lay-men living their entire lives in accordance with the precepts of Islam. But as human life has to be lived in this world, the Muslims could

---

[10] A well-known *hadīth*, which says, "The learned among my people are like the prophets of Israel."

[11] A ruling by a jurist becomes binding only if it is enforced by a judge or by the state. If it is accepted by the individual, it is binding upon him, because then it becomes a part of his belief. There is no other method of enforcing it.

[12] For the functions of the Muslim community, see Ibn Tumart, *Kitāb*, ed. Luc-iani, (Alger, 1903), pp. 245 ff.

[13] Rosenthal, *op. cit.*, p. 23, where he says, "There are no two swords, a spiritual and a temporal, in Islam."

not be different in their mundane needs from non-believers, and for
that reason many matters which are looked upon as merely secular
by other communities would be included within the functions of the
organized Muslim community.   There is no religious community,
not even of monks and hermits, which has no mundane matters to
look after; but in Islam the secular element had to be much greater,
because it was the total community and not only a section of the
community which was thus organized.   Besides, Islam is not otherworldly in its approach to human problems.[14] It is, however, necessary to mention here that Islam does not recognize the division of
human activities into two segments of religious and secular; it thinks
that all human activity has a spiritual significance because it springs
from a spiritual personality and in turn affects it.   Actions are not
of equal significance in the development of our total personality; but,
from the point of view of Islam, they are of considerable importance.[15]   With this basic philosophy and with the absence of a
priesthood, Islam could not provide separate organizations for religion and worldly matters.   The pattern, therefore, was provided
fundamentally by the Muslim community in the lifetime of the
Prophet of a society of laymen living together for religious ends
but taking care of its mundane needs.

When the Prophet died, the community did not change the pattern of its life.   There was one great change: revelation had stopped
and the Prophet was no longer available for guiding them where
they could not see the light clearly.   They, however, had a body of
revelation, which they believed to be the word of God and therefore
infallible.   They had the sayings and the example of the Prophet
which they believed to be of great value in leading a righteous life,
and they had their own reason to apply to this body of teaching.
This was the basis of their law and theology alike, and it was to
be enlarged into all the complexities of legal thinking.   These teachings were their heritage, but the problem which confronted them at
the time of the death of the Prophet was to carry on the life of
the community and to prevent it from falling apart.   Their sorrow
at the death of the Prophet was so great that their senses were

[14] Rosenthal, *op. cit.*, p. 8.
[15] The Qur'ān almost invariably commends those "who believe and do righteous
deeds."   However, belief is given precedence, because it is the source of righteous
deeds.

stunned for a while. Credit goes to the Prophet's disciple and
friend Abū Bakr for seeing the situation clearly and for facing it with
foresight and courage. He said, "O people! If you worshiped
Muḥammad, then he is dead. But if you worship God, He is
eternally alive." Then he recited the verse of the Qur'ān which
says, "And Muḥammad is but a prophet; there were other prophets
before him. If he is killed or dies, will you return to your ignorant
ways?"[16] In this way Abū Bakr brought vividly to the mind of the
Muslims assembled there that they had to continue their existence as
believers in the faith and to discharge the duties which they had
undertaken. These duties had, in their essence, been defined for
them in the Qur'ān and the teachings of the Prophet. And in the
life of the Prophet they would also find the need of keeping the
organization of the believers alive, as quite a large proportion of
their religious duties were communal in character and required association and organization.[17] Now that the Prophet had died, who
would keep this organization alive and functioning?

The need of association and organization is implicit in the
faith of Islam and also found explicit support, at least indirectly, in the Qur'ān and the traditions of the Prophet, but the manner in which it was to take shape and function has been left to the
Muslims themselves.[18] The Muslims who assembled to ponder over
the situation which had arisen as the result of the death of the Prophet approached it in accordance with their knowledge and experience. The first thing that the community needed was a man in
the place of the Prophet to act as the head of the community for
ordering its affairs and looking after its interests. It was plain to
them that he was not to be a prophet;[19] he would be one of themselves, open to being questioned regarding his actions, which were
to be judged not only on the basis of their justice but also in accordance with the teachings of Islam, which according to the Mus-

[16] He was reciting the Qur'ān, iii, 144. The literal translation of the last clause
is, "Will you return to what you have left behind?"
[17] Qur'ān, iii, 102-104, emphasizes the need of organization and unity.
[18] 'Ali 'Abd-u'r-Rāziq has laid great emphasis on the fact that the caliphate has
no basis in the Qur'ān or the Sunnah in *Uṣūl-u'l-ḥukm fi'l-Islām*, (Cairo, 1925).
There are no references in the Qur'ān or the Sunnah regarding the forms of organization.
[19] Because of the *ḥadīth*, "There shall be no prophet after me." Also, because
he has been called "the Seal of the prophets" in the Qur'ān. The seal was put at the
end of a letter by the Arabs.

lims was the criterion of all human behavior. Thus their idea of organization was to elect or agree upon a person whom they could trust, who was to act in accordance with the principles already given to them by the Prophet. It followed that within the limits of Islam and of justice in general he had to have high authority, which was to be obeyed, but not in preference to the dictates of Islam and one's duty to God.[20] This man had to be one who would command respect as well as obedience, through his seniority, piety, and personal qualities. For determining these factors they could not always rely upon heredity; in any case their long tribal experience and their Islamic ideas of the dignity of man prevented them from looking upon monarchy with favor, nor did the neighboring great monarchies of Iran and Byzantium inspire them with any great respect for their systems. This was so because at least in their peripheries they were misruled and their administration was oppressive. Thus left to their own experience they did what a body of Arabs would do when confronted with such a situation; they elected, without taking into consideration his relationship to the Prophet, one who seemed to be suited for the office. To their minds it was not a question of a man succeeding to a patrimony, rather it was the problem of finding a man for a position which was concerned with their welfare and the security of their beliefs and ideals.[21] They elected Abū Bakr for the office. In the course of the discussion it was suggested by one of the Ansārs that there should be two men, one for the Quraish and the other for the Ansārs. This was ruled out—and this is of great significance—because the community was considered to be one and indivisible. Abū Bakr took up the title of *khalīfatu Rasūl-u'llah*, "successor to the Prophet of God," which subsequently came to be shortened into just *khalīfah*, found in the form of caliph in the English language.[22]

It has been necessary to devote all this space to this first election because it set a precedent and the Muslim jurists have taken it to

[20] Qur'ān, iv, 59.

[21] This is clear from the reports of the discussion which ensued at this time. The Shiah traditions do not agree with these reports in all their details; historical probability, however, seems to support the earlier tradition, only on the basis of which can the acceptance of Abū Bakr by 'Alī and the community be explained.

[22] E. Tyan, in *Le Califat*, I (Paris, 1954), raises doubts about "the proper election" of Abū Bakr, but he is probably searching for procedures which could not have been defined at that time.

be the fountainhead of their arguments and thinking. Broadly speaking, the procedure adopted established the principles of election by a number of people who commanded respect and then acceptance by the community through universal acclaim.[23]   It was not based upon any definite verse of the Qur'ān or any tradition of the Prophet. It was not a premeditated act of constitutional experts; those who participated in this simple act did not claim that their action in any way bound their successors, and indeed, the method was varied by them in accordance with the circumstances, but through all these variations the general principles of election by the few and acclaim by the many persisted.[24]   It was but a partial expression of the democratic ideals and instincts of Islam; nevertheless, it was an expression.   In the atmosphere of Medina, with its strong flavor of Islamic ideals and its traditions of tribal democracy, the institution might have developed some robust characteristics, but when it was transported to Damascus, it began to wither.[25]   In the hands of the Muslim jurists it became the target of legalistic hair splitting and lost its original democratic tendencies.[26]   The basic assumptions in the minds of those who elected Abū Bakr were correct in view of the teachings of Islam; it is, however, patently clear that they were not clearly understood by many among the community.   This is evident from the suggestion that more than one caliph could be elected to look after the interests of the different sections, which would have split the community from the very beginning.[27]   The understanding of the ideals which inspired Abū Bakr was particularly weak among some of the outlying tribes.[28]   They refused to pay taxes to the central exchequer.   This act of theirs has been misunderstood by the historians of Islam and its full significance has become clouded.

---

[23] S. Khuda Bakhsh, *The Orient under Caliphs* (Calcutta, 1921), p. 9.

[24] Some orientalists do not accept the statement of Muslim historians regarding 'Umar's election. It is difficult to understand how they can dismiss the fact of his finding acceptance in the community. It is highly improbable that he, without considerable support and in the absence of a paid professional army, could have simply "seized power."

[25] Brockelmann, *op. cit.*, p. 73, says, "Mu'āwiyah did not rule his Arabs like an Oriental despot but like an old-time tribal Sayyid." He was, however, responsible for establishing a dynasty. See Rosenthal, *op. cit.*, p. 33.

[26] S. Khuda Bakhsh, *The Orient under Caliphs* (Calcutta, 1921), p. 264.

[27] Muhammad Hamid-u'llah, *Muslim Conduct of State* (Lahore, 1945), p. 83.

[28] E.g., Ibn Jamā'ah, in *Taḥrīr-u'l-aḥkām fī tadbīri ahl-i'l-Islām*, ed. and trans. by Hans Kofler in *Islamica*, VI, 357, justifies usurpation; so does Māwardī in *Aḥkām-u's-sulṭāniyah* (Cairo, 1928 A. H.), pp. 8 ff., though less blatantly.

There is no mention that they wanted to go back to their pagan ways; this was no revolt against Islam as a religion; it was a rebellion against the central authority in Islam. It was not a challenge to the doctrine; it was the indivisibility of Islam. Indeed so widespread was this revolt that for some time even the stern disciplinarian 'Umar counseled postponement of any action against the tribes, because, so soon after the death of the Prophet, action by the caliph might have led to a prolonged and disastrous civil war. Still Abū Bakr saw the consequences of hesitation so clearly that he refused to compromise. In fact the question was of such importance to him that he said that he would fight against the offending tribes even though he might be the only fighter. His courage was, however, rewarded; he successfully established the doctrine of a united Muslim community under single leadership, working together for common goals.[29] The difficulties that arose under 'Uthmān and 'Ali were due to the fact that some of the Arab leaders were not able to understand the full significance of Abū Bakr's conception of the political organization needed by the young community of Islam; it was for this reason that his ideals were frustrated so soon.

However, as time passed, the implications of the principles underlying the early political behavior of the community under the guidance of the immediate disciples of the Prophet came to be understood within some limits; but those who undertook to investigate those principles were bogged down in their legal aspects to such a degree that they lost sight of the political possibilities inherent in the attitudes that had been taken by the earliest caliphs, especially Abū Bakr. The legal aspects were not unimportant; in the greater bulk of Muslim law, the jurists were able to achieve remarkable profundity and insight, but they were unable to guide the community on the path of political growth. Before undertaking an analysis of the causes underlying this phenomenon, it would be useful to have a look at the development of Islamic law, because it is relevant to the political thinking in Islam.

It has already been mentioned that the Muslims look upon the Qur'ān as revelation; as such, it is the word of God and, therefore, infallible. Theoretically all Islamic laws are derived either directly or indirectly from it. The Qur'ān itself draws attention to the fact

[29] This point is discussed a little more fully in I. H. Qureshi, *The Administration of the Sultanate of Dehlī* (Karachi, 1958), pp. 22, 23.

that the book contains some injunctions which are clear and which do not admit of any elaborate interpretation and there are others which are not so clear.[30]   There is, however, one good guide for the understanding of the Qur'ān, its understanding possessed by the Prophet. This can be gauged from what the Prophet said at different times and his actions and behavior on various occasions.   The Prophet, however, was human and, therefore, not infallible; hence the Prophet himself said that if the believers found any discrepancy between any of his observations and the Qur'ān, they should adhere to the Qur'ān and reject his observations; indeed, where the Prophet was not dealing strictly with spiritual matters based upon revelation, he did consult his disciples and often accepted their advice and even acknowledged his errors, if he found that he had not seen something in its proper perspective.   Therefore his sayings and actions called the Ḥadīth and the Sunnah occupy a secondary place in the sources of Islamic law.[31]   The Qur'ān and Ḥadīth or Sunnah can not give crystal-clear guidance on every legal complexity of human relations and activity; hence guidance can be obtained by a process of deduction, the application of human reason to these texts.[32]   However, a multiplicity of deductions would create chaos in public affairs; even in such intimate matters as public and congregational worship, there would arise difficulties.   The remedy has been provided in the doctrine of *ijmā'* or consensus.   Thus there is provision within the bosom of the law itself for its growth.   There are various ways in which human effort—*ijtihād* in the language of the Muslim jurists—can be applied to a problem, and each one has a technical term for itself, but we need not go into these details.   It is important, however, to remember that the conclusions reached by *ijtihād* have only the status of a recommendation, unless the *ijtihād* be embodied in a decision on a particular case before the *qāḍī*, when he, in his capacity as a judge, enforces it.   Of course his *ijtihād* can be upset by a higher court in the same case or not accepted by other judges in similar situations.   To be universally binding, there should be consensus, *ijmā'*, on an interpretation.[33]   In the legal sense, *ijmā'* is the con-

---

[30] Qur'ān, iii, 7.

[31] Zaki Ali, *op. cit.*, p. 43.

[32] Shāh Walī-u'llah, *'Iqd-u'l-jīd fī aḥkām-i'l-ijtihād wa't-taqlīd* (Delhi, 1310 A. H.) deals with the question of *ijtihād*.

[33] Von Grunebaum, *op. cit.*, p. 3.

sensus of those who are capable of understanding the issues involved and are familiar with the Qur'ān, the Ḥadīth and the *ijtihād* of the previous thinkers. Thus it would be clear that the main components of Muslim jurisprudence are the Qur'ān, the Ḥadīth, *ijtihād*, and *ijmā'*.

Ijmā' is a process which, in the absence of a church or an organized authority in matters legal and theological, takes time in formulation. During the time that this process is taking place and opinion has not crystallized, the acceptance of an opinion arrived at by *ijtihād* is dependent upon the conscience of the individual who is confronted with a similar problem; in other words it has no common validity. If the state is in a situation where it must accept or reject an interpretation, it has to depend on its own resources of thinking and knowledge.[34] It has, therefore, been accepted by the jurists that where a just ruler is confronted with differences of opinion among the doctors of law, he can choose any one of the interpretations put forward by them.[35] A word of explanation is needed here for the jurists' conception of a just ruler. He should not only have the desire to be just but also be capable of understanding justice; in other words, his motives should be righteous and his knowledge of the law adequate for discerning the virtues of every interpretation which is offered.[36] In the course of Islamic history the earlier Arab rulers were qualified because of their experience and knowledge and familiarity with Arabic, the language of the texts, but the Turkish and other non-Arab rulers were generally little qualified to understand the hairsplitting of the jurists. They therefore overcame the difficulty by appointing a learned theologian, mostly one known alike for his learning and piety, to advise them on legal and theological matters.[37] In this manner the officers of *shaikh-u'l-Islām* or *Ṣadr-u's-ṣudūr* came into existence.[38] Legally the political authority never gave up its right of enforcing the interpretation which it considered to be right, but there was established the convention that the advice tendered

[34] Rosenthal, *op. cit.*, pp. 35, 36.

[35] Qureshi, *op. cit.*, p. 44.

[36] Māwardī, *op. cit.*, p. 5.

[37] This was approved by Ghazzālī. Rosenthal, *op. cit.*, p. 40.

[38] For the further elucidation of the technical terms used here, consult the *Encyclopaedia of Islam*. The functions of the *Ṣadr-u's-ṣudūr* have been discussed in Qureshi, *op. cit.*, pp. 159, 160, 175.

by the expert was accepted. If any attempt was made to upset this arrangement, it created discontent and ill will.

This discussion would show that the state was not above the law. The _shar‘_ which contained the accepted interpretation of the Qur'ān and the Sunnah was supreme.[39]   Indeed, in the legal sense, it was the sovereign and not the will of a mundane sovereign.   As it was considered to be the embodiment of the will of God, He was the sovereign in this sense.   Therefore, some have held that an Islamic polity is a theocracy, the rule of God; but this may be a source of misunderstanding and, therefore, the term should not be applied to Islamic polity.[40]   All terms, whatever their derivations, come to be associated with certain ideas, and theocracy generally connotes the rule of a church, a body of priests or others specially ordained as the agents for carrying on the government of God.   There are no such implications in the classical Muslim conception of a polity.   This is a government by laymen, not only because there are no priests in Islam, but also because the Muslim law does not envisage that all rulers will be learned.   It is ideally a polity based upon righteousness and governed by the principles of Islam.   The Islamic law, being a part of Islam and being based upon its teachings is to be the law of the Muslim society and government, but it is to be administered by men who are not necessarily learned in law, except when legal matters are to be decided.   No country is governed solely by lawyers even though all its activities must be in accordance with law. There is, however, one peculiarity of a Muslim polity which is not shared in the same degree by the modern secular state.   An Islamic state is much more limited in its legislative authority.   It cannot legislate against the _shar‘_.[41]   This is a limitation which needs detailed examination.

It has already been stated that where there is _ijmā‘_ and opinion is unanimous, or where the dictates of the Qur'ān and Sunnah are explicit and clear, the state has no authority to overrule them.   This does cover a large area of legislation; but there are important spheres where the state has considerable scope for legislation.[42]   The jurists recognize a neutral area of human activity, technically called _mubāḥ_,

---

[39] Khuda Bakhsh, _Essays, Indian and Islamic_ (London, 1912), p. 5.
[40] Also, Rosenthal, _op. cit._, pp. 8, 9; Zaki Ali, _op. cit._, p. 40.
[41] Khuda Bakhsh, _Essays, Indian and Islamic_, p. 51.
[42] This has always been recognized. See Qureshi, _op. cit._, p. 44.

which is covered neither by what has been enjoined nor by what has been forbidden. In this field the state can legislate for the public good; it can also create procedures of government which are in the spirit of Islam and not against any of its express provisions. Besides, in so far as progressive *ijtihād* is permitted and the doors are not closed upon fresh interpretation, the state has considerable elbow room.[43] The *sharʿ* is capable of change and expansion under the pressure of new needs, and this process can be accelerated by the state.[44] The question of interpretation, however, poses a serious problem, because, in the course of history, four orthodox and a few heretical schools of interpretation have been crystallized and some of them do not believe in "unlimited *ijtihād*"; they limit the scope of new interpretation within the school itself, so that the body of interpretation built up within it cannot be ignored to find solutions which are in contradiction to previous findings.[45] This was found necessary to bring some consistency into interpretative thinking in order that the system might hold together. This was even more necessary because jurisprudence and theology are interrelated in Islam through the common process of interpretation; indeed the word used is *fiqh*, understanding, and not law or theology. This was necessary, at least when the need was felt to prevent anarchic thinking, but the idea has certainly been carried too far. Modern thinking in Islam is painfully conscious of the need of releasing interpretation from the overpowering authority of the layers of traditional thought related to conditions no longer existing in their entirety.[46] If such an attitude finds concrete expression in new interpretation, the Islamic state, which binds itself close to the Qur'ān and the Sunnah, will have much more legislative freedom, especially when a re-examination of the old thinkers and new techniques of scholarship will prove that many reports regarding the Sunnah are not

[43] Zaki Ali, *op. cit.*, pp. 45, 46.

[44] There are schools of thought which have always recognized the principles of necessity and general good in matters where a more lenient view of the *sharʿ* is possible. The latest advocate of this principle was Iqbal. See his sixth lecture, "The Principle of Movement in the Structure of Islam" in *The Reconstruction of Religious Thought in Islam* (London, 1934), in which he gives a wider conception of *ijtihād*.

[45] This is *ijtihād-i-muqayyad* or *ijtihād fi'l-madhhab*, Shāh Walī-u'llah, *Al-inṣāf fī bayān-i-sabab-i-ikhtilāf*, Urdu trans. by Ṣadr-u'd-din Iṣlāḥī under the title *Ikhtilāfī masā'il men i'tdāl kī rāh* (Lahore, n.d.), pp. 124 ff.

[46] Iqbal, *op. cit.*, sixth lecture.

trustworthy and therefore not binding in any sense. If the liberal-
izing tendencies noticeable throughout the Muslim world are di-
verted into constructive channels, the Qur'ān and the reliable body
of Sunnah will have the same role as a basic law has in any society;
they will be inviolate, but they will leave plenty of room for legislation. There is another angle from which this problem can be
viewed. In the last resort the legislative functions of a government
are exercised in accordance with the moral conceptions of the legislators, which, in their turn, are colored deeply by the religious
traditions of a community. Muslim legislatures would, in any case
to the extent they are Muslim, be guided by their notions of right
and wrong, and these will be inspired by their religious thinking,
whether they give it that name or not. It must, however, be admitted that there is considerable difference between the teachings
of a religion working in the background and their finding sanction
in the legal system of a people.

This discussion of the place of the Muslim law in a Muslim
polity has taken us away from the chronical order in which
political ideas and constitutions developed in Islam. Once the caliphate had come into existence, even though it was not based on any
express command of the Qur'ān, it came to be recognized as a religious institution.[47] We have seen that it fulfilled what would
in other systems be called a secular need, the need of government
in a community to fulfil its basic mission in the context of its ideals.
It was not the Muslim counterpart of the Holy See; it was a Muslim
institution of government. However, according to the thinking of
the Muslims it fulfilled a religious need because to the Muslims
Islam was inconceivable without a Muslim community. Therefore an
institution for the governance and the maintenance of that community
was as much religious as the gathering of Muslims for worship.[48]
When the jurists began to discuss whether the caliphate was a political or a canonical institution, after some controversy, they reached
the conclusion that it was canonical.[49] This was not a discussion
about the authority upon which it was based; it was a question of
determining the nature of the obligation of a Muslim towards it.

[47] Māwardī, op. cit., p. 3.
[48] Rosenthal, op. cit., p. 29.
[49] H. Laoust, Le Califat dans la Doctrine de Rashid Rida (Beyrouth, 1938),
p. 16.

Even the historian and social thinker Ibn Khaldūn was emphatic that the caliphate was a canonical necessity and that the Muslims were under a religious obligation to establish it and to maintain it.[50] This illustrates how politics and religion are considered to be but two facets of the faith in Islam.

The jurists look upon the thirty years of the Republic after the death of the Prophet, when the "rightly guided" caliphs ruled, as the true precedent for their rulings regarding government.[51] Later, it is their belief, the caliphate lost its truly Islamic characteristics and became an empire not run in the best traditions of Islam.[52] Many of the orthodox historians are extremely harsh in their assessment of the role played by the Umayyads, except, of course, 'Umar ibn 'Abd-u'l-'Aziz. It is possible to understand the change which took place if we take into consideration the difference in the atmosphere of Medina and that of Damascus. At Medina there continued to exist the atmosphere of piety based upon the ideals inspired by the Prophet; at Damascus the demands of running an empire, now consisting of peoples which had been long under the dominance of strong monarchies, were felt more pressingly. Medina still thought in the terms of the democratic ideals of Islam and the inherent democracy of a tribal and, to some extent, nomadic life.[53] Medina believed in plain living and high thinking; Damascus had the luxuries of Byzantium to tempt it. Medina was religious and more concerned with matters spiritual; Damascus was worldly and enmeshed in politics. The dichotomy which developed in Islam at this stage was never cured.

It had serious results in the spheres of active politics as well as political thinking. Its devastating effects on the realm of religion itself were no less important. Mu'āwiyah was deeply influenced by the political tradition of imperialism and sought to establish an imperial dynasty by claiming the caliphate for himself and later nominating his son Yazīd as his successor. His claim led to the conflict with 'Alī and thus created the great schism within the body of Islam. It was Mu'āwiyah's revolt which was

[50] Ibn Khaldūn, *Muqaddamah* (Beyrouth, 1879), pp. 165, 166.
[51] Māwardī, *op. cit.*, pp. 6 ff.
[52] Rosenthal, *op. cit.*, p. 33.
[53] Brockelmann, *op. cit.*, pp. 67, 68.

ultimately responsible for the rise of the Shiah sects.[54]   The pious
residents of Medina were unhappy at the turn which events had taken
and, finding themselves helpless, established the tradition among
some theologians and religious persons of withdrawing from the
affairs of the Muslim state and depriving it of the services of the
most sincere men of learning.[55]   The learned were themselves divided; one section was of the opinion that they should not abandon
the state to its fate and deprive it altogether of their advice and counsel, and, therefore, continued to accept public responsibility; there
were others who thought that political contacts would corrupt them
as they had corrupted the pure ideals of the Islamic state and therefore adopted a policy of severe aloofness and persuaded others to
follow in their footsteps.[56]   Those among the former who had sin-
cerely hoped to keep the government on an even keel found themselves weakened by the attitude of those who decided to keep aloof,
because not all who frequented the courts and co-operated with the
state were sincere and some were only too eager to support the rulers
in whatever they chose to do.   This is perhaps one of the reasons
why the lawyers and theologians in Islam never developed a satisfactory theory of constitutional safeguards against the misuse of
authority.[57]   The precedents of the early years of the Republic were
interpreted to establish the principles of election by the elect and
acceptance by universal acclaim, but little was done to prevent these
principles from degenerating into mere legal forms, losing all their
substance.   Thus the philosophy of obedience to authority was
strengthened without the provision of its necessary counterpart, an
effective check against the misuse of power.   The jurists recognized
the right of rebellion against illegal and unjust orders; indeed, the
Muslims were told that it was their duty to rebel whenever they
saw that the rulers had become tyrannical or unjust;[58] but this was

---

[54] *Ibid.*, p. 76.   [55] *Ibid.*, pp. 67, 68.
[56] This trend was strengthened later by the mystics.
    [57] Rosenthal, *op. cit.*, p. 22, praises the jurists for their success in reconciling
theory with fact.
    [58] This is a well-recognized principle and finds mention in numerous authori-
ties, e.g., A'n-Nuwairī, *Nihāyat-u'l-irab fī funūn-i'l-adab* (Cairo, 1926), p. 5.
The caliph 'Umar asked even non-Muslims not to submit to unjust treatment at the hands of his officials. Abū Yūsuf Yā'qūb, *Kitāb-u'l-kharāj* (Cairo,
1346 A. H.), p. 66; for French version, see Abou Yousof Ya'koub, *Le Livre de
Impôt Foncier (Kitab el-kharadj)*, traduit et annoté par E. Fagnan (Paris, 1921),
pp. 177 ff.

admittedly the last resort.[59]   In the use of the right of rebellion, they had been asked to be extremely cautious, because the creation of disorder without adequate justification was characterized as a mortal sin.   It is obvious that rebellion is an extreme measure and the patriotic citizen generally finds it distasteful; besides, it involves too great a risk and demands tremendous public spirit.   The net result was that if the rulers did not openly act against the basic principles of Islam, there was little incitement to rebellion in misrule and misuse of authority.

The entire phenomenon, regretted as it has been by all writers on Islam in one way or another, was, in a sense, inevitable.   It was the price of rapid growth.   The Islamic society did not grow up gradually in the entire area which within the first thirty years of the death of the Prophet became its habitat.   Medina was the only place where the people had seen the growth of the Muslim society from small beginnings; it was there that the experiment of living a life in accordance with the growing volume of the teachings of the Prophet had been worked out, and the people of Medina understood its significance fully and knew its spirit.   In the rest of the *Dār-u'l-Islām*, the religion had spread too swiftly for its finer points to be assimilated to the extent where they could work for the creation of a new political form based upon the spirit of Islam.   Therefore at an early period in the history of Islam, influences crept into its political thinking which, though not in fact in accord with its innermost urges, nevertheless, because of their early association with the new faith, came to be considered a part of its philosophy.[60]   While the religious teachings of Islam were capable of holding their own against the rival religions which it overthrew, the simple and tribal form which the democratic urges of Islam had adopted in the political

[59] This is based upon the Islamic injunction to respect and obey all legally constituted authority if it does not indulge in tyranny and subvert the Islamic purpose of organization.   The source is the Qur'ān, iv, 59, which enjoins obedience to God, the Prophet, and to "those in authority from amongst you."   This has been interpreted to mean that one's duty to God comes first, then his duty of obeying the commandments of the Prophet, and lastly, obedience to the state.   In case of conflict between any one of these, they take precedence in the order listed.   An injunction to obey the state was not to be lightly set aside in view of a clear injunction of the Qur'ān, and disobedience was to be the result of a clear call of the conscience.

[60] Brockelmann, *op. cit.*, pp. 72, 73; Shaikh Muhammad Hilmi Tumara, "La Souvrainte Islamique et La Khilafat," *Review du Monde Musulman* (Paris), LXIX (First Quarter, 1925), pp. 85-112.

sphere was incapable of surviving against the imperial traditions which it sought to replace.   In the days of slow communications the vast distances of large empires were not conducive to the emergence of democratic forms of government and the newly acquired Muslim Empire was no exception; the forces which converted the city-state of Rome into a monarchy asserted themselves more rapidly in the world of Islam, as the imperial tradition had already been deeply entrenched in the areas which came under its sway.   The Umayyads maintained the forms which had been developed under the tribal traditions of Medina, but their democratic spirit was dissipated under dynastic rule and the political exigencies of a far-flung empire ruling peoples to whom the tribal concepts of Medina were meaningless.

Medina, however, continued to exert its influence in the world of Islam through its learning and piety, but this was in the fields of theology and religious tradition.   Besides, it was not able to define its disappointment with the Umayyads in constitutional or legal terms.   The theologians attacked the spirit of Umayyad rule rather than its form.   The main reason perhaps was that the forms had been kept.   The discontent was not without its victory; the Abbasids took advantage of the unpopularity of the Umayyads in the eastern and southern peripheries of the Caliphate and ousted them.[61]   This, however, proved to be, from the constitutional point of view, but a change of dynasties.   The Abbasids, in their days of glory, showed greater regard for the tenets of Islam;[62] the Islamic injunction that the Muslims should order their affairs with mutual consultation was given a little more concrete form;[63] but the Abbasids clung to their power as much as the Umayyads had done before them.   They even emphasized the doctrine of hereditary succession, which had been discarded by the pious caliphs of the Republic.   The emphasis now was on good rule, and no mention was made of the right of the community to participate in the business of the government.   On the contrary, even such tribal democracy as the Umayyads had unconsciously maintained was lost in the more autocratic traditions of Iran.[64]   For instance, the Umayyad caliphs had felt the need of

[61] *Ibid*, pp. 103 ff.

[62] *Ibid*, pp. 110, 111.

[63] By the creation of a synod of theologians.   The injunction is contained in the Qur'ān, xlii, 88.

[64] Brockelmann, *op. cit.*, pp. 109, 110.   Also, H. A. R. Gibb, "Al-Māwardī's Theory of the Khilāfah," *Islamic Culture* (Hyderabad), Vol. IX, No. 3 (1937).

explaining their policies to the people while addressing the congregations of the Faithful in the great mosque on Fridays. Yazid III had told the congregation that they should refuse to obey him if he went against the law or the dictates of justice.[65] We do not read of similar statements by the Abbasid caliphs. Though the Umayyads had limited the succession to their own line, yet there was more consultation in the choice of a caliph under them than under the Abbasids. Thus, though the Abbasids had come to power by directing the discontent against the Umayyads into channels favorable to themselves, they were not loth to adopt those features of the Umayyad rule which were advantageous to the concentration of power in their hands.

With the decline of the Abbasid power, a new phenomenon came into existence. Hitherto the conception of the unity of the Muslim world had received only one setback; with the overthrow of the Umayyads, the world of Islam had been divided into two. There was the Western Caliphate of Northwest Africa and the Eastern Caliphate of the Abbasids. Under the latter, the Turks came to the forefront; and with the weakening of the hold of the Abbasids over their empire, new dynasties grew up which held only a nominal allegiance to the Abbasids. There emerged kingdoms which were independent in every respect, except in name.[66] In this manner the caliphate itself became a shadow instead of the reality. Rulers held the caliph almost as their prisoner, showing all outward respect but giving him little freedom of action.[67] Distant chiefs and monarchs received letters patent without having in the first instance been appointed or approved by the caliph. In short, the caliph was reduced to the status of a monarch *de jure* while all the *de facto* power was in the hands of others. What the Abbasids lost in political power, they tried to regain in the shape of religious prestige and they assiduously built up a myth of religious sanctity behind the institution, thus unconsciously divorcing it more and more from political effectiveness and reality. As the *raison d'etre* of the institution was

[65]Muhammad Ṣāliḥ, *Tārīkh-i-Banī Umayyah* (Meerut, 1847), p. 59.
[66] Maḥmūd of Ghaznih sought recognition from the caliph, but he was so independent that he sent letters containing threats to the caliph. Al-'Utbī, *Tārīkh-i-Yamīnī* (Teheran, 1271 A. H.), pp. 214-216.
[67] Jurji Zaidan, *Umayyads and Abbasids*, English trans. by D. S. Margoliouth (Oxford, 1913), p. 258.

political, even though it had been brought into existence by the doctrines of a religion, it could not but lose its significance in the course of time.[68]

The most famous writer of this period, whose *al-Ahkām-u's-sultāniyah* is the Bible of all writers on Muslim political institutions, portrays the situation under the later Abbasids without in any way trying to remedy it.[69] It is an effort to give a legal garb to all the irregularities which had crept into the body politic. The right of the rulers of the provinces who had seized power was recognized under the myth of governors "by the right of power." All that they had to do to obtain the sanction of the law was to maintain the institutions of Islam in their dominions. The caliph could, if he so desired, appoint prime ministers and governors with absolute authority, which means that he could abdicate his powers and delegate them to others. Māwardī does not stop for a minute to examine the disastrous consequences of such legal theories.[70] In trying to maintain a respect for the law, he weakened the law to such a degree that its main purpose was lost. He was no Jeremiah discontented with the decline in the institutions which had set in; he assigned to himself the function of removing the friction between the theory and the practice of politics in his age. Whatever might have been his shortcomings, he at least was a realist; he was not like several other writers who still talked in terms of a city-state, having been inspired by the classical Greek writers.[71] It is strange that the ideas of Aristotle should have been current without any critical examination of their validity in the environment. The general principles of good government were all that mattered to the writers of this period. Later, under the Turkish dynasties, the writers were not even interested in the legal or political aspects of government; the

[68] To illustrate how the word lost its significance and came to be used for any state or reign may be mentioned the Hindu work *Rājawalī*, which speaks of "the caliphate" of the Hindu heroes of the *Mahābhārata* and of the legendary Bikramajit. Qureshi, *op. cit.*, p. 39.

[69] Abu'l-Hasan 'Alī al-Māwardī, *al-Ahkām-u's-sultāniyah* (Cairo, 1298 A. H.). A French version is also available: *Les Statuts Gouvernementaux ou Regle de Droit Public et Administratif* par Māwardī, traduit et annoté par E. Fagnan (Alger, 1915).

[70] Māwardī, *op. cit.*, pp. 21-32.

[71] Such views were quite common in the writings of the medieval Muslim writers. A good example is *Kitāb-u's-siyāsat fī tadbīr-i'r-riyāsat* which is based upon Aristotle. Cambridge University Library MS Qq 293. Fārābī, Ibn Bājjah, Ibn Rushd, al-Dawwānī, all use the term *madīnah*, "city."

study of political institutions as such received only cursory treatment and all effort was directed towards an efficient and benevolent exercise of authority.[72] The institutions, good, bad, or indifferent, were taken for granted. The assumption in these writings is that the monarch has certain duties towards the people and towards God, but there was no question of his sharing his authority with the people.[73] The most barren field in the history of the intellectual achievement of Islam is that of political science. In a way this is surprising, because the Muslims developed their legal thinking to a remarkable degree, and law played a most vital role in their society. It is also surprising that Ibn Khaldūn had no successors in his attempt to understand history with reference to social factors and his study of society itself. His analysis of the basis of the Islamic polity did not lead to further thinking on the methods to make the theory behind the Islamic polity more effective.

There can be many explanations why there was no constitutional and political development not only in the Islamic world but also in the entire East, but none of them is entirely satisfactory.[74] In Islam there are strong democratic trends in social, legal, and religious matters; that these trends should have been frustrated in politics at such an early stage of its history needs some explanation. Perhaps the very fact that these trends found an outlet in other institutions did not make them strong enough to break through political barriers. Being in possession of a society which seemed to give them the opportunities that they were seeking, the people did not attach the same importance to political expression. Another reason may be that the idea of good government was so prevalent that the parallel notion of self-government found no support. It needs higher political maturity to realize that good government is no substitute for self-government. The disgust with which the early Medinites came to look upon the entire business of government may have been responsible for this at-

---

[72] There are a good many books of this nature; the most famous are Niẓām-u'l-mulk Tūsī, *Siyāsat-nāmah*, ed. Charles Scheffer (Paris, 1897) and ʿUnṣur-u'l-Maʿālī Kaikāʾus *Qābūs-nāmah*, ed. Saʿīd Nafīsī (Teheran, 1933). These two books are cited only as examples.

[73] One of the most philosophical of Turkish treatises is Ḥājjīʾ Khalīfah's *Dastūr-u'l-ʿamal*, in which he asserts that "God entrusts people to sultans and amirs." See Rosenthal, *op. cit.*, p. 229.

[74] Claude Cohen, "The Body Politic," Part III in Von Grunebaum, *op. cit.*; see especially p. 158.

titude to some extent. The long traditions of autocratic rule in the areas where Islam spread might also have been responsible for the phenomenon. It should be remembered that the age of benevolent despots did not come to an end in Europe so very long ago. A good deal of the nationalism and political consciousness of today is a matter of improved communications. The possibility of the association of the population with government in large empires with slow communications would have seemed absurd in the early days. Later, when popular government made real strides in the West, the Islamic world had already sunk into a state of stupor and decay. This decline is not so difficult to explain. The Mongol inroads of the Middle Ages, especially the destruction of the towns and cities along with which went the demolishing of libraries, seminaries, and colleges, and the dispersal of men of learning, were responsible for arresting the growth of Muslim thought.[75] Then the Muslims lost the control of the sea routes, which ultimately destroyed their commerce. This brought about economic adversity and sent the Muslim world into the abyss of poverty and backwardness. These factors raise yet another question: Why did the Muslims not make any efforts to revive their intellectual activities and their prosperity? As a matter of fact they did make efforts and the recovery of Islam after the Mongol disasters was remarkable; but somehow the intellectual excellence of previous ages was not recaptured. There are some great names in the realm of learning in the period after Islam had recovered from the worst consequences of the Mongol holocaust, but they do not shine as brilliantly as the earlier stars in the firmament of Islamic learning. Conservatism, rigidity, and too great a dependence upon authority proved effective barriers against progress. These are only indications, and none of them, as has been mentioned earlier, provides a really satisfactory explanation of the absence of political thinking.

There may perhaps be a real clue in the Muslim attitude towards law. There grew up such a regard for legal methods, thinking, and processes that there are few parallels in the world. Especially in the field of education, law came to occupy the central position. The Muslim word for theology and law, which are inter-

---

[75] All histories of the area that deal with the period contain some account. See especially Brockelmann, op. cit., pp. 244 ff.

twined, is *fiqh*, understanding. They are based upon the interpretation of the sacred texts. All legal thinking flows from them, hence
the ultimate dependence upon authority. The Muslim jurists have
reached great heights in interpretation and have evolved sound legal
principles, yet their thinking has been based upon authority and not
pure intellect. As *fiqh* was considered to be identical with religious
education, its importance in a religious society can be understood.
Law has a natural tendency to be conservative; it seeks to protect
the ideals of society rather than improve them. That is the reason
why some societies have been driven to change their structure through
methods which lay outside the scope of law. In Islam in particular,
fiqh is judge-made law. Even where it is theoretical, it
is akin to it. Hence Muslim legal thinking was bound to be even
more conservative and therefore less creative. The situation de-
teriorated when the four orthodox schools came to be so firmly
established that their doctors enunciated the doctrine of limited
interpretation, giving the interpreter freedom only within the four
corners of his school. This created even greater rigidity. As *fiqh*
became the most important subject in higher education, it began
to condition minds in other disciplines as well.

It has been mentioned that writers on politics devoted much space
to the need of just and benevolent government. They were supported by writers on ethics as well as law. On the whole, Muslim
governments generally tried to live up to these ideals. There are
some instances of tyranny, but these are few. The people did not
find much cause for discontent. Matters which were of the greatest
importance to them were sometimes outside the scope of direct
governmental activity, for instance the administration of justice and
ḥisbah was in the hands of learned and pious men, and monarchs and
their agents seldom interfered with them. Theoretically the theologians who were in charge of these departments were under the
monarch, but they were not looked upon as the servants of the state;
they were supported by the government, but they were expected to
look upon their duties as a form of worship, and many did act in
accordance with these ideals. The people expected them to be pious
and fair, and they responded. The administration of justice is a
well-known function of government and needs no further explanation,

but *ḥisbah* does require a word of description.[76]   It covered a good many functions of modern municipal government, and its purpose was to make the life of the citizens more convenient by the provision of communal facilities and the removal of all forms of public nuisance. It ranged from price control and prevention of adulteration of food-stuffs to seeing that school children were not awarded too heavy a punishment.   There was hardly any aspect of life in a town which did not come within the jurisdiction of *ḥisbah*.   The villagers did not expect too much from the government; they wanted only protection and a reasonable assessment of the dues they had to pay.   Very often these had a tendency to become traditional and life seemed to flow easily in its charted courses.   There was no pressing burden of feudal duties or obligations, no repressive game laws, no divisive lines which could not be crossed by a turn in fortunes.   The central governments were inclined to be sympathetic, because leniency towards the peasants had come to be the very basis of good administration and a healthy economy.   This was repeated in every textbook and became deeply engrained in the mind of the rulers, who generally found it to their advantage to insist upon equitable agrarian regulations.[77]   In short, there was little pressure upon the common people to demand any share in the government.   Islam had no hereditary aristocracy; the system evolved by its rulers was bureaucratic and not feudal; the mighty hereditary nobles of Europe had plenty of incentive to secure their position *vis-à-vis* the crown; in these efforts they saw the good of their progeny.   In Islam the mighty were the servants of the monarch; they did not form a hereditary class; how could these servants, having merely a transient interest in their relationship with the monarch, think of securing for themselves rights which would help them in days of adversity?   Their prosperity depended upon the pleasure of the monarch, whom they would not like to displease for vague and remote ends.   The Magna Carta could be extracted only by feudal nobles, because the king was not too far removed from them.   A body of public servants could not think of forcing the monarch to declare their rights, because theirs was a different kind of relationship.

[76] For a full discussion of this institution and its working, see Ibn-u'l-Ukhawwah, *Maʾālim-u'l-qurbat fī aḥkām-iʾl-ḥisbah*, ed.   Reuben Levy (London, 1938).   A shorter discussion is available in Qureshi, *op. cit.*, pp. 164-173.

[77] E.g., Nizām-u'l-mulk's *Siyāsat-nāmah*, ed. Charles Scheffer (Paris, 1897), p. 18.

One might perhaps also go back to the early formative period to discover the causes of the absence of the germs of growth of political institutions. The problem in early Islam was to curb the anarchic tendencies of the Arab tribes, who showed dangerous signs of lack of cohesion; hence the emergence of the tradition of a strong executive was a foregone conclusion. In the later history of Islam as well, the disruptive elements of a multiplicity of ethnic and cultural groups living under the same government needed the curb of a strong and powerful executive. With a well-developed system of legal institutions which gave the citizen considerable immunity from official highhandedness, the power of the executive was not resented; it was even welcomed, because the dread of anarchy is universal in the East, and to this the Muslims were no exception.[78] The need of a government for the protection of the society is a recurring theme in the writings of Muslim thinkers.

This attitude of indifference towards any attempt to control the power of the executive or to have a say in its constitution did not change until it was modified by contacts with the West. The urge for democracy did not come because democratic institutions were considered to be desirable for their own sake; it was not the liberalism of the governmental organization of the democratic West that inspired emulation; the demand for reform was not the outcome of a sense of oppression that had to be fought; it was not the result of endeavors to curb the highhandedness of tyrannical governments. It was born of the desire for gaining the strength to resist the ever-increasing aggression of the European powers. With the first defeats came the realization that the Muslim peoples were not adequately equipped to fight the West and thus safeguard their liberty; the most obvious need was to make up the deficiency in arms. This in turn involved a study of the methods of using the new weapons and the principles of strategy dictated by them. These were the first educational contacts with the West; with the growing need in the field of diplomacy, Western education became necessary and a number of students went to Europe. During the period of decline the efficiency of the government had also been impaired, and the young men who went to the West could not but be impressed by the efficient

---

[78] Compare *Mahābhārata*, Sāntiparva, section 59; Manū, *Dharmasāstra*, vii, 3; and writings of Moh-ti, the Chinese thinker of the 5th century B.C.

methods they saw there. When they came back and advocated the
new methods, they were not able to influence the administrators of
the old school and their superiors. Their impatience increased and
they thought that the people would be more willing to hear them.
If they could establish a system by which the growing enlightenment of the educated classes could be harnessed into the service of
the state, there might be a better chance of stopping the rot. They
had seen with their eyes the growing corruption, which sometimes
undid the valor of the troops on the battlefield.[79] They had also
witnessed diplomatic reverses as the result of an indifferent understanding of the issues involved. They became more than ever convinced that the new class of men educated in the West should be
in control; but this was not easy, because the old class was still
entrenched in power. The pressure of international diplomacy was
so great that the younger men just could not afford to wait for the
older people to die; therefore sustained effort for the establishment
of democratic institutions was necessary. The new institutions were
rightly considered a part of the program of progress and the realization of national integrity and independence.

When the need for these institutions came to be felt strongly, the
Muslims began to search for sanctions in their religious literature.
In the history of the thirty years after the death of the Prophet, they
found precedents for election, which had only to be enlarged and
defined in legal terms. In the Qur'ānic injunction to the Muslims
regarding the ordering of their affairs with mutual consultation, they
found the sanction for the establishment of parliamentary institutions.[80] As a matter of fact this verse was displayed prominently
in the chamber of the Turkish Parliament in the days of the sultans.[81] Iran also established a parliament, and thus the Islamic world
started on the path of the adoption of Western democratic institutions. These were only the beginnings; that the path is long and
difficult has been demonstrated by the setbacks which many Muslim
countries have received in their quest for democracy. Some of these
setbacks were due to long and deeply ingrained habits of thought
which go back several centuries. These will change in course of time,
but they could not change overnight. This should cause no undue

[79] E.g., Turkey, Brockelmann, *op. cit.*, pp. 383 ff.
[80] Qur'ān, xlii, 88.
[81] L. Stoddard, *The New World of Islam* (New York, 1922), pp. 22-24.

pessimism; the tempo of change in the Muslim world is so great that the waiting cannot be too long. Political institutions are deeply related to the social conditions of a country, and with the emergence of greater equality as the result of agrarian reforms, either enforced or in the process of enforcement, the growth of industry and urbanism and the spread of literacy, the environment is being made more congenial for the development of healthy democracy.

There are, however, dangers as well. There is a growing impatience at the slow rate of progress. There are countries in the East which are demonstrating methods of socio-economic modernization and of increasing the fighting strength of an underdeveloped nation through means which are not democratic. Would, for instance, the example of Communist China prove more attractive than the slower processes of democracy? There are two disturbing factors in the situation. The first is the desire to catch up with the more developed nations, of which the chances seem to be remote, because with all the efforts of the Eastern countries, the lag is increasing and not decreasing. If China demonstrates that it is possible to come up to the level of the West within a short time, the appeal of Communism may prove to be irresistible.[82] If this happens, the long tradition of a strong executive may help the spread of Communism. After all, the initial inclination for democracy came from the fact that at that time it seemed to be more fruitful in strengthening the Muslim countries and enabling them to withstand the challenge of the West more effectively. That feeling is still not dead. The deterrents in the spread of Communism may be the basic philosophy of Islam, which is opposed to materialistic dialectics, and the principles of individual liberty and dignity as embodied in the Islamic doctrine and law.[83] One should, however, not think that Islam makes people immune from the acceptance of any other doctrine: what could prevent the Muslims from being converted to a different philosophy except their faith? But it is faith which is the first martyr in Communism. The challenge, however, need not come in that extreme form. The conflict might be made easier through a process of reinterpretation and an emphasis upon the methods of

[82] Walter Z. Laqueur, "Appeal of Communism in the Middle East," *Middle East Journal*, Vol. IX, No. 1 (1955), pp. 17-27.
[83] Zaki Ali, *op. cit.*, p. 390.

Communism rather than its basic philosophy, which, after all, is not Communism's strong point.

There is yet another danger. Democracy may prove a cohesive force in some circumstances; in others it may prove disruptive. Democracy increases the feeling of nationalism. This may prove cohesive in communities that are well integrated and possess characteristics which strengthen the consciousness of unity, but where there are divisive influences at work, it intensifies them. One of the indirect results of the introduction of parliamentary government in the Ottoman Empire was the growth of Arab-Turkish differences, which brought in their wake not only the dismemberment of the Empire, but also a host of other problems. The larger Muslim countries have populations which are not ethnically uniform, and, if they want to escape disintegration, they will have to adapt the democratic forms to their special needs. It would not have been such a disaster if the various groups had been large enough to constitute modern states with sufficient economic and human resources to be viable and capable of defending themselves against their powerful neighbors. There has been no thinking upon this problem, and therefore no real solutions have been discovered. The menace has been fought only by negative means; too often there has been a denial of the existence of the problem instead of a correct appraisal of the situation and a search for proper remedies.

The rise of nationalism in the world of Islam has posed problems which should have given a headache to Muslim political thinkers. It has been accepted without any realization of the impact it is likely to have upon the loyalty of its adherents to Islam. The first Muslim to see clearly the lack of compatibility between nationalism and Islam was Iqbal, the national poet of Pakistan.[84] He devoted a good deal of his effort to counteracting its effects, but he was sailing against the prevailing winds. If we have a close look at the concrete results of nationalism in certain parts of the Muslim world, we shall at once see the dichotomy between nationalism and Islam. It has already been mentioned how the growth of nationalism created the rift between the Turks and the Arabs. Gradually impelled by their nationalistic feelings, the Turks at last di-

[84] There is a growing volume of literature upon Iqbal. For a short note, see de Bary, ed., *Sources of Indian Tradition* (New York, 1958), pp. 749-751.

vorced their polity from its affiliations with Islam and declared
Turkey to be a secular state. This was not only a break from tradition
but also the rejection of the spirit of Muslim political organization,
because a Muslim polity has for its aim the discharge of these duties
which are imposed upon its followers by Islam. It also was a revolt
against the demand of Islam for total loyalty. It also militates
against the idea of the indivisibility of the Muslim world, which had
been dead as a fact for centuries, but which was alive as a doctrine.

The results of nationalism in the Arab world have been
no less astounding. To a good many Arabs, Arabism and Islam
are identical. They see no difference between the two; even when
their ire is directed against a sister Muslim nation, they seem to think
that Islam cannot be on the side of the non-Arab. This process,
however, has gone further, and some Arab writers now look upon
Islam as a by-product of Arab nationalism, or, because this would be
a grave anachronism, of Arab resurgence.[85] From this point of view
Muḥammad was a great Arab rather than a prophet who rose above
the notions of race and country, and men like ʿUmar were great
Arabs rather than great Muslims, and, what is more, they followed
politics which were meant to advance the interests of the Arabs
rather than the cause of Islam. It is interesting to note how nationalism tends to change the accepted conceptions of history. These
attitudes, however, are not likely to strengthen Islam, because to the
extent that loyalty to Islam occupies a secondary place in the hearts
of its followers, its hold will be weakened. Even when it is made
to share the affection of which it had a monopoly, its hold is not
the same.

The question arises: Why should Islam find itself in conflict
with nationalism? The main reason is the doctrine of the brotherhood of all believers irrespective of their ethnic origins. To the
extent that nationalism divides the Muslim community in the world
into opposing camps or sectors likely to come into conflict with one
another, it is against the teachings of Islam. War among Muslims is
one of the most heinous sins in Islam and nationalism may and does
bring it about. The classical example is the revolt of the Arabs
against the Turks when they were engaged in a mortal conflict

[85] H. Z. Nuseibeh, *The Ideas of Arab Nationalism* (Ithaca, 1956), pp. 25, 26,
82.

during the First World War. The other reason is the doctrine of the indivisibility of the Muslim world, a doctrine which has been violated by forces other than nationalism as well in the course of history. When Abū Bakr decided to bring the Arab Bedouin tribes back to their allegiance to the central authority in Islam, he was considered by the jurists to assert the principle of the indivisibility of the Muslim community. So long as the lands of Islam were united under a single government, the principle was respected in fact. After the rise of the Abbasids, the establishment of the Western Caliphate violated the doctrine, but in the Eastern Caliphate, it was still valid. Towards the end of the Abbasid regime at Baghdad, this was reduced to merely a legal fiction. In the course of time there arose powerful dynasties which claimed to be the caliphs within their own territories, and there grew up even a little literature to justify this idea, though it was mostly accepted without much argument.[86] There was no use fighting against facts which had asserted themselves in spite of the original doctrine. As the scriptures were not positive on this point, there was not much controversy. The not too infrequent wars within the body of Islam were more difficult to justify because they ran against clear texts of the Qur'ān. At times some justification was found like the suppression of heresy or even the bolstering up of the authority of Islam where the rulers had failed in their duty, but not all wars could be justified on these grounds, and, whatever the theologians might have felt on these occasions, one does not come across any vehement denunciations of such violations of the injunctions of Islam. There can, however, be no doubt that such wars were against the letter as well as the spirit of the teachings of Islam. If Islam could be disobeyed for furthering the interests of dynasties, it is more conceivable that its principles will be set aside for the furtherance of national aims. As such conflicts are abhorrent to Islam, those who still believe in its values are suspicious of nationalism.

There has been a little thinking on this problem which has resulted in hitherto abortive attempts to create organs of consultation and co-operation among the Muslim nations. They have been unsuccessful because at present the national feeling is too strong and

[86] The Mughul Emperors claimed to be the caliphs in their dominions, but the precedent was set much earlier even in the subcontinent. See Qureshi, op. cit., pp. 32, 33, 38, 39.

some of the conflicts too deep to admit the utility of such bodies. But then the injurious effects of nationalism have not yet fully asserted themselves. Hitherto there has been only the exhilaration of a newly found conception of society. The reaction may come when its inadequacies have been discovered. The main source of disillusion may come from the economic limitations of the peoples which have embraced it and the pressing need for co-operation. Another force may be the pressure of greater powers in the shape of attempts to gain greater control over a strategic area of such importance.[87] These are merely possibilities at present; the stark reality is that nationalism is gaining ground at the expense of Islam in the larger part of the Muslim world.[88] If this trend continues, Islam will have to do some basic rethinking of its position to survive at all.

[87] A recent example is the increased Islamic orientation of Egyptian propaganda with the growth of Communist influence in Iraq.

[88] S. N. Fisher, *Social Forces in the Middle East* (New York, 1955), p. 258.

7

Islamic Elements in the Political Thought of Pakistan

Ishtiaq Husain Qureshi

There has been such vociferous insistence upon Pakistan's being an Islamic state[1] that the complexity of its political thought patterns has not received the attention of the students of Pakistan affairs. It is true that the large majority of the Pakistani people are Muslims and that Pakistan was ostensibly established on a religious basis. This is, however, only one side of the picture; religion explains a good deal so far as the *raison d'etre* of Pakistan and its thinking is concerned, but it does not explain everything. It is, therefore, necessary to probe a little deeper and see what part Islam has really played in bringing Pakistan into existence and in developing its outlook.

To start with, it is necessary to see what were the implications of being a Muslim in the Indian subcontinent; was the Muslim, for instance, just an Indian with a different religious belief, or did his differences with other Indians go deeper than religion alone? Was he, for instance, just as different from his Hindu neighbor as the Roman Catholic Englishman is from his compatriots who belong to the Church of England? This may not seem to be a fair comparison, because, after all, the Roman Catholics and the Protestants are alike Christians. Was then the difference the same as between the American Jews and the followers of other religious denominations in the

---

[1] The sentiment was crystallized in a provision of the constitution of 1956, which prescribed that the country would be called "The Islamic Republic of Pakistan," Article 1, *The Constitution of the Islamic Republic of Pakistan* (Karachi, 1956). Under martial law declared on October 7, 1958, the name was changed to "Republic of Pakistan."

United States? Here again the parallel does not hold good for two reasons: the Jews and the Christians share a good deal of the Semitic tradition as embodied in the Old Testament; and the Jews, through their association with the West and having lived so long in Europe and in America have adopted a good deal of the same cultural tradition as their Christian compatriots. Indeed, but for differences in religious doctrine and practices arising from those doctrines, there is no difference in the way of life and culture of the Jews and the Christians in the United States of America or in the United Kingdom. Was this also true of the Muslims and the Hindus in the subcontinent?

Even a cursory examination would show that the differences were much deeper than mere religious ones. They manifested themselves in such significant things as cuisine; dress; furniture; domestic, religious, and public architecture; names; social customs; vocabulary, even where the language happened to be the same; script in certain instances; and general outlook upon life.[2] Their view of history was different, the glory of one being the humiliation of the other. A good deal has been written upon the Muslims of the subcontinent being merely converts from Hinduism; but this view is erroneous. There is a fair proportion of the descendants of migrants from other Muslim lands, especially Central Asia, Iran, and Arabia.[3] The converts in the two Muslim majority areas now included in East and West Pakistan were overwhelmingly from Buddhism and not from Hinduism. The important feature of the conversions to Islam in the subcontinent was that it was not merely conversion to a religion, it was the adoption of the mores and the entire way of life of the Muslim community. It is not without significance that in certain areas of the subcontinent the words *Turk* and *Muslim* were synonymous until quite recently. If a Hindu was converted to Islam, his former coreligionists would talk of his having turned a Turk.[4]

[2] For an examination of the differences between the Muslims and the Hindus, see chap. v in Percival Spear's *India, Pakistan, and the West* (Oxford, 1952), pp. 76-91.

[3] The earlier British writers spoke of the Hindus and the Muslims as two different races. See James Mill, *The History of British India* (London, 1820), I, 132; G. A. Herklots, *Islam in India* (new edition revised by William Crooks, London, 1921), pp. xi, xii. All Muslims are not racially different from the Hindus, but a fairly large number are; it is this section which has given its peculiar characteristics to the Indo-Muslim culture.

[4] This has been the general practice in the countryside for many centuries. This

There is a cogent reason for this. The Muslims, whether Arab, Central Asian, or Iranian, were organized into separate communities from the very beginning. This was partly due to the general attitude of the Hindus towards all foreigners who were styled as *yavanas* or *melechchas*. The first word is a Hindu corruption of the term "Ionia," used in the East for the Greeks and was first applied to them; the second means "unclean." Both the words implied contempt and put the foreigner beyond the pale of social dealings like interdining, intermarriage, or participation in common festivals. Thus the foreigners were left very much to their own resources and organized their life separately. In a religious-minded community many of its traditions and customs had become identified with religion and converts generally picked up the entire culture of the community whose religion they chose to accept. Outside that community they had no social life; hence conversion to Islam meant really adoption into the Muslim community. There were instances of entire groups being converted who were able to keep some of their own customs, but a large number of people were converted in small batches or individually; even those who were converted in large numbers found it more attractive to adopt the customs and the culture of the Muslims. In this manner the Muslims preserved many of the characteristics of foreign origin in spite of adding large numbers of converts to their community. No community can live in a habitat for centuries without being influenced by it; the Muslims were no exception, and they adopted many conceptions and customs from the subcontinent, but these were assimilated with their original culture in such a manner that they seemed to be a part of it. This would be apparent to everyone who has studied either Indo-Muslim architecture or art. With a few exceptions, the buildings are dominantly "Muslim," but there are a few features, carefully assimilated and subordinated to the main style, which are the contribution of the Indian style.[5] Similarly the Mughuls created a

---

is not surprising in view of the large migrations from Central Asia throughout the Muslim period.

[5] For the main characteristics of Indo-Muslim architecture, see chapters on architecture in *Cambridge History of India*, Volumes III and IV. For greater details, see James Fergusson, *History of Indian and Eastern Architecture*, rev. and ed. by James Burgess and R. Phene Spiers, (London, 1910). A brief account is available in Ikram and Spear, *Cultural Heritage of Pakistan* (Karachi, 1955).

school of miniature painting which was so deeply influenced by Iran that it has been called by some 'Indo-Persian' as if it were a branch of the Persian school. Yet, by the absorption of some Indian features, it is distinct and different to a degree that the critics are no longer inclined to consider it merely an offshoot of the Iranian school.[6]

The Muslims of the subcontinent absorbed layers of immigrants from Arabia, Iran, Central Asia, and the Afghan mountains; the greatest impact was made by the Central Asians, because they seem to have been the most numerous and also because the ruling dynasties were overwhelmingly Turkish. Nevertheless, all the migrants contributed to its culture, as did India.[7] Thus the Muslims of the subcontinent were molded into a new community, distinct from the other Muslim communities and nations of the world, but also distinct from the people of their habitat. This community was neither Arab, nor Turkish, nor Iranian, nor Afghan, nor Hindu; it was the Indian Muslim community. It never lost its contacts with the rest of the Muslim world, nor did it ever permit itself to lose its affection for the world Muslim community. This is not the appropriate place to go into its history; but it is necessary to mention that it was faced for the greater part of its history with the colossal task of maintaining its separate entity; its greatest fear was that it might meet the fate of many other communities, foreign in origin, which had been swallowed up by Hinduism. Whenever it felt that its entity or beliefs were in danger of being absorbed into the local milieu, it reacted strongly and threw up movements to counter such a possibility.[8] It never reconciled itself fully to being

[6] *Ibid.*, chapter on painting. There are several works on Indian painting; Percy Brown is the leading authority on Mughul painting, on which he has a well-known book.

[7] Only two dynasties of Dehlī were Afghan, one claimed to be Saiyid on rather flimsy grounds, all the rest including the Great Mughuls were Central Asian. The non-Turkish dynasties were short lived. There are numerous references in early European writers about the Muslims of the subcontinent being Tartars. For reference to the separate racial entity of the Muslims, see James Mill, *The History of British India* (London, 1820), 132; also, G. A. Herklots, *Islam in India*, revised by William Crooks (London, 1921), pp. xi, xii. The religion and religious scriptures are of Arab origin; the literature has a strong Iranian flavor and originated in Iran; many of the mores and customs are Central Asian.

[8] The most important of these was the movement of Shaikh Aḥmad of Sarhind, whose influence came to be felt strongly in the reign of Jāhangīr, and the forces released by him became a mighty torrent in the subsequent reigns. The Ghair

Indian; one has only to examine its poetry to see how, while living in the tropical climate of the Indian subcontinent, it still dreamed of the cooler lands where roses bloomed and nightingales sang, where lilies made the air fragrant and tulips carpeted the forests, where the plane trees brightened the autumn with their red leaves and cypresses stood sentinel on the running springs.[9]   Look at the paintings of Chughtai and see how from his subconscious flow the images of Central Asia in their classical draperies and ecstatic looks.   Their great thinker Shāh Walī-u'llah called them travelers sojourning in a foreign land,[10] their poet Hālī compared them to a caravan which had fallen on evil days in a strange land;[11] their last great thinker and poet, Iqbal, condemned nationalism in all its forms and identified himself and his people with the world community of Islam with the entire world as their country.[12]   How could a people like this be completely Indianized to the extent of considering itself a part of the Hindu world?

The community, however, did not choose a distinctive name. It just continued to call itself "Muslim."   Sometimes the people would call themselves Indian Muslims, but the more common term, when used to distinguish themselves from other Muslim communities in the world, was "Muslim in India."   The emphasis on "Muslim" in these terms as well as otherwise is significant.   It arose out of the fact that after the community had been established in the subcontinent it began to absorb within itself the various layers of migrants from other countries, whose peculiar characteristics were shed in favor of the mores and customs of the local Muslims.   It

---

Muqallid movement, which is known to Western writers by its misnomer of Indian Wahhabiism, also had a facet of fighting against customs which had crept into the mores of the Muslims from Hinduism.

[9] The imagery even today is entirely Iranian; but for its greater subtlety and the difference in the language, Urdu poetry is not different from the poetry of Iran. Most of the great poets wrote in both the languages, Ghālib and Iqbal being outstanding examples.

[10] Shāh Walī-u'llah, al-Balāgh-u'l-mubīn (Lahore, 1897), p. 1.

[11] Hālī has a famous ode in which the following couplet occurs:
"Wuh dīn jo niklā tha barī shān se ghar se,
Pardes men wuh āj gharīb-u'l-ghurabā hai."
The English translation would read as follows: "A faith which left its home with so much glory is now reduced to being a stranger of strangers in a foreign land." The ode is on the plight of the Muslim community in the subcontinent.

[12] Muhammad Iqbal, The Mysteries of Selflessness, trans. into English by Arthur J. Arberry (London, 1953), pp. 32. ff.

was a process not too dissimilar to the Americanization of the immigrants from the different European countries. Like America, the
subcontinent was a land of new opportunities for the migrants, because here men of their own faith and possessing a basic stratum of
the same culture had established their rule and were short of man-
power. Throughout the history of Muslim rule in India and indeed in the Nizam's dominions before their absorption into the Indian
Union, migrants from other Muslim countries were encouraged by
all possible means. Unlike America, however, the older population of the subcontinent was highly civilized and, when properly
led, was capable of putting up a strong resistance. The Muslim
settlements necessarily started as armed camps in the midst of a
hostile population after the Muslim conquest; the earlier trade settlements of Arabs do not fall into that category, though even the latter
were not entirely free from a sense of insecurity. In the earlier days
when the Muslim Empire had been newly established, apart from
the big cities, a large number of small townships were created where
Muslim colonies were planted to keep peace and to insure the safety
of communications.[13] These colonies were sometimes beleaguered
and had to fight back to save themselves from annihilation. Gradually with the growth of the power of the Empire and the con-
ciliation of the native population the situation improved, but the
sense of insecurity never disappeared. The reason was that several
times when the power of the state, for one reason or another, suffered
an eclipse, the Muslim communities were subjected to plunder,
massacre, and all the horrors of war or insurrection. The last such
outrages came just before the establishment of the British Empire,
when the Maratha, Jat, and Sikh depredations resulted in misery
and loss of property and life to many Muslims where they were not
strong enough to defend themselves.[14] In this there was no distinction between the newly converted and those who were older Muslims
or between the older residents and fresh migrants. There is no greater
factor in uniting men into a community than a sense of common
danger; this integrated religious, social, and cultural group emerged

[13] I. H. Qureshi, *The Administration of the Sultanate of Dehli* (Karachi, 1958),
pp. 214, 216.
[14] Ghulām Husain Ṭabātabā'ī, *Siyar-u'l-mut'ākhrīn* (Lucknow, 1276 A. H.),
III, 892; Khaliq Ahmad Nizami, *Shāh Walī-u'llah ke Siyāsī Maktūbāt* (Aligarh,
1950), pp. 49, 89.

as the Muslim community of the subcontinent. The common factor among all the elements composing it was that they were Muslims; therefore, this was the name by which the community called itself. In that context this seemed to be adequate. It was sufficient to distinguish them from the other sectors of the population, especially from the Hindus.

And yet this name was not adequate. It described only one characteristic of the community, its religion. It is true that religion is an important factor in the life of a Muslim people, but then there are so many racial, cultural, and geographical groups among the Muslims of the world that every people has to be described further. In the days of modern nationalism the other factors have become all important, but they were always present. The Arabs, the Turks, the Iranians, and other Muslim nationalities already existed at the time when the Indian Muslim community came into existence. This community, like the Arabs and the Turks, was Muslim, but it had its own entity as well. It began to develop its own culture and in course of time came to have a separate language, a body of its own literature, its own architecture, its own art, and its own mores and social customs. It became a distinct entity in the world of Islam.[15] These embodiments of its culture were different in spirit from the culture of the land which they occupied. It had a flavor of the habitat, but only a flavor; in its roots it was still Arab, Iranian, and Central Asian. The Muslims of the subcontinent were not fond of calling themselves Indians, partly because of the continuous stream of fresh migrants and partly because of their pride in their own foreign ancestry;[16] besides, the word "Hindu," given to the native population by them, had a geographical significance. The Muslims of the subcontinent were strongly aware of their spiritual ties with the Muslims of other lands and never ceased to think of them with affection and a certain amount of wistfulness.[17]

[15] I. H. Qureshi, *The Pakistani Way of Life* (2d ed.; New York, 1957), pp. 8-11.

[16] Muslim family names very often, like the present writer's, show their foreign origin and are held as a source of pride. The example has been catching and in course of time some families of native converts have adopted names to show a foreign origin. This shows the pride in foreign ancestry and is a good psychological indication.

[17] Many a popular song is of that nature, sung on many a social occasion; the following is a good example:

Apart from their differences in culture and outlook with the Hindus, their nostalgia for other Muslim lands, their continued sense of insecurity, the foreign content in their traditions, and the non-Indian racial constituents of their politically conscious classes made the Muslims much more than just a religious community.[18] They had all the characteristics of a nation; only they were living with other nationalities in a common land. This last feature of their life was not peculiar to them; there have lived many nationalities alongside others under the protection of large empires.

The point of this discussion hitherto has been that the Muslims of the subcontinent were a nation, not merely a religious community.[19] They were throughout conscious of their separate entity, though not of their nationhood. In the beginning when thinking in terms of nationhood would have been a grave anachronism, the question of their realization of their true status did not arise; later they were themselves misled, thinking of themselves only as Muslims and not discovering any other description. The tyranny of a word can be immense; their description of themselves as Muslims was not sufficient to lead their thinking of themselves into clear channels; in this way they misled themselves and confused others. Their own confusion was tremendous, as can be seen from their confused policies in the beginning of their political struggle. They wanted to be free, but saw dangers for themselves

---

"Dikhāde mujhko, yā Mawlā, Madīna kaisī bastī hai,
    Jahan din rāt, ai Allah, tīrī raḥmat barastī hai."
The following is an exact translation: "Show me, O Lord, what is the town of Medina like, where Thy grace showers day and night." A common song sung in the streets during the late twenties and the thirties was:
"Mere Mawlā bulāle Madīne mujhe,
      * * * *
    Nahīn Hind men denge yah jīne mujhe."
This can be translated as follows: "My Master! Call me to Medina; they will not leave me alive in India."

[18] Various authors have discussed the political and economic causes of the tensions between the Muslims and the Hindus, e.g., C. Manshardt, *The Hindu-Muslim Problem in India* (London, 1935), pp. 35-51; Beni Prasad, *India's Hindu-Muslim Question* (London, 1946). All authors, whatever their point of view, recognize the fact that it was not merely doctrinal difference which was at the root of the problem.

[19] W. C. Smith in his recent book *Islam in Modern History* (London, 1957), like many others, has missed the point, where he discusses the phenomenon of the demand for Pakistan. The Muslims were not merely "a religious community." Such oversimplification of a complex problem only clouds the issues.

in the victory of the Indian National Congress; they wanted to identify themselves with the rest of the population considering themselves to be a part of the Indian nation, and yet they were afraid of this process and shrank back at every turn from the prospects of losing their identity. Ultimately in a flush of self-discovery came the realization that they were a nation and the popular support for that idea struck all observers as being phenomenal. The Muslims discovered the truth about themselves, but the world is still a little confused. That is the reason why there has not been a total acceptance of the emergence of Pakistan as an independent nation. The West in particular does not understand the full significance of Pakistan. So long as it continues to think of the Pakistanis as only Hindus with a different religion, it will continue to be unsympathetic to Pakistan and doubt its necessity. It is unfair to expect a knowledge of all the historical processes from an average Westerner, be he a politician or a journalist, which would justify in his eyes the existence of Pakistan. It becomes more difficult because of the prejudice which exists against Islam.[20]

This long history of the Muslims of the subcontinent calling themselves Muslims has also conditioned their thinking. When they achieved Pakistan, there were many sections of the nation which thought that the struggle had been to keep aloft the torch of Islam; this was not unexpected because to many of them Islam stood for all that was noble and good in their ideas. It was the idealization not only of their philosophy but also their way of life, all the constituents of which were not religious. When many of them spoke of Islam, they thought more of their own mores and culture than the doctrines embodied in the scriptures. There were a few who thought clearly and saw that Islam did not necessarily demand the revival of political traditions which were no longer relevant in the conditions of today; there were quite a few to whom it was of vital importance that the ancient precedents should be the sole guide in developing the new polity. As the consensus, with only negligible exceptions, was that Islam must play an important role in the life of the nation, it was certain that Pakistan would be an Islamic state. With Pakistanis calling themselves only Muslims and having no other name up to the time of the establishment of their state, it was natural

[20] K. J. Newman, *Essays from Pakistan* (Lahore, 1950), pp. 1-7.

that there should be so much insistence upon Islam. A clear understanding of the issues involved was a different matter. The Pakistanis were soon to realize that as a nation they were not just Muslims
but a separate political entity with interests which were peculiarly
their own and for which they would have to contend as other nations did. For instance when Afghanistan voted against the admis-
sion of Pakistan into the United Nations and staked its claim for
Pakhtunistan, or when the other Muslim nations did not receive
Pakistan with the enthusiasm which the Pakistanis had expected,
the realization came soon enough that nationalism was the gospel of
the greater part of the Muslim world and not the classical Islamic
conception of the brotherhood of all believers and the unity of the
Muslim world.

These disappointments, however, did not deter the Pakistanis.
They could not be the mentors of the rest of the Muslim world,
but they could at least base their own polity on the teachings of
Islam. When they started work on writing their constitution, they
realized that the nation was by no means unanimous upon its understanding of the nature of an Islamic polity. It is not surprising that
there should be differences regarding the application of the principles of Islam to the constitution of a country like Pakistan, where
all levels of conservatism and radicalism exist side by side. There
are secularists who think that the main function of Pakistan is to
safeguard and foster the cultural traditions of the people and that
therefore it should leave religion strictly alone. Their existence in
Pakistan and their work and sacrifices in fighting for Pakistan is an
indication of the fact that it was not religion alone which was responsible for the partition of the subcontinent. On the other extreme are the people who think that Pakistan must revert to the
institutions of the early days of the pious caliphs.[21] In between these
extremes there are many layers of thought which all struggled for
expression during the days when the Pakistanis were trying to influence the writers of the constitution. At last it was possible to
create a synthesis of these ideas and produce a constitution which
was generally acceptable.[22]

[21] Leonard Binder in his "The Islamic Constitutional Theory and Politics in
Pakistan" (Unpublished doctoral dissertation, Harvard University, 1956), discusses
the different groups.

[22] For a history of the writing of the constitution and the different issues which

This was possible because of the long tradition of liberal thought among the Muslims of the subcontinent.[23] It is necessary to discuss this background in somewhat greater detail.

With the establishment of the rule of the Turks in the subcontinent, the school of jurisprudence and theology which found favor increasingly among the people was the Ḥanafīyah. Ultimately, but for some coastal areas where the tradition continued to be Shāfi'-iyah, Hanafiyah became the prevalent school of thought. As this school gives greater importance to *qiyās*, the application of human reason to the problems which need determination or adjudication, there grew up a tendency to look upon questions in a less fundamentalist manner.[24] This tradition gradually developed and ultimately produced a thinker of the caliber of Shāh Walī-u'llah. He was born in 1702 when the Mughul Empire had started on the course of rapid decline; he therefore lived in an age when a diagnosis of the maladies from which the Muslim society and state were alike suffering was the greatest service a thinking mind could render to his people, and Shāh Walī-u'llah undertook that task with remarkable assiduity.[25] He has left behind voluminous works which show the encyclopaedic character of his knowledge as well as the clarity of his vision. In his writings he has not limited himself to a survey of the religious field, though religion was his main concern.

arose and the way in which they were decided, there is an excellent study by G. W. Chowdhury, *Constitutional Development in Pakistan* (Lahore, 1959). For a more detailed study, the debates in the Constituent Assembly of Pakistan provide excellent material.

[23] This thesis will seem a little strange to those who base their opinions on W. C. Smith, *Modern Islam in India* (Lahore, 1943). Smith used the yardstick of Marxism and found Indian Islamic aspirations and policies reactionary. He ignored the long tradition of liberalism in Indian Islam in his analysis and also failed to understand the real motive force behind Muslim attitudes in the subcontinent.

[24] For the development of Islamic jurisprudence, see A. A. A. Fyzee, *Outline of Muhammadan Law* (London, 1955); Joseph Schacht, *The Origins of Muhammadan Jurisprudence* (Oxford, 1953), pp. 295-310.

[25] Very little has been written in English on this remarkable thinker of the eighteenth century. The following articles will give the reader some idea of his work: Al-Ma'ṣūmi, "An Appreciation of Shāh Walī-u-'llah al-Muḥaddith al-Dehlavī," *Islamic Culture* (Hyderabad), IX (1947), 340-352; K. A. Nizami, "Shāh Walī u'llah Dehlawī and Indian Politics in the 18th Century," *ibid.* (Jan.-Oct., special jubilee number, 1951), Part I, pp. 133-145; M. Abdul Baqi, "Theories of State and Problems of Sociology as Expounded by an Indian Divine of the 18th Century," *Islamic Review* (London, 1950). There are two good chapters in *The History of the Freedom Movement* (Karachi, 1957), I, 491-542.

He has explored the political, economic and social conditions which were responsible for the malaise and has suggested remedies which do credit to his understanding of politics, sociology, and economics. He also had a good conception of the need for cultivating public spirit and social ethics. It would thus be seen that his approach was not merely that of a theologian who under such conditions was likely to bemoan the decline of religious virtues and do little else. Shāh Walī-u'llah explored mundane and scientific causes for what had been happening. He was the founder of a tradition and a school; his influence upon the religious thinking of the Muslims of the subcontinent was profound. His influence upon the religious circles was even greater. Indeed the credit for keeping alive the sense of his importance goes to the great Muslim theological seminaries of the subcontinent, and those educated in the modern tradition have awakened only recently to the magnitude of his learning as well as his greatness.[26] Through him was built up a tradition of looking upon political and economic problems in a broader perspective than just examining the legal implications as had the earlier jurists. As the difference may not be clear, it is necessary to point it out. For instance, when Māwardī was looking upon the institutions of his age he was not concerned with the fact that they were really intended to serve some purpose other and higher than that of satisfying legal requirements.[27] He showed no anxiety at their decline; he never put to himself the question whether they were real or had been reduced to a mere fiction. He was more anxious to fit into a legal pattern what he saw than point out that the law was actually being reduced to impotence and even absurdity by the interpretations which had been put on it. This was the attitude of a man to whom the sanctity of the law meant only that if the facts did not fit into the law, the law should be twisted into fitting the facts. Walī-u'llah, on the other hand, was not concerned with the superficial and apparent conformity with the law when its spirit was being sacrificed. The Mughul Emperor was still recognized as the *de jure* sovereign by those who had reduced him to a mere shadow. Many jurists of Māwardī's line of thought were satis-

---

[26] His works have been published mostly by the Seminary at Dabhel; 'Ubaid-u'llah Sindhī did good work in making him better known among the Muslims; his influence was considerable in Deoband, another famous seminary.

[27] Māwardī, al-Aḥkām-u's-sulṭāniyah (Cairo, 1298 A. H.).

fied, but not S̲h̲āh Walī-u'llah, whom no legal fiction could reconcile to the decline of the Muslim power and the peril in which he saw his Muslim compatriots at that time.[28]

This attitude was in consonance with his philosophy. He did not look on Islam as a body of laws imposed by God upon the believers without any purpose.[29] With this assumption, he examined the teachings of Islam and tried to find their social and political justification and their impact upon human welfare. It is true that this was simply an angle of scholastic philosophy, but its implications were broader than a mere rational explanation of the tenets of his faith. Two of these implications deserve mention. The first was the recognition of the basic importance of the welfare of the individual and the society, not only in the spiritual sense but also in mundane matters.[30] The other was that if some teaching was not producing this result, our understanding of it must be mistaken. In this manner theology and jurisprudence were taken out, to some extent, from the realm of the embellishment of the classical interpretations and brought more into the field of rational examination and reinterpretation, a process in which instead of logical deductions alone, sociology, economics, and political principles were to play a vital role. The earlier jurists and theologians had not been entirely oblivious of their importance, but S̲h̲āh Walī-u'llah laid much greater emphasis upon them.

Another important stage in the development of Muslim thinking was the movement of Syed Ahmed Khan.[31] He was one of the earliest modernists in Islam. His acceptance of the values of Western thought was enthusiastic because he thought that without it his people could never better their prospects. He started his movement after the suppression of the great rebellion of 1857, when the Muslims had been completely crushed in the subcontinent and were being punished terribly for their part in it. Though they were not the

---

[28] See Nizami's article in *Islamic Culture, loc. cit.*

[29] S̲h̲āh Walī-u'llah, *Ḥujjat-u'llah-u'l-bāligẖah,* Urdu trans. by Mawlana 'Abd-u'r-Rahim (Lahore, 1953), I, 128.

[30] It was this approach which took him into the realm of politics, economics, and sociology.

[31] The best biography is in Urdu by Alṭāf Ḥusain Ḥālī, *Ḥayāt-i-jāwid* (Agra, 1903). See also C. F. I. Graham, *The Life and Work of Syed Ahmed Khan* (Edinburgh and London, 1885), and Bashir Ahmad Dar, *Religious Thought of Sayyid Ahmad Khan* (Lahore, 1957).

only ones to revolt, the British, with some justification, held them responsible, and crushing indeed was the blow which fell upon them. Even before 1857 they had fallen deeply into the morass of decay and had lost all hope of prosperity. With the establishment of the Mohammadan Anglo-Oriental College at Aligarh, which ultimately developed into the well known Muslim University, Syed Ahmed Khan made it easier for the Muslims to take to modern education. He took upon himself the task of interpreting Islam in accordance with the new knowledge. In these two ways he started the work of reorienting the Muslim mind. This had far-reaching results. On the one hand the loyalty of the Muslims to their faith was not impaired; on the other, they took advantage of the new tendencies of human thought as developed in the West. One disadvantage was that the theological seminaries continued in their traditional manner and were not affected by Western thought. This was a serious disadvantage, because thus there grew up two traditions of education divorced from each other. The rift between the theologians and the classes receiving modern education went on increasing and ultimately there grew up significant differences in understanding the principles of their common faith.

The gap would have become wider if there had not been conscious efforts to remedy the situation; besides there were some natural factors at work. The Mohammadan Anglo-Oriental College and later the Muslim University of Aligarh scrupulously avoided teaching Sir Syed's interpretation of Muslim theology; indeed the departments of theology were in the hands of conservative theologians. Aligarh depended upon the general atmosphere of the institution and its secular branches of teaching to modernize the thinking of the Muslim students rather than upon changing the content of its theological teaching. This was also true of the other Muslim schools and colleges which were established in various parts of the subcontinent. Indeed the establishment of educational institutions became the fashion among those Muslims who wanted to demonstrate their patriotism. These institutions all followed the pattern of Aligarh in theological training or even religious instruction. The reason was that the parents of the students were mostly pious Muslims and did not want any interference with the religious beliefs of their children. The theological seminaries also began to make some concessions. They made arrangements for teaching English as a language, but this proved to be merely a gesture, because the departments of English were given a secondary position and were neglected. However, Shiblī, who had been a lecturer at Aligarh, conceived the idea of combining the best of modern education with a more thorough training in Islamic learning.[32] The idea was well conceived but in its execution Shiblī's conservatism was so dominant that, in the course of time, modernism was almost thrust out of the institution, which became a stronghold of orthodoxy. However unsatisfactory might have been the results of the attempts of the theological seminaries to modernize themselves and bring their thinking into line with the new demands, they do demonstrate a change in outlook. Nor can the seminaries be blamed entirely for their failure in this field, because they were not fully equipped to assess the nature of the problem and to provide the facilities for solving it. The realization of a necessity is often the beginning of sound reform. Those who were educated in the Western tradition were the foremost in efforts to understand their faith in the context of a new-found knowledge. Sir Syed Ahmad Khan had made it easier for them by showing the way.[33] All that he said was not accepted, because he had too profound a respect for the discoveries of physical sciences, whose postulates necessarily change every day. His acquaintance with Western thought and Western knowledge was merely second hand. His main thesis, however, that Islam was a rational religion and could be understood with the help of human reason, however crippling, was accepted. Syed Ameer Ali took it upon himself to continue the work of interpreting Islam to the West and also to the rising generations of Muslims educated in the same tradition.[34] The impact of such writings was considerable, and there grew up a class of men who were aware of Western thought as well as of their own heritage and valued both sufficiently not to discard either. Pride in the Islamic heritage was reinforced also by the writings of men like Shiblī and Abu'l-Kalām Azād, who created a romantic feel-

---

[32] For Shiblī's life and work, see Saiyid Sulaimān Nadwī, *Ḥayāt-i-Shiblī* (Azamgarh, 1943).

[33] His review, *Tahdhīb-u'l-akhlāq*, continuously published articles trying to prove that there was no conflict in the teachings of science and the scriptures of Islam. Also see his *Essays on the Life of Mohammed* (London, 1870).

[34] His best-known work is *The Spirit of Islam*, originally published in London (1891), which has gone through several editions.

ing about the Muslim contributions to the culture and civilization of the world. Indeed the trend was so strong that it could not have been resisted.

Three great poets used their talent for the same purpose. Hālī sang of the Muslim past; Akbar ridiculed absurdities which always arise when cultures reorient themselves; he was merciless in his satire and served the dual purpose of keeping the Islamic mores alive and preventing the excesses of the ultra-modernists.[35] Then came Iqbal, who cast Islamic thought into almost new molds.[36] He preached a renewed effort in the revival of Islamic values, of which he gave a most inspiring interpretation. The clock had turned a full round; Iqbal was familiar with the West and was not so overwhelmed with its superiority. Indeed he found a good deal to criticize in it and warned the Muslims against its weaknesses. He warned them in particular against the destructive role played by nationalism in human affairs.[37] He found both capitalism and communism wanting and asked his people to understand the fullest significance of the teachings of their faith. And yet Iqbal was far from being a reactionary. He believed in the necessity of what he called "a reconstruction of religious thought in Islam."[38] He quarreled with the conservative theologians for their rigidity, their farfetched interpretations, their distortion of the doctrines of Islam, and their general lack of understanding. And the surprising phenomenon was that he earned the respect of the theologians as well. Iqbal was a graduate of Western universities in philosophy; he was fully familiar with the Western thinkers and writers; he was at home in English and German; he was intellectually all that a modern Muslim could desire to become. But he was also well read in Islamic philosophy, mysticism, and literature; he wrote in Persian and Urdu as well as in English; he was deeply steeped in the knowledge of the Qur'ān, the exegesis of which he understood bet-

---

[35] For short biographies and accounts of their works, see Ram Babu Saksena, *History of Urdu Literature* (Lucknow, n.d.).

[36] For literature on Iqbal see *A Select Pakistan Bibliography* (Karachi, 1958), pp. 17, 18. There is a short note in de Bary, ed., *Sources of Indian Tradition* (New York, 1958), pp. 749-751.

[37] This is a common theme with him. See *Mysteries of Selflessness*, English translation of *Asrār-i-bīkhudī* by Arthur J. Arberry (London, 1953), p. 32.

[38] See his book, *The Reconstruction of Religious Thought in Islam* (Lahore, 1944).

ter than many a known scholar. He exercised the most profound influence upon the Muslims of the subcontinent, far more profound than the influence of any other modern thinker or writer. And this influence was in the direction of strengthening a living faith in the validity of Islam not only as a religion but also as a social and political philosophy. This was something different from the forms of Muslim theology and jurisprudence, something beyond the ken of the theologian and the jurist, yet spiritually much more powerful. He strengthened allegiance to the inner spirit of Islam, which could not be captured by mere adherence to forms and could not be contained within the rulings of the theologians and jurists. This was a new force, which we shall find active in the subsequent history of the Muslims of the subcontinent. And it was this element in the political thinking of Pakistan which many found difficult to understand.

The Khilāfat Movement, in which the Ali brothers played such an important role, was the next step in adding to the Islamic content in the political feelings of the Muslims.[39] Its purpose was political; it was to save the last stronghold of the political power of Islam from complete annihilation by putting pressure upon the British to desist from imposing too harsh a treaty upon the Turks. Its importance, from the point of view of strengthening the Islamic trends in the political thinking of the Muslims of the subcontinent, was considerable. It made the masses familiar with the political theories and institutions of Islam; the educated classes developed a new attachment to them.[40] Another outcome of this movement was the emergence of the theologians as a factor in politics. They worked side by side with those who had been educated in the Western tradition, and new avenues of discussion and understanding were created. Those Khilafatists who had no grounding in Muslim theology were deeply impressed with its liberalism and rational outlook; their activities now took a more religious bias. In certain instances the

[39] There is no good biography of Mohamed Ali and his brother, who was also a co-worker, Shawkat Ali. There is a biography in Urdu by Ra'īs Aḥmad Ja'frī, *Sīrat-i-Muḥammad 'Alī* (Lahore, 1950). See de Bary, ed., *op. cit.*, for a short note on Mohamed Ali, pp. 768-772.

[40] It was during this period, as the result of the decline of the Khilāfat, that Muslim intellectuals devoted considerable attention to the legal and religious basis of the institution. In the subcontinent, Abu'l-Kalām Āzād came out with his *Mas'alah-i-Khilāfat wa Jazīrat-u'l-'Arab* and Khuda Bakhsh wrote his *Politics in Islam*. Both were published in Calcutta in 1920. Arab writers like Rashid Riḍā and 'Alī 'Abd-u'r-Rāziq also came out with their writings on the subject.

metamorphosis was striking. The Oxford-educated Mohamed Ali, one of the best writers of English prose which the community has produced, began to dress in long flowing clothes of Arabia and came to be styled as Mawlānā, a term used for Muslim theologians.[41] The influence upon the theologians was also remarkable; Abu'l-Kalām Āzād, who later became the minister of education for India, became such an ardent Indian nationalist that he was perhaps the most secular-minded theologian in contemporary Islam.[42] Gradually all his ideas were transformed; his conception of Islam became only a Muslim version of theosophy; his earlier insistence upon the desirability of maintaining the individuality of the Muslim community and creating stronger bonds with the rest of the Muslim world gave way to his enthusiasm for identifying it more completely with India. Even the conservative Husain Ahmad said in the course of a religious discourse that nations were made by geography, for which he was severely rebuked by the poet Iqbal.[43] These are extreme examples; but they do indicate the general trend towards a bringing together of the graduates of the two kinds of institutions and of creating a synthesis in Muslim thinking. This synthesis is by no means complete; it would be incorrect to think that there are no differences between the conservative theologians and the Western-oriented Muslims in Pakistan; there are not only differences but sometimes even tensions. The extremists in the two sections are quite far apart indeed; but fortunately this division does not run through the rank and file. And, what is more significant, there is a class of moderates who understand the point of view of the two sections and are not swayed by the extremism of either.

[41] For an insight into Mohamed Ali's mind, read his *My Life, a Fragment*, ed. Afzal Iqbal (Lahore, 1942), and also the collection of his speeches and writings edited by Afzal Iqbal and published at Lahore in 1944. His review, *The Comrade*, is, of course, the best source.

[42] For his life, see Mahadev Desai, *Maulana Abul Kalam Āzād* (London, 1941). There is sketchy biographical material in Abu'l-Kalām Āzād, *Tadhkirah* (Lahore, n.d.). Since Āzād's death in 1958, a fuller autobiography has appeared: Abu'l Kalam Āzād, *India Wins Freedom* (Calcutta, 1959). It gives considerable attention to his activities as an Indian nationalist leader and naturally seeks to justify his views and policies. See also a memorial volume edited by his secretary, Humayun Kabir, *Azad* (Bombay, 1959).

[43] In the following lines:
"How strange is it that Deoband should produce a Husain Ahmad,
  He chanted from the pulpit that countries make nations;
  How ignorant is he of the position (on this point) of Muhammad of Arabia!"

It is this class which, perhaps not quite as articulate as the others, really helps the people make decisions. It is this class, once again, which puzzles the outside observer. Its views are not quite logical many a time, but this does not mean that they are not wise, because human affairs are not always fashioned by logic. It is progressive without being destructive. Its loyalties are deeply Muslim, even though, in certain instances, there may be considerable laxity in its conformity with the ritual and observances so strongly emphasized by the theologians. It has been this class which has provided the leadership to the community during the last few decades. The reason is that this class consists mostly of the intelligentsia, which is in a position of advantage in formulating public opinion. Outwardly in their appearance, practices, and even some ideas they might not seem to differ from the extremists who have little faith in the validity of religion, but they are essentially different because they have in their hearts deep springs of faith so that in times of crisis they come forward and through their loyalty and devotion capture the imagination of the community. In this process they do not discard their education or their liberalism; indeed they bring these to bear upon the task which lies ahead of them. The best example of these men was Mohammed Ali Jinnah, certainly not the picture of orthodoxy from the point of the exacting criteria of the theologians. As a matter of fact he did not belong to the orthodox school of thought at all. Still he was one whose loyalty to his faith and his people knew no limitations of self-interest or fear of looking inconsistent with his previous positions.[44] He had the greatness to change his policies and views when he thought they had lost their validity. Men like Earl Attlee misunderstand him and fall foul of him because they think that only those can have a feeling for Islam who not only meticulously follow the rulings of the medieval jurists but who also dress and behave like them. For men like Attlee the world of Islam has not only not moved at all but also has no business to move.[45] It

[44] For a short biography, see Hector Bolitho, *Jinnah, the Creator of Pakistan* (London, 1955).

[45] Earl Attlee said in a filmed television interview that he had never liked Jinnah; the main reasons for his dislike as conveyed by the interview were that Jinnah had insisted upon the partition of the subcontinent to which Attlee as the presiding prime minister of the United Kingdom was vehemently opposed, and he thought that "Jinnah was not genuine," presumably because he did not expect a modern man like Jinnah to be such an ardent Muslim. The film was shown on

is, however, obvious that the thinking of this class will be of the greatest significance in the future history of Islam. It was the thinking of men of this class which was of the greatest importance in the Islamic trends in Pakistani political thinking at the time of the writing of the constitution. They had to make concessions to conservative sections because the constitution was intended to satisfy the largest sectors of public opinion, but the basic thinking was from these moderates. And, what is more important, their thinking also affected the opinions of the conservative theologians.

There was considerable agreement that Pakistan was not to be just a state peopled by Muslims, but it was also to reflect their ideals and beliefs. This is what was meant by the desire to have an Islamic state in Pakistan. There were a few secularists who differed, but they did not carry much weight because they had no following. It was easier to set the goal than to define its implications. The less educated extremists among the religious minded thought that in an Islamic state its coercive power would be available for making the Muslims of Pakistan conform to their idea of what Islam was. Fortunately these men also formed a very small minority. There were others who thought that the ideal Islamic state had existed under the Pious Caliphs; therefore the institutions of government under them and the methods adopted by them were the pattern of a truly Islamic state for all time and should be re-created in Pakistan.[46] This also did not represent the enlightened opinion of the learned among the theologians, who, because of their association with the Western-oriented political leaders were sufficiently well informed about the needs of a modern state.[47] It was not in the recognition of these needs but in their proper assessment that the differences lay. However, there was sufficient common ground to make a compromise possible.

What were the main characteristics of an Islamic state which

BBC television on Jan. 3, 1959. The details of the interview appeared in *Dawn* (Karachi), Jan. 4, 1959. A report on the reaction of Pakistan's newspapers appeared in the *Times* (London) Jan. 5, 1959, p. 7, and in Pakistan *News Digest* (Karachi), Jan. 15, 1959, pp. 1, 3.

[46] Syed Abu'l A'lā Maudoodi, *Islamic Law and Constitution* (Karachi, 1955), p. 100.

[47] This is illustrated by their suggestions for incorporation into the constitution contained in a resolution of a conference held by them for this purpose. They have been quoted verbatim in de Bary, ed., *op. cit.*, pp. 861-864.

the theologians wanted to be introduced in the constitution of Pakistan?[48]   Curious as it may seem to the Western reader, there was no demand for the declaration of Islam as the official religion.   As a matter of fact, thoughtful theologians were opposed to such a move. Those among the Western-oriented politicians as well, who were close to the theologians in their approach to the constitutional problems of Pakistan, did not advocate this.   The introduction of the nomenclature "the Islamic Republic of Pakistan" had no thought or pressure behind it.   In none of the reports of the various committees appointed for making recommendations for the approval of the Constituent Assembly did this term occur.   It was first proposed and carried by almost a snap vote in a meeting of the Muslim League party just before the recommendations in that chapter were to be considered, and it was passed because of the discipline of the majority party in the house.   There was no design behind it.   Even those who were responsible for this—and they certainly were not theologians—were not thinking in terms of an official religion, because they did not follow up their move by providing for the administration of religious affairs in the constitution.   Pakistan never had a ministry for religious affairs, nor is it likely to have one under the present climate of public opinion.   In private discussions the theologians shuddered at the idea of a ministry for religious affairs, because they did not want religion to become a plaything for the politicians to be bandied about in controversies and election campaigns.   Thus in the matter of keeping religion out of administrative control there was no difference of opinion.   For the same reason the institution of religious courts for the administration of the personal law or the adjudication of cases having any religious significance was never proposed.   No one even thought of the matter.   This attitude was different from the practice in certain other countries where Islam is recognized as the state religion.[49]   The explanation is that the supporters of the idea of Pakistan as an Islamic state did not believe that religion was capable of being contained in

[48] Also see S. M. Ikram, *The Role of Religion in the Political Life of Pakistan*, a paper read in the Seminar on Religion and Politics in Pakistan at the Institute of Islamic Studies at McGill University, Montreal, Canada, in the summer of 1958.

[49] R. C. Ghosh, *Constitutional Documents of the Major Islamic States* (Lahore, 1947); H. M. Davis, *Constitutions, Electoral Laws, Treaties of States in the Near and the Middle East* (Durham, N. C., 1953).

a water-tight compartment of its own, either in the life of the individual or of the nation. This was in accord with the classic conception of the Muslim society in which Islam regulated the entire life, not just a part of it.

The most interesting discussions from the point of view of the students of politics as well as Islam were those relating to the positions of the head of the state and the legislature, because they were responsible for some original thinking and even suggested departures from the classical views. Despite the preponderance of politicians educated in the Western tradition in the Constitutent Assembly and in the political life of the country, it is interesting to note that the more radical views did not always win; indeed the advantage was on the conservative side. Despite this, Pakistan's administrative institutions and methods produced an impression upon the observer that it was no different in nature from any secular polity. Indeed when India persisted in calling Pakistan a theocracy—and this was not done with any charitable motives—the Pakistanis resented such statements. In fact, the impressions of the observers were quite right, because there was no difference between the government of any secular state and that of Pakistan, for the simple reason that the government was secular, run by men who were educated in secular institutions imparting education in the modern secular tradition. There are many who confuse the ulema—the theologians—with priests. The ulema are simply men who have received a training in Muslim theology. They are not ordained and do not constitute a church or a priesthood.[50] In the entire administration of Pakistan not one of these theologians could be seen, though, of course, there was nothing to bar them as citizens if they had entered through the prescribed channels. And this was the essence of the thinking behind the constitution which described Pakistan as an Islamic republic. It was not to be run by a privileged religious class or by doctors of Islamic theology; it was to be a modern state functioning in the twentieth century, but it was to be based upon the principles of Islamic teachings. In the light of these the positions of the chief executive and the legislature were to be determined.

[50] S. R. Shafaq, "The Clergy in Islam," chap. x in S. N. Fisher, ed., *Social Forces in the Middle East* (New York, 1955).

The Constituent Assembly appointed a committee of experts to recommend to the Basic Principles Committee, another committee of the Assembly, such provisions as they considered necessary to be introduced into the constitution for making Pakistan an Islamic state. Among other recommendations, they expressed the view that a presidential form of constitution represented the Islamic traditions of an effective and stable executive better than the parliamentary method. This view was rejected, because the unanimous opinion of the politicians at that time was that a presidential system was too complicated to be worked in a country where all progress in the direction of self-government had been towards parliamentary responsibility. Such experience as the people of Pakistan had, like that of the people of India, had been with parliamentary institutions. The record of Latin America was discouraging. The writers of the constitution were too afraid of the emergence of a dictatorship to try the experiment of a presidential form of democracy. The committee gave up its insistence upon the presidential form when it saw that its views were not likely to find favor and concentrated upon those matters which, from its point of view, were of a fundamental nature. They said that the distribution of the powers of government between the Parliament and the president was a matter of political and constitutional adjustment, but there could be no doubt in their mind that the president of the republic must be a Muslim.[51]

The moderate section of the members of the Constituent Assembly was averse to such a provision being inserted in the constitution. Some of them thought that it was unnecessary; an overwhelming Muslim majority was not likely to elect a non-Muslim for a long time to come.[52] Others were of the opinion that they had put so many curbs on the powers of the President that he was the chief executive only in name. They argued that if the prime minister who was envisaged in the constitution to exercise all real authority could be a non-Muslim under the constitution—and to this the *ulema* never objected—there was no reason why the president could not be a non-Muslim. The theologians put forward precedents and legal

[51] The recommendations of this committee were not published, but they form part of the archives of the Constituent Assembly of Pakistan.

[52] American readers would be interested to know that it was argued that, in spite of the absence of a legal bar, no Jew or Roman Catholic had been elected President of the United States of America.

arguments to support their point of view. They insisted that there could be no question of their agreeing to the legal possibility of a non-Muslim becoming the head of the state. In reply it was suggested that so long as the power rested in the hands of the people and their representatives in the Parliament, the majority of them would be Muslims.[53] This majority would have effective power of the state under its control and thus there was no danger of the liberty of the Muslims being bartered away by even a treacherous non-Muslim—and there would be at all times non-Muslim citizens just as loyal as any Muslim; but these arguments made no impression and the moderates had to give way. Judging by the roles played by Ghulam Muhammad and Iskandar Mirza in the politics of the country and the power they gathered in their hands, who can say that the ulema were wrong in thinking that immoderately ambitious persons could set constitutional safeguards at nought and become all powerful through clever maneuvering or intrigue? The tradition of a strong and stable executive seems to have asserted itself in the popularity of General Muhammad Ayub Khan's regime in the country. Whereas the Muslims have shown great hostility to any government by aliens, they do not seem at present to be so fond of self-government as to prefer it to efficient and good government by their own people even though they may not have been elected by constitutional means. This is the picture not only in Pakistan; it is true of other Muslim countries as well.[54] Whatever may be the forms, the real situation is not very different in other Asian lands either. This tendency may change with the growth of education and experience or it may persist and seek other constitutional forms in the future. At present the people want efficient methods to draw them out of the mire of poverty and ignorance, and democratic methods seem too slow and ineffective in their eyes. The merits of a system of government are not seen so clearly by people who are perennially hungry.

The point which raised the greatest controversy was the legislative authority of the Parliament. It was a well-established prin-

[53] This was based upon Qur'ān, iv, 59 where Muslims are enjoined to obey "God, the Prophet and those in authority from amongst you." This interpretation, however, was contested; the views of the earlier jurists and precedents could not easily be disregarded.

[54] Charles Issawi, "Economic and Social Foundations of Democracy in the Middle East," *International Affairs* (London) XXXII (1956), 27-42.

ciple in the classical Islamic polity that Islamic law was above all instruments of government—no one was above it.[55] It could not be otherwise, because the *raison d'etre* of an Islamic polity was that it should enable the Muslims to discharge their individual and social responsibilities as laid upon them by Islam without let or hindrance. Indeed the Muslim society was organized for the purpose of facilitating the Islamic way of life. In such a society the teachings and principles of Islam were necessarily of supreme importance. Hence it was recognized that the function of the Muslim polity was the enforcement of the principles of Islam as laid down in the Qur'ān and in the teachings of the Prophet through his precept and example. Islamic law and theology, called the *shar'*, were based upon these authorities, but they had developed through the thinking of scholars and judges who had to adjudicate on the questions of their application. A body of universally accepted interpretations had been built up through the ages; four systems of orthodox interpretation—all of them considered to be equally orthodox—have come into existence. There are other systems as well which are looked upon as more or less heretical. All interpretation and addition to theology as well as law has been through deduction; fresh legislation has no place in such a system of law. If all law is to be of this nature, what is the function of a modern elected legislature?

In the course of the long centuries when vigorous Muslim polities had existed, it came to be realized that there was a considerable area where the Islamic law was neutral. In this area the state had authority to legislate for the public good. This was conceded by the theologians and thus there was no difficulty in agreeing upon the principle that the legislatures had a function to perform in Muslim countries.

The vast majority of the Pakistani Muslims are Ḥanafī Sunnis, but there are many Shiahs of different schools of thought and among the Sunnis as well there are many who are not Ḥanafīs. Therefore, there was never any question of adopting any particular system of *fiqh*. This was made clear in the Objectives Resolution which speaks of the Qur'ān and the Sunnah and not of *shar'* or *fiqh*.[56] It was thus made clear and no one objected that

[55] Khuda Bakhsh, *Essays, Indian and Islamic* (London, 1912), p. 51.
[56] The Objectives Resolution with minor changes (none in this regard) was in-

Pakistan was not tied to any school of interpretation. Here again much more elbow room was gained, because the *fiqh* is naturally much more detailed. For this liberal attitude which enabled the ulema as well as the politicians to rise above sectarian prejudices credit goes equally to both. It was further made clear by the leaders on the floor of the Constituent Assembly that in the matter of the application of the principles of the Qur'ān and the Sunnah, the interpretation which was accepted by a particular sect would be held valid in its application to the sect concerned. The non-Muslims had been already assured their rights through the incorporation of fundamental rights which guaranteed them freedom in practicing and preaching their religious beliefs.[57]

In spite of these provisions, the main question remained. How was the relationship between the principles of Islam and the Parliament to be defined? After some discussion, not only in the committee rooms of the Constituent Assembly, but also from the platform and in the press, it was decided that a limitation on the powers of the legislature could be set by laying it down that the legislatures will have no authority to pass any legislation which is against the injunctions of the Qur'ān and the Sunnah. But then, how was such a provision to be made effective? Who was to decide whether a piece of legislation had violated the provision? In the beginning there was a strong feeling that such decision should not lie in the hands of a body outside the legislature, so that the legal authority of the legislature should not be impaired. The method recommended by the Basic Principles Committee—and one may reveal now that it was suggested by my lamented friend Sardar Abd-ur-Rabb Nishtar—was a complicated one. It laid it down that if a number of members raised the question that the proposal before the House contravened the Qur'ān or the Sunnah, the speaker would refer it to the President, who might then seek the opinion of a standing body of theologians appointed for this purpose. If they ruled that the proposed legislation did contravene the Qur'ān or the Sunnah, their opinion would be placed before the House, which would make the final decision. In this manner an opportunity was given to the legislature to ac-

corporated in the constitution and can be read on pages 1-3 of *The Constitution of Islamic Republic of Pakistan* (Karachi, 1956).
[57] *Ibid.*, pp. 11, 12.

quaint itself with the learned expert opinion on a question, from the point of view of the principles of Islam. This recommendation did not find favor, because though the final authority was placed in the hands of the legislature, it was feared that it would in effect give a veto to the theologians and make them superior to the parliament, as it was feared that after the expression of such authoritative opinion, the legislators would not have the courage to throw it overboard. The ulema did not like it because legally the Parliament was still empowered to legislate in defiance of the Qur'ān and the Sunnah.

In an address to the Political Science Association of Pakistan, I put forward a theory which excited some interest but which was not accepted.[58] It was an elaboration of a well-known principle of politics in Islam. Where the injunction of the _sharʻ_ is not clear and the interpreters are divided in their opinions, the head of the state has the right to choose the interpretation from among those offered which he considers to be the best. It was argued in this address that in the ancient days the head of the state was vested with this authority because he represented the authority of the community; in the present context it was the Parliament which was the repository of that authority.[59] Hence where there was a difference of opinion, the matter should be discussed in public and ultimately when opinion crystallized, the Parliament, sensitive to public opinion, being an elected body, should accept one of the interpretations and legislate accordingly. Even if it went wrong, the matter could be corrected later when a new House was elected. This, it was pointed out, would make the people participants in the acceptance of an interpretation which would become a part of their consciousness and their conviction. No state can be more or less Muslim than the people who constitute it. This was a democratic method of solving controversial matters, but it must be conceded that the public is not the best judge of legal niceties; but then the people were not being asked to judge cases on the basis of recognized law; they were only being asked to accept or reject some legislation as being in accordance with or abhorrent to their beliefs. And then no plebiscite was suggested, nor referendum; the legisla-

---

[58] This address has been incorporated in a small book, *Pakistan, an Islamic Democracy* (Karachi, 1951). One of the addresses has been reproduced in de Bary, ed., *op. cit.*, pp. 865-876.

[59] A. K. Brohi, *Fundamental Law of Pakistan* (Karachi, 1958), chap. viii.

ture, as the representative of the people, was asked to decide matters and to take responsibility. In short it was suggested that the question whether a proposal before the Parliament was in contravention of the basic teachings of Islam could be discussed—indeed it was bound to be discussed—outside the legislature as well as inside it. The doctors of Islamic theology could participate in the discussion and their opinions would carry weight in accordance with their reputation for learning and piety and the force of their arguments. But the legislature was to be the final authority. After all if it went wrong, its successors could change its decisions. This was a political solution and in my opinion in accordance with the spirit of the previous tradition, but, as has been mentioned before, it did not find favor.

The First Constituent Assembly ultimately decided to make the Supreme Court responsible. Just as it was to decide if the constitution had been violated by any action of the government or the legislature which was *ultra vires* of it, the court had also to be the judge whether the Qur'ān and the Sunnah had been violated by any act of the Parliament. Superficially this seems to have been a wise decision, but there were grave shortcomings in it. It was not fair to load the Supreme Court with a responsibility like this, as it was not equipped for it. The judges of the Supreme Court are selected for their legal learning, but they are not experts in Muslim theology. Their decisions were likely to be criticized and the prestige of the court might suffer in consequence. Being judges they would have a conservative outlook and Islamic theology would still be tied to the apron strings of law and lawyers, whereas the great need today is to free it from the rigidity which has crept into it as the result of continued legalistic interpretation. And the new legalism would not even have the advantage of opinions steeped in Islamic tradition of thought. For a court to sit down and examine the validity of a tradition of the Prophet is to try to achieve the impossible. Muslim scholars have been the first to condemn the Anglo-Muhammadan Law of British India, which had been developed in the same way as the constituent Assembly now wanted the *shar* to develop.[60] Earlier as well there had been judges of the highest

[60] The Anglo-Muhammadan Law was the Muslim personal law which was applied by the British Indian courts to the Muslims in connection with matters like marriage, divorce, and inheritance.

standing and probity, some of them Muslims, who had built up this corpus of mostly judge-made law. All the judges of the Supreme Court are not likely to be Muslims; indeed even today one of the best respected judges of the Supreme Court is a Pakistani Christian.[61] To ask non-Muslims to interpret Islamic theology for the benefit of the Muslims is to put them in an extremely embarrassing situation. The difficulty, however, would not really lie in some of the judges' being non-Muslims as in the fact of all of them having been educated in a different tradition of law and jurisprudence, which is mostly Anglo-Saxon in Pakistan. All the elements of flexibility and progress which are the result of honest and open public discussion would have been eliminated.

The Second Constituent Assembly was wiser. It provided for the appointment of a commission for making recommendations for bringing the existing laws into accordance with the Qur'ān and the Sunnah.[62] This commission was also "to compile, in a suitable form, for the guidance of the National and Provincial Assemblies, such injunctions of Islam as can be given legislative effect." This was done on the positive side; on the negative side it was laid down that "no law shall be enacted which is repugnant to the Injunctions of the Holy Qur'ān and the Sunnah." A careful study of the constitution reveals the fact that no one except the legislatures themselves were responsible for deciding whether they were contravening the injunctions of Islam. The Supreme Court had no jurisdiction in the matter, because the manner in which this clause would function had been defined and in that definition there was no mention of the Supreme Court. The legislatures were absolutely free in the matter; the only restriction would be the democratic one of public opinion by which the actions of all legislatures should be governed. This effect was achieved by a clever use of legal language; but the attempt succeeded. Public opinion was taken in. There was no agitation against these provisions; not even did the Jamā'at-i-Islāmī protest and it seemed to be satisfied. This attitude may be explained partly by the fact that there had been such delay in framing a constitution and such unwelcome signs had appeared on the scene that people were relieved that there was a constitution which promised them rights and general elections and they also knew that they could

[61] Recently he has become the Chief Justice of Pakistan.
[62] *The Constitution of the Islamic Republic of Pakistan*, Article 198.

remedy any shortcomings later. In fact there is no real remedy against legislation contravening the principles of Islam except the good sense of the legislators and their regard for their faith. In the ultimate analysis it boils down to the classical theory. Where the injunction is clear, there is no choice; but then if it is so clear, the Muslim legislators would be digging their political graves if they violated it against public protest. Where there is doubt and difference of opinion, these differences can be aired in public and the people's representatives can accept such interpretation as seems to be most in accord with the public interest and popular opinion.

And this raises a fundamental question. Is there, can there be, such a thing as an Islamic constitution? Whatever the writers of the various drafts in Pakistan might assert, the experience in that country has proved that there is no such thing. There are precedents from Islamic history; there are Islamic laws, if the injunctions of the Qur'ān are given that name; there are Islamic principles; there is also an Islamic way of life; all these do exist, even though some of them may not be easy to define, but there is no such thing as an Islamic constitution. The quest in Pakistan was misdirected; the search should have been for an Islamic way of life in this twentieth century, not for an Islamic constitution. A constitution, after all, is only the framework which a people finds suitable for ordering its affairs; it is merely an instrument, at best; it may be molded by the spirit which urges a people, but it does not mold that spirit. The Pakistanis might have learned a lesson from the life of the Prophet, who did not include in his teachings any instruction regarding the form of government they were to establish.[63] He left them principles which were to govern their polity; even these were not too many; he undertook to mold their character, but left the business of building up political institutions to their intelligence, because he was aware that institutions are made by the spirit and it is the spirit which is important and needs training so that what it builds may prove beneficial. An Islamic state will be different in spirit from other polities, if an Islamic state is achieved, but not in form. The need is to find a true outlet for the democratic tendencies of Islam through the spirit of the government. The forms should be designed to make this outlet possible; that is all that matters and little else is possible.

[63] Le Gardet, *La Cité Musulmane* (Paris, 1954), pp. 126-128.

There is an important question which should be answered before this chapter comes to a close. How will the abrogation of the constitution and the establishment of a new regime affect Islamic thinking in the politics of Pakistan? It is not easy to answer a question regarding the future. The President has said that the next constitution will be a simple one, by which perhaps he means that the institutions will be of a nature that their functions can be easily understood by the people. It is difficult, however, to see how the complexities of constitutional law can be avoided. Besides, one hopes that the writers of the new constitution will not confuse simplicity with brevity. In a country like Pakistan it is necessary to have a detailed written constitution, because healthy conventions are not easy to establish. The troubles in Pakistan did not arise because the constitution was unworkable or too elaborate. The sole cause of the malaise was that the spirit of the provisions was violated by selfish and self-seeking men. They respected neither the principles underlying the constitution nor the well-understood conventions of democratic government. The ills of Pakistan were caused by men, not institutions. The next constitution of Pakistan should not be a brief document, because a law in which the details are left undefined gives greater opportunities to unscrupulous men. Therefore, the constitution will necessarily have to be an elaborate document if it seeks to curb the propensities of selfish and unpatriotic elements. General Muhammad Ayub Khan has indicated that he would like to have a constitution of the new French pattern. The Islamic frills will perhaps disappear; they were in any case unnecessary, because they sought to achieve so little. What the Pakistanis seek to gain can be gained in other and better ways. Thus the constitution will, in all probability, not wear its Islam in its button hole. The love which the Muslims of Pakistan have for Islam and their loyalty to it are a different matter. Islam is deeply embedded in their sentiment; it is the warp and woof of their history. Pakistan can not exist without Islam. Its loyalty to Islam is enduring and will last. Nothing has happened to change that. This loyalty will continue to fashion its political thinking policies.[64]

[64] The reader will notice certain discrepancies in transliteration. These have crept in for two reasons. Where an English work has been cited, its transliteration has been reproduced. Names of persons knowing English have been reproduced as they spelled them. Many family and other names came to be written before the adoption of any scientific system of transliteration.

8

Political Dimensions of Foreign Aid

John D. Montgomery

Perhaps the most neglected aspect of foreign aid as a factor in modernization is its political dimension. This is surprising enough, since its influence is exercised so much more obviously upon national than upon village and family traditions.[1] But the importance of this political dimension is all the greater because foreign aid is being offered at decisive moments in the history of the underdeveloped world, before these states have yet developed a stable political tradition and when colonialism is yielding to national independence, the functions of government are broadening, many unitary administrative patterns are becoming multi-centered, and the political forces in the national community are beginning to reflect the emergence of rival elite groups. In one way or another substantial programs of foreign aid affect all of these essentially national problems.

Foreign aid is, therefore, unavoidably political, at least in this sense. Although this aspect of foreign aid is sometimes overlooked by the United States and its friends, the neutral powers are wise enough to recognize this fact even though the aid appears to them in its most politically sterile forms. "It is true that [American] aid

[1] Agricultural credit, farm organization, and community development projects are, of course, intended to affect village traditions, including local political behavior. Such projects are for the most part, however, carried out through a national ministry of agriculture, health, or education. Cf. Edward C. Banfield's argument that "most of the people of the world live and die without ever achieving membership in a community larger than the family or tribe. Except in Europe and America, the concerting of behavior in political associations and corporate organizations is a rare and recent thing." *The Moral Basis of a Backward Society* (Glencoe, 1958), p. 7. The backwardness of an area is said to be principally caused by "the inability of the people to cooperate for a common purpose." Robert Waelder, "A Hypothesis about the Nature of an Archaic Society," *World Politics*, XII, No. 1 (1959), pp. 92-102, 94.

has no [objectionable] strings attached," an editorial stated in a Burmese newspaper a few years ago, "but we overlook the fact that foreign aid is itself a string."[2] At the November 1959 Colombo Plan Conference President Sukarno warned the delegates, "Do not think that assistance will produce a nation in your own image.... The Indonesian nation is an ancient nation, a nation with proud memories. ... The Indonesian nation has its own traditions. It will develop in accordance with those traditions." In spite of this natural desire to protect the integrity of Indonesian statehood, Sukarno acknowledged that "development must, then, be an overall process touching the life of men at all its points," and conceded that "any scheme of pure economic development can be no more than an irritant in the body politic and the social organization of the nation."[3]

If schemes of purely economic development are an irritant in the body politic, those of technical advancement may be even more so, since they directly affect men's ways of doing things. Foreign aid accumulates in its operations the properties of both economic and technical assistance; and since both its purposes and its environment are politically charged, it provides some painful irritants (as well as ointments) in the processes of social change.

These factors will be considered below as suggesting four political dimensions of foreign aid:[4] the international, domestic, and administrative factors relating to the beneficiary government, and internal politics in the United States. Most of the specific examples below are drawn from American programs in Asia, but this is not intended to imply that similar experiences and typologies may not exist elsewhere. On the contrary assumption, several tentative conclusions can be drawn from them relevant to Africa, the Near East, and Latin America, and to other donors from the West.

I. INTERNATIONAL POLITICS AND FOREIGN AID

The international setting of foreign aid involves a complex of relationships: East-West alignment, regional activities and in-

[2] *The Nation*, Rangoon, Aug. 17, 1951, p. 2.
[3] *Address by His Excellency President Sukarno of the Republic of Indonesia to the Colombo Plan Conference on November 11 1959.* (Embassy of Indonesia, Washington, D. C.), pp. 7, 13, 5.
[4] Foreign aid is here discussed as including economic and technical programs. Military assistance presents additional problems not yet opened to public analysis.

terests, and bilateral agreements and understandings of the receiving nation with the donor and its allies. The main impact of foreign aid in each of these relationships has been to strengthen existing tendencies. Foreign aid does not often change a government's international posture fundamentally, although it may be used to reduce bilateral tensions and it may inadvertently weaken existing friendships.

Two principal factors appear to be at work in determining the amount and use of foreign aid in relation to questions of East-West alignment. The first of these is the closeness of the alignment; the second, the importance of the military and strategic considerations involved.

Countries that are in close alignment with the United States and the Western bloc receive large amounts of aid. American military or other strategic objectives are also important. The aid programs in countries where both these conditions prevail, such as those in Korea, Taiwan, Turkey, and Viet Nam, are relatively unitary and well co-ordinated in terms of their national economic and strategic objectives and the general program balance. In other countries whose alignment is equally decisive, but whose strategic claims are less urgent, the level of aid is lower and other justifications for economic and military assistance must be found. The resulting program may appear diffuse and even haphazard by comparison. Thailand, for example, is committed to the West, but it can demonstrate no urgent economic needs and no immediate Communist threat. American aid has nevertheless been offered it in fairly substantial amounts because of the international posture Thailand has taken, creating an implied obligation on the American part to befriend a loyal partner even if he is not suffering from military insecurity or economic distress. But American aid programming in Thailand has never had as sharp a focus as that in Viet Nam. In still another context, smaller, less-committed countries like Cambodia and Laos have sometimes claimed disproportionately large amounts of aid because of urgent military need, though for lack of mutuality of purpose the program has been relatively ineffective.

Finally, neutralist countries like Burma or India have solicited aid for their economic needs without offering any form of military or political alignment. Aid to neutralists usually rests on purely humanitarian grounds, on bargaining based upon a balancing off of favors from the opposing bloc, or on the proposition that the progress of these countries is important to the West. Countries of the neutralist spectrum tend to develop a relatively wide selection of aid programs because military strategy plays no unifying role in their requests and because they can usually evoke competitive offers of aid from several sources. But the total amounts of aid from the West have probably been less than if they had chosen to be allies. Aid to Burma has never equaled that received by equally strategically situated nations that were fully committed, and the resulting programs have tended to have a much less clearly focused concentration in their design than those of the other three types.

Aid to neutralist countries may be accompanied by vigorous internal political controversy about its usefulness and its danger to the neutralist position, but it usually has achieved only a relatively superficial penetration into the political and technological framework of the host society. It is noteworthy that the economic and political impact of American aid was greater in the Marshall Plan countries, Greece, Taiwan, and Viet Nam, than in countries representing other basic international settings for foreign aid.

Although these considerations are clearly the dominant international factors in establishing American aid levels, others have recently become important, as well. Regional relationships in particular have taken on a critical relevance to the East-West conflict. Even where foreign aid has not actually served as a mechanism for inducing membership in regional alliances as it has in Pakistan or Iraq, it has encouraged extensive regional involvement in projects serving mutual objectives throughout the world. The development of regional interests and "good neighbor" cooperation has had other values than encouraging participation in a SEATO or a CENTO.[5] Improving relationships within a region for mutual economic advancement and political stability has long been an end of American foreign policy entirely apart from questions of Communist penetration or subversion.[6] Offers of aid in regional development have not succeeded in affecting relations between Israel and its Arab

[5] See Senator Hubert H. Humphrey, *The Middle East and Southern Europe* (Washington: U. S. Senate Committee on Foreign Relations, 1957), pp. 6-10.

[6] Council on Foreign Relations, *Basic Aims of U. S. Foreign Policy*, U. S. Senate Committee on Foreign Relations, Study No. 7, 1959.

neighbors, where mutual suspicions were too powerful to yield to such blandishments, but Cambodian-Thai suspicions based on a long series of border incidents have demonstrably relaxed as a result of their joint participation in the Mekong River Development Project. In the former Indochinese states of Laos, Cambodia, and Viet Nam, as well, after their separation into independent nations, the former imperial community of interests gave way to nationalist suspicions, varying degrees of Communist subversion, and political emphasis upon cultural differences that seriously impeded economic progress. Here the United States deliberately used foreign aid as a device for reviving or creating a sense of community on a project-by-project basis. Thailand, which desired strong regional co-operation in the interests of its own national security, took the lead in encouraging co-operation in regional development in spite of its historic suspicions of Burma, Cambodia, and Malaya. Other regional projects in the fields of communications, education, and technical and resource development in Southeast Asia were created by the ICA missions in the hope of reducing political barriers and establishing cultural exchanges. While the promise of foreign aid has not actually induced the lion and the lamb to feed at the same trough, it has attracted different species into joint endeavors and has quieted some natural suspicions.

A third group of international problems relating to foreign aid involves bilateral relationships outside the region and unrelated to East-West alignments. Among the most troublesome of these are the ties between former colonies receiving U. S. aid and the former mother country. Some colonies—Cambodia and India, for example—achieved independence while retaining a deep cultural affection for the mother country, whose technicians and administrators continued to perform useful services during the period of transition. In others, a total rejection of the colonial status, especially when independence was achieved by war and nationalistic struggle, has brought about rejection of the cultural influence of the former imperialists as well. Indonesia and Viet Nam at one time considered any cultural or technical assistance from Holland and France an interference. In countries where independence has lost its connotations of violence, an ambivalent attitude toward the former mother country tends to produce alternating whims of nostalgia and resentment. American aid has had to adjust to these fluctuating political sentiments, serving as foster parent when the need dictated, and standing patiently aside when the French, the Dutch, or the British ways were preferred as technically or culturally superior. Because of the sensitive and volatile character of these relationships, international considerations have had more pronounced effects on foreign aid within the Western world than in the relatively homogeneous Communist bloc.[7]

Most of the international relationships developing out of the foreign-aid context are transient. It would be unrealistic to assume that national traditions developing in the early years of independence will continue to dominate the foreign policies of these countries. The scrapbag of history is well filled with discarded treaties and records of wars among former allies. Moreover, foreign aid is often administered in a crisis atmosphere or one of suspicion between the host government and the donor. Foreign aid has nevertheless succeeded in influencing international co-operation in specific directions at least temporarily. Doubtless this phenomenon can be further exploited in the interests of a world order as American policies develop in precise enough form to make it feasible.[8]

II. PROBLEM OF MUTUALITY: FACTORS RELATED TO THE INTERNAL POLITICS OF UNDERDEVELOPED COUNTRIES AND UNILATERAL AMERICAN PURPOSE

International factors shape the design and conduct of the aid program in underdeveloped countries more significantly than the domestic politics within the host countries do, but the ultimate suc-

[7] It is possible that even in the Eastern bloc elements of international "gamesmanship" in the relationships between satellites and the solar center have produced varying responses from Russia and China. It is almost certain that the complexities of neutralism in Burma, India, and Indonesia have influenced Soviet aid policies just as they have those of the United States; and similarly, the relatively high degree of independence allowed East Germany or Poland and the ambivalence of Yugoslavia have influenced the economic relationships that are the Soviet equivalent of foreign aid. It is even possible that in certain satellite nations compelled by the fortunes of war to accede to the political dominance first of China and then of Russia, or vice versa, there may be developing divided loyalties between the cultural claims of the two principals, resembling those of ex-colonies to the mother country.

[8] See Robert C. Tucker, "Russia, The West, and World Order," *World Politics,* Vol. XII, No. 1 (1959), pp. 1-23, for a discussion of the need for such a policy.

cess of the program depends upon the internal rather than external affairs. Foreign policies in underdeveloped countries (and perhaps elsewhere) are more often a function of the political orientation of the host government than of objective international circumstances as seen by others.

Aid programs which the donor and the host government undertake out of strong mutual interests obviously enjoy more impetus from the joint efforts of the two governments than those accepted with apathy or misgivings. In the long run, however, programs representing the greatest mutuality may not be the most important to the country's welfare or development. Their acceptance may represent a bilateral "lowest common denominator" rather than a theory of economic development that would be acceptable to either party. Conversely, severe tensions may also arise in the execution of programs representing high and genuinely mutual priorities.

Even where projects enjoy an undoubted mutual support, they may engender political frictions. A principal political objective of foreign aid, and a basic requirement of statehood in most parts of the underdeveloped world, is the achievement of an adequate degree of internal security, especially in areas threatened by Communist subversion. Where instability plagues the leadership of a newly developing nation, the establishment of security, under a Hobbesian law of survival, takes precedence over any other political or economic ambition. Politically, however, the process of achieving stability with foreign help may offer severe challenges to a new and sensitive sovereign government. In establishing governmental relationships where they have not previously existed, and in gaining popular acceptance of the legitimacy of foreign assistance, new governments may be embarrassed to ask for such aid in asserting their authority. No alternative may exist, however, if dissident internal groups offer a powerful military challenge to the government. The dilemma is then posed in its severest form: inviting the West to help create the conditions essential to political survival may require sharing with an outsider some of the most fundamental decisions of sovereignty. The choice may be between legitimacy and survival.

In 1955 the internal security of Viet Nam was an international concern. France, the United States, and Communist Viet Nam and China were all directly concerned in one way or another; and even

as late as 1959 assassinations of local government officials were occurring at the rate of nearly one every working day of the year, and
sabotage, terrorization of the peasants, and night raids were not
infrequent in the plains south of Saigon.[9]

An American police team in Viet Nam recommended that a national civilian village-based police force be organized to protect the
rural countryside against Communist raids. The only existing organization capable of serving this purpose in 1955 was the 50,000 to
60,000-man Civil Guard, a poorly organized and ill-equipped relic
of the civil wars whose functions consisted mainly of semi-military
skirmishes within province boundaries, and which was overmanned
and underorganized, being denied even the authority to cross a provincial boundary in the pursuit of outlaws. But to reorganize the
Civil Guard as the American technicians recommended would have
meant releasing 20,000 to 30,000 of its least effective members, thus
perhaps creating unrest among a group of hardened soldiers of
fortune. On the other hand, it would establish a national agency
with stronger permanent roots in the villages than those of any other
government agency. Adopting civilian rather than military leadership would develop a new and unpredictable elite, and abandoning
military tactics and armaments might weaken the national defense
(American support to the Army limited its total strength to 150,000).
It is small wonder that the American suggestions were ignored and
the Vietnamese pressed the large sums for the purchase of heavy
artillery and other purely military equipment. The Americans refused this request, and the Vietnamese government in turn declined
repeatedly to endorse the proposed reorganization.

Another set of objectives bearing a similar mutual Asian-Ameri-
can priority is that of economic development. The point of time at
which this can become a dominant purpose depends upon an existing condition of internal order and upon a specific economic and
social vision on the part of the national leadership.

One project bore the label of internal security and economic development at the same time, and was thus doubly mutual in purpose.
Yet it encountered serious political obstacles as every major decision
was reached. In 1956, U.S. and Vietnamese authorities agreed jointly

[9] See Wesley R. Fishel, "Vietnam's War of Attrition," *New Leader*, Dec. 7, 1959,
pp. 16-21 for a recent discussion of the security problem.

to undertake a large-scale land-development project as a security measure and for economic purposes. The American statement of objectives[10] emphasized its humanitarian and economic aspects, but also referred to it as a means to the "promoting of security in areas now vulnerable to anti-government propaganda and activity." It was this aspect, building what President Diem called a "wall of humanity" against subversion and disloyalty, that constituted its major purpose in Vietnamese eyes. On this basis, the Vietnamese measured the success of land development in terms of the speed with which unemployed or underemployed city dwellers and others were resettled in the new centers, while the American technicians preferred an evaluation based on the economic viability of the centers themselves. Nevertheless, the project was a mutual one, and in 1957, $10 million was allocated to it. The administrative and policy difficulties that followed—and they were numerous—were all related to these differences in purpose and priority. Many sites were ill-chosen and ill-prepared, equipment was roughly handled and diverted from agreed tasks, and some centers served as political re-education camps rather than development projects. Repeated efforts to persuade and even force the Vietnamese government to act more cautiously were of no avail, and finally, in 1958, $5 million of American funds allotted to the project were cut off entirely. Because total aid level for Viet Nam was already determined, however, this cutoff meant only the reprogramming of the same amount for military purposes, and the Vietnamese government was able to transfer funds from military to land development projects in order to continue operations unimpeded by American advice. The American position was heavily influenced by fear of a Congressional investigation of the land development project; and it is noteworthy that American and Vietnamese cooperation improved immediately after the fund transfers of 1958, which relieved the agricultural technicians of responsibility and enabled them to appreciate the political and the physical achievements of the program. The Director General of Land Development later reviewed these collisions of purpose in a public speech:

According to the President . . . land development must be started first in areas having few favorable conditions for the development, regardless of

[10] United States Operation Mission Vietnam, Project Agreement 30-12-144, April 20, 1957

how remote they are, or whatever difficulties may exist in order to create attractive centers and develop them later. . . . The American technicians did not agree with these views; they wanted to work slowly but surely, with careful preparation in light of purely economic considerations. . . . They welcomed land development in areas where operations were easy, sure of success, and without risking loss, even those losses that are known in advance but sustained for the sake of experience—calculated risks.[11]

An even more vigorous dissent was uttered by the President's brother and chief political advisor, Ngo Dinh Nhu. In an interview for *La Vie Francaise* on May 15, 1958, he launched a vigorous attack on the American aid program, which was reprinted in Saigon in the *Journal d'Extrême Orient*, June 3, 1958. Speaking of the American hesitancy to support the Vietnamese land development, he said:

The Americans distrust those projects which they have not thoroughly studied. In agricultural affairs, they want to venture only into those projects which return 100 per cent the first year. But on the high plateaus it is obviously necessary to wait a certain time before being sure of success. USOM, which is charged at the same time with studying projects under their financial administration, is always afraid of criticism from the American Congress. . . . I am speaking of the high plateaus, but I could say the same thing for the development of the rice paddies of the Cochin-China. We find that the development of our economy suffers from American slowness. We should prefer to form a committee of experts from all nations, in which USOM would have nothing but financial control of the funds rather than, as now, having USOM first develop and then financially control projects. Having all responsibility in one single body paralyzes it.

Even where the long-range purpose is identical and the differences are merely those of timing, the force of politics may predominate over technical considerations. In still another context—that of economic development—American purposes in Viet Nam clearly paralleled those of the host government in principle, leaving only what appeared to be technical and administrative problems to be resolved. But economic development is not a purely technical process. The $451 million spent on the U. S. commercial import program in Viet Nam in the first two years of independence were intended to

[11] Quoted in USOM, Division of Agriculture and Natural Resources, *Land Development* (Saigon, 1959), p. 5.

prevent inflation and supply foreign exchange needs at the same time. The political question of what these "needs" were led to agitated and continuing debate. As late as 1957, when a moderate dollar balance had begun to form, the Vietnamese government decided to continue issuing licenses for imports that would satisfy new consumer demands rather than to encourage capital imports. This decision arose from the judgment that the rising class of technicians, entrepreneurs, professionals, and civil and military servants whose living standards were involved might otherwise become dissatisfied with the efforts of the regime on their behalf. The American advisors favored using the commercial import program for what they considered more productive purposes. Eventually the aid mission had listed hundreds of items as ineligible for dollar support, with the Vietnamese government continuing to press for permission to import luxury items.[12] Its own foreign exchange holdings, though more carefully husbanded than the massive resources of the commercial import program, were still not used for a systematic encouragement of industrial development.

Industrialization has not by any means been universally accepted in the underdeveloped world as the most desirable way of achieving economic development: agriculturally viable Burma, Viet Nam, and Thailand were much less inclined to give industrialization a high priority than was Taiwan, where in ten years a virtual economic revolution had taken place.[13] And in all of these countries, moreover, a serious controversy over public versus private enterprise raged whenever economic projects were under discussion.[14]

[12] *Current Situation in the Far East*, Hearings, U. S. House Committee on Foreign Affairs, July 27-Aug. 14, 1959, p. 38.

[13] The Department of State, *The Republic of China*, Publication 6844 (Washington, 1959), p. 3; *Department of State Bulletin*, Nov. 30, 1959, p. 779.

[14] The violence of Asian hostility to private capitalism is sometimes overlooked in the United States. In an off-the-record, unpublished speech to civil servants, Ngo Dinh Nhu, brother and chief political advisor to President Diem, stated that "democracy without a morsel of private ownership is a false democracy," adding that "This sort of democracy is seen in the free capitalist countries of Europe, and in Communism." President Sukarno of Indonesia, rejecting the types of Western aid that would encourage the growth of a wealthy class of capitalists said, "We could not adjudge ourselves prosperous if we established a prosperity of the elite, even if that is prosperity in the eyes of much of the world." *Address by . . . President Sukarno . . . to the Colombo Plan Conference. . . . Loc. cit.*, p. 6. Nehru stated that "the political aspect of democracy, good in itself, was not adequate. . . . Political freedom under economic pressure is very limited freedom." These remarks were made in a context in which the importance of state ownership in eliminating

If mutually designed programs inspired collisions between the donor and host governments, political disturbances of a different type occurred where specific projects were accepted with reservations or reluctance by one party or the other. The elements of mutuality in specific fields have differed greatly from place to place in Southeast Asia. This becomes increasingly evident as one descends from the generalities to the particulars of binational purpose. In Buddhist countries a psychological atmosphere of mutuality may be generated by the doctrine that the act of giving is a means of acquiring "merit," and therefore the receiver confers a benefit upon the donor by opening this channel of virtue to him; while an equal sense of well-being may be derived by Western donors from the Christian ground that it is more blessed to give than to receive. On the basis of such a psychological parity of receiving and giving, Burma having decided again to accept U. S. aid after refusing it for a number of years, has succeeded in creating the impression that the good will and moral purpose of the United States is being "tested" by the size and nature of its aid program. Since all the projects offered to Burma are requested by the government and are given voluntarily, a high degree of mutuality might be anticipated. Unfortunately, however, this has not been the case. The piecemeal projects, sound enough in themselves, have represented compromise rather than a mutuality of purpose and planning.

Most newly established governments in Southeast Asia lack both a development planning apparatus and the will to impose austerity in order to achieve economic progress. Dramatic but premature or unrealistic programs like steel mills where no iron or coal are found, atomic reactors where no physicists are available, electronic computors, cancer research institutes, and similar developments have had an almost irresistible appeal, whereas handicraft development centers, secondary school laboratories, bookkeeping courses, and village health stations have often seemed unexciting. Even technical assistance projects designed to stimulate collateral improvements in techniques and public policies[15] are seldom sufficient without supporting insti-

the objectionable economic pressures was obvious. *Future of Asian Democracy: Report of a Symposium on 'Problems and Prospects of Democracy in Asian Countries'* (New Delhi: Indian Bureau of Parliamentary Studies, 1959), pp. 4, 5.

[15] See "The Decision to Introduce Mechanical Accounting to the National Budget," in John D. Montgomery and the NIA Case Development Seminar, *Cases*

tutions sometimes requiring far-reaching changes in governmental administration and organization. Sometimes, proceeding in advance of such developments in the "social infrastructure," the pacing of foreign aid has become too fast for absorption, vehicles and equipment being brought in before operators and especially maintenance technicians have been trained, and schools and hospitals being built faster than teachers and doctors and nurses become available. Both Americans and Asians have been accused of moving too fast on occasion, or persuaded to accept unwelcome preliminary projects to achieve a desired agreement. This form of reciprocity is something less than mutuality, but it sometimes serves to minimize internal political criticism.

In addition to political controversies incidental to the aid programs, there are also conscious and basic collisions of purpose encountered overseas. Each party engaged in setting up the aid programs is subject to complex internal tensions and pressures in formulating its policies regardless of the position of the other. The American position is often rigid as a result of U. S. legislation or other domestic factors having little to do with the situation in the receiving countries. Because the resolution of certain of these tensions has been impossible, the public exposure of binational differences has also become unavoidable. Among these, the sharpest conflicts have arisen from the paradoxical desire of U. S. private enterprise to see that the governmental agencies dispensing aid use it to foster private capital entrepreneurship abroad. Similar preoccupations on the part of the farm bloc, U. S. shipping interests, and small business have also greatly complicated aid administration. Pressures against offering technical assistance to rice growers abroad have arisen out of concurrent policies designed to protect American farm surpluses from competition from other parts of the world. Laws protecting U. S. shippers against more favorable prices for delivering aid goods have forced costs up, sometimes to an uneconomic point. Finally, regulations protecting American small business in bidding against more efficient procurement arrangements offered by large industrial concerns have so complicated the purchasing of aid goods and services

in Vietnamese Administration (East Lansing, MSU Viet Nam Project, 1959), pp. 20-30.

that the programs themselves have suffered from excessive costs, slow deliveries, and a resultant waning of enthusiasm.

U. S. aid has even supported programs where clearly antagonistic purposes were in the background. In extreme cases these have been resolved only by the application of sanctions or implied threats, such as the removal of a program or the withholding of funds on the U. S. side and a refusal on the part of the host government to participate in or permit doubtful projects. The laws passed on behalf of American shipping require that U. S. commercial import aid be withheld if less than half of the imports are carried in American vessels, unless none are available. In other cases American funds have been withheld or withdrawn from projects that were corruptly administered. At the same time, certain projects that seemed desirable from the American point of view have been vetoed in underdeveloped countries because they were considered contrary to the national policy of the host government. Community development projects, for example, have been rejected in order to keep American technicians out of rural areas.

Not all of the unresolved issues of public policy arise from conflicts of interest. Differing social theories have also contributed to tensions in the development of mutually acceptable programs in both the United States and the host countries. They include the concept of public versus private enterprise; technical versus political considerations; the values of "undemocratic stability" versus "democratic disorder"; "large" versus "small" U. S. aid programs, both in resources and personnel; and the problems of "interference" versus "noninterference" in requiring basic reforms in civil service administration and fiscal management in order to maximize the benefits of aid.

Most programs are neither completely mutual nor wholly antagonistic, but are subject to negotiation. Improvements in public administration, for example, may be desired in varying degrees by both parties, at least in theory; but political considerations may impede the adoption of a specific project if it would threaten the cohesion of the civil service or jeopardize the prestige of the regime. Mutuality of purpose is identified in terms of specific projects, times, and places, rather than an assumed coincidence of national objectives.

Identity of national aspirations in the host government and the United States does not guarantee the acceptability of an aid program in their support; nor can the threat of withdrawing foreign aid serve as a lever of American policy to engineer acceptance of our will. This limitation is dramatically demonstrated in the problems of *withdrawal* and *termination* as alternatives to the indefinite continuance of foreign aid. Withdrawal is here considered a tactical maneuver, usually made for political reasons involving the cold war, while termination takes place when a program has fulfilled its economic or technical objectives.

Withdrawal is usually a temporary, localized action. It may be undertaken at the initiative of either party. In Laos the United States used the threat of withdrawal in 1958 as an instrument to force the government to undertake fiscal reforms; in Burma it was the host government that asked the U. S. mission to withdraw in 1953 as a moral protest against American sponsorship of Kuomintang activities within its borders. Total or partial withdrawal might theoretically take place at any time cold-war or other conditions alter sufficiently to permit it, although the United States has seldom actually indulged in a unilateral withdrawal. If disarmament permitted major reductions in certain types of aid, therefore, it is probable that for political reasons other forms might be increased. Lesser shifts in international alignments or military strategy may also bring about partial, local, or temporary withdrawals and changes of emphasis.

Termination of aid implies a planned scaling down as program objectives are achieved. Because of the difficulty in measuring economic "recovery" or "development," a decision to terminate because of the achievement of such goals might be made politically rather than on technical grounds, but the rational and orderly manner of terminating a program would be distinguished readily from the politics of withdrawal.

The possibility of withdrawal is weakened by the political and administrative forces favoring continuity in the aid program. Any decision against the forces of inertia requires extraordinary justification. Foreign aid, like any governmental activity in motion, automatically produces self-perpetuating factors creating a presumption in favor of its continuation. Large-scale, world-wide aid operations have necessarily involved something approaching a permanent commitment in technical personnel: thousands of technicians representing scores of specializations have been recruited and given career status in one form or another in ICA. Technicians generate programs and programs require technicians: in order to recruit personnel this circular logic has been applied to the development of a career service, whose ingenuities are then directed to program development requiring more, and also permanent, personnel. After Parkinson it is no novelty to say that government bureaus seldom tend to be self-liquidating unless some political force intervenes.

Certain economic factors also tend to perpetuate the program. The "revolution of rising expectations," both stimulated and appeased through foreign aid, creates the same kinds of insatiable demands that have motivated the continued growth of the American economy.[16] Moreover the gap between "underdeveloped" and "developed" countries is widening rather than narrowing. Nowhere in the underdeveloped world is there a convergence rate that would permit a forecast of economic equality with the industrialized countries. There will be "underdeveloped" economies in a relative sense for an indefinite period of time; there will also be some moral argument for technical economic aid indefinitely. At the same time, political arguments for termination will continue to find expression both in the United States and among the underdeveloped countries. A tension between economic and political demands will be an indefinitely prolonged result.

Economic aid now being given for specific projects does not ordinarily contain terminal provisions for the program as a whole. On the contrary, certain types of aid carry clear economic implications

[16] The "droit au dollar" as a psychological reaction of the receiver of aid needs no demonstration. A. G. Dickson cites a resolution of the Asian Conference of the Socialist International in Tokyo, November 1954: "Assistance is at once a right and a claim created by past and present exploitation of the Asian countries by the developed countries." "Technical Assistance and Idealism: Misgivings and Mistakings," in *The Yearbook of World Affairs* (New York, 1958), p. 207. Large donors of economic aid to have not yet been able to find a means of explaining that their action does not come out of a sense of what George Kennan called a "cosmic guilt." He argues that it is the obligation of the host government to assure the donor that aid will not be interpreted as a "sign of weakness or fear" or a "desire to dominate." "Any form of benevolence, if prolonged for any length of time, comes to be taken for granted as a right and its withdrawal resented as an injury." Quoted, *ibid.*, p. 209 n. Unfortunately, no formula has yet been offered by which "the dignity of the Western position in Asia and Africa" can be restored.

of continuance. Most loans to industrial banks or corporations, for example, are repayable in soft currencies that will presumably be redirected to the same country for further economic or technical assistance. While this does not necessarily require the commitment of further dollar aid, it presumes a continuing program involving the services of a certain number of technicians and administrators, hence of an aid mission.

The psychology of giving, another perpetuating factor in the environment of foreign aid, is probably more strongly at work among embassy and aid mission personnel than in Washington. The conscientious technician tends to regard "his" projects with an avuncular affection, offering them the degree of jealous overprotection afforded by an indulgent uncle. Technical projects are psychologically the mission chief's or ambassador's to give and the technician's to defend. All of these participants are concerned with the integrity of a project, both technically and financially. They may threaten to withhold funds that are in danger of being misspent; or to refuse advice they think will be misused or ignored anyway; or to suggest that money that has been wasted be refunded so that it may be better used. They may also be willing to encourage a good performance by promising further gifts, or to subsidize projects designed to protect an investment made earlier. Sometimes they are tempted to gain acceptance of a mooted point by "offering" aid projects in "exchange." The psychology of giving, like that of receiving, invites an attitude of inertia. The influence of such factors on the views of the country team is, of course, incalculable; but it is noteworthy that a mission rarely recommends a reduction of its own total program for internal reasons short of grounds for "withdrawal."

The reasons for continuing the aid programs thus seem to be stronger than those that impelled it in the first place: the cold war continues, hunger and poverty still create political and economic unrest and deny humanity a decent chance for self-fulfilment, and the need for developing economic interchange between the United States and the underdeveloped third of humanity is as great as ever. All of the assorted motives that led to the establishment of the foreign aid program in the first place, from the most altruistic to the ignoble, are joined today by powerful administrative, economic, and psychological considerations favoring its continuance.

There are, however, limiting and partially self-liquidating factors at work in the ambiance of the aid program. Even though they may be overwhelmed by contrary forces most of the time, they are important, especially those adopted as a matter of policy. The yearly funding and programming cycle provides an occasion for review and justification of existing projects, placing a burden of proof, at least in theory, upon the spending agency.[17] The short-term assignment of technicians to the field—two to four years—encourages the design of projects that can either be completed during that period, or carried out in segmented phases coinciding with budgetary cycles and tours of duty. Moreover, new programming procedures require the justification of each project in terms of mission objectives and call for painstaking annual reviews that could provide the machinery for termination, if such became U. S. policy.

Other limiting factors include the absorptive capacity of the host country's economy, an indeterminate sum in total but a practical and continuing consideration in specific areas. Hospitals and schools cannot be built faster than contractors can assemble men and materials, and even after construction, they may lie idle until doctors and teachers can be recruited and trained. As we have seen, these considerations do not always impede requests from the host government, or suggestions by ICA technicians, but they inhibit their acceptance in Washington. Sometimes pure economics also limits the rate of dollar input in a country, especially when inflationary results become unavoidable or the aid budget is cut.

Politically there are also braking forces at work on the program which may conceivably tend to force it in the direction of a planned scaling down or a termination. The high degree of ICA vulnerability to public and Congressional criticisms of white-elephant projects renders the agency sensitive to the possible dangers of excessive or prolonged activity. Moreover, there is a strong desire on the part of the host government's agencies for constantly greater managerial and technical independence from supervision and post-audit responsi-

[17] Many administrators believe that the principal effect of the Congressional budgetary hearings has been to terrorize the aid agencies and inhibit long-range planning, including that leading to termination. This is a psychological rather than a logical effect, however; the history of aid appropriations does not justify the conclusion that aid as such is actually in jeopardy every year. Long-term planning remains possible in spite of the inconveniences of the annual program review.

bilities. Both of these political factors tend to move successive segments of the program from American to native sponsorship, even though U. S. aid funds may still be required.

The possibility of terminating American aid programs depends not so much upon the manner and degree of planning as upon overriding political considerations. Defining goals in measurable terms can make termination feasible technically, and can help produce a sense of accomplishment as each objective is reached. But in programs that are mutually agreeable, as well as those reflecting politically antagonistic purposes, conflicts in execution may be expected to arise. Many of these reflect administrative procedures as well as basic political objectives.

III. ADMINISTRATIVE RELATIONSHIPS AND THE POLITICS OF FOREIGN AID

The theoretical separation of "policy" from "execution" in American foreign relations is difficult to maintain in the administration of foreign aid. Most aid programs in Southeast Asia are actually carried out by the host government or its designated agencies, with American technicians performing advisory and supervisory functions. This relationship carries at least three implications of political importance: first, that administrative decisions and operations will both reflect and influence other relationships between Americans and Asians; second, that the processes of administering aid will probably have a centralizing effect upon the governmental structures in the host country; and finally, that the presence of large numbers of American technicians and their families will influence public opinion toward the United States, the West, the capitalistic system, and democracy.

The administrative relationships between the host government and the ICA mission fall into three general patterns: joint relationships, the counterpart system, and the liaison approach. To some extent, all of these relationships may exist in a given situation, but for purposes of generalization it would not be too misleading to characterize the relationships in Taiwan as joint, those in Viet Nam and Thailand as counterpart, and those in Burma as liaison.

Joint planning and administration is the closest of these relationships. Jointness arises out of mutuality and confidence, and both of these qualities are reinforced by the processes of joint decision-making. The Joint Commission on Rural Reconstruction on Taiwan is the classic example of this approach. Since its organization in 1948, its membership has consisted of three Chinese (including the chairman) and one or two Americans, each with one vote on the disposition of funds and the design of programs for rural development. It is part of both the Chinese government (under the Executive Yuan) and the U. S. government (the American commissioner being appointed by the President and responsible to the "administrator" of ICA). The entire technical staff is merged, no distinction in rank or function being made between Chinese and Americans. There have been some minor difficulties on the Chinese side because of national relationships with the provincial agricultural agencies in Taiwan, and on the American side because the international character of the organization placed it outside the normal pattern (where a technical division of agriculture operated within the aid mission). Neither of these, however, has influenced Chinese-American relationships.

The counterpart relationship involves parallel organizations in the aid mission and the host government, each with its own technicians working separately but exchanging information, advice, and criticisms. At higher levels, policy and program decisions are made independently and ratified or amended by the other party. Working relations among technicians are close, but political factors at work in the higher echelons of decision-making are exerted upon only one side, and no jointness in resolving them is possible normally. In the effort to establish a national police force in Viet Nam described above, technicians on both sides were in substantial agreement, but domestic politics forced the Vietnamese government into an open split with the American position, and many months of negotiations were necessary before a compromise could be reached. The administrative apparatus of the counterpart approach strengthens technical relationships but places greater strains on the binational processes of foreign aid.

The liaison approach implies a separation at the technical as well as the policy layers of the agencies involved. In Burma, for example, proposals are worked out by the host government, submitted to the American Embassy, and referred to technicians who are brought in on temporary duty for the purpose. American proposals, if any, would be prepared unilaterally or with unofficial advice from Burmese authorities and submitted to the planning agencies of the host government. Programs are subject to negotiation both technically and politically; no mutual establishment of priorities or national objectives takes place, and the sovereignty of the host government is thus preserved in appearance as well as in fact. This administrative pattern is frustrating to technicians interested in enriching project implementation by a genuine exchange of information and advice, and it prevents the projects themselves from contributing to the development of a national planning apparatus that might emerge out of mutual discussions.

Binational relationships of planning and administration are not simply a matter of alliance, alignment, or mutuality of purpose. They are related as well to domestic politics in the two countries.

The centralizing tendency of foreign aid arises partly out of its nation-to-nation basis and partly out of added functions and resources it may confer upon the host government.

Throughout the underdeveloped world a powerful and seductive myth accepts the new national governments as extensions of village traditions. Beyond the roads and telegraph lines in Guinea, jungle drums are said to transmit tribal and village sentiments to the center. President Sukarno denied that there was an "elite" in the capital city:

The dynamic of this nation is safely imbedded in the villages, in the countryside, in the houses of the workers, amongst those to whom cooperation and the full consideration of man for man are [the] real and unquestioned way and purpose of life. . . . We rediscovered a vast and healthy and infinitely potent democracy of our own in all our villages and districts, a democracy which had withstood the impact of generations of colonialism and years of error by our own Republic. . . . It is a system of great democracy which involves everyone in the process of making decisions and of implementing those decisions.[18]

[18] *Address by . . . President Sukarno . . . to the Colombo Plan Conference.* . . . *Loc. cit.*, p. 11.

Whatever the merits of this analysis might be when viewed in terms of the realities of political behavior, the increasing centralization of governmental administration in the newly independent world is easily demonstrated.[19]   U. S. aid reinforces this trend.   Aid to education is delivered by way of a national ministry, as is that in fields of health, public works, and even, often enough, community development.   Even if the aid programs themselves are decentralized, as they often are in agriculture and some other technical fields, detailed consultations with national officials is necessary in order to gain permission to operate, and important local relationships tend to be arranged and sometimes controlled by the national government.   New functions to be performed by the central government, including police, fiscal administration, business regulation, social services, and others, are often made possible or strongly influenced by foreign aid.

The very existence of an American technical and economic mission of any size introduces a third set of administrative and political changes.   The most important accident of aid administration may well be the presence of scores or even hundreds of American administrators and their families in the capital city and the countryside.[20]   In Viet Nam, 2,405 officials, contract personnel, and dependents were in Saigon and other centers representing or carrying out American policy in the summer of 1959.   Issues ranging from the effects of this "American presence" on housing costs[21] to resentments against their living standards[22] arose and were interpreted as evidence that Americans are "unpopular."[23]   This in turn becomes the basis of an argument against foreign aid as a tutor of anti-Americanism, and possibly of authoritarianism or socialism.   In large missions overseas, an effort is made to minimize "la présence améri-

[19] The Guy Pauker thesis that this process is taking place under military leadership was recently stated in the Conlon Report to the U. S. Senate Committee on Foreign Relations (Study No. 5, Nov. 1, 1959), pp. 55-62. See also his "Southeast Asia as a Problem Area in the Next Decade," *World Politics*, Vol. XI, No. 2 (1959), 325-345.

[20] *Situation in Vietnam*, Hearings before a subcommittee of the U. S. Senate Foreign Relations Committee, July 30, 1959, p. 48.

[21] *Ibid.*, pp. 50-52.

[22] *Ibid.*, pp. 57-64.

[23] The political significance of such "unpopularity" is easily exaggerated, just as that of individual heroism is. "Anti-Americanism" has not become a political theory or program in Southeast Asia, perhaps largely because it is associated with personalities rather than national aspirations.

caine," and the authorized strength of aid missions and embassy staffs is planned with these considerations in mind.

The administrative requirements of aid sometimes induce changes in governmental operation as a condition of grants of funds or even the rendering of technical assistance. Not many newly established governments possess an apparatus of administration and planning adequate to performing even the functions of colonial administration once borne by the mother country on its behalf, to say nothing of assuming the added functions imposed by independence and by the necessity of introducing economic change. Since the speed of the latter may be directly influenced by foreign aid, the burden may become all the greater as the amount and scope of the aid is increased. Institutional and technological innovations presumably occur faster where there is economic and technical assistance, but this in turn requires planning agencies in or out of the government, as well as statistical and data-gathering bureaus, proper methods for retaining control over public and aid funds, and other administrative supports. No government wants to turn the planning function over to an outsider, however benevolent. Projects designed to develop data-gathering and planning institutions and personnel in the host government have seldom received strong domestic support; on the contrary, they are often resented as an interference with the very essence of government.

The legislative requirements of the aid program require its administrators to exact promises from the host government affecting its own internal operations. These relate to procedures involved in accounting and auditing aid funds and in purchasing aid commodities. Resistance to administrative change is a classical characteristic of bureaucracy,[24] and this tendency is enhanced when traditional privileges (including informal accounting systems and unmentionable perquisites of ministerial purchasing agents) are endangered.

Still more sensitive nerves are exposed if questions of basic public finance are touched by foreign aid. The threat of withdrawal of aid was used in Laos to induce the government to abandon a wasteful and corrupt exchange rate that was enriching an influential

---

[24] Max Weber's statement of this characteristic is, at any rate, a classic. "Essentials of Bureaucratic Organization: An Ideal-Type Construction," in R. Merton, *Reader in Bureaucracy* (Glencoe, 1951), pp. 18-27.

segment of the population. Less direct efforts were used (with less success) to suggest the same change (though under much less desperate circumstances) in Viet Nam. After much negotiation, a similar lever in Taiwan raised power and railroad rates to an economic level in spite of the resistance of certain public enterprises that suffered slightly from the price rise. Important social policies have been involved when American tax experts have begun inquiries to determine how much the local economy can be expected to contribute to its own governmental costs. In Viet Nam, for example, more than half of the governmental revenues are directly contributed by American aid, and most of the rest comes from taxes levied on the U. S.-supported commercial import program. Yet of the 12,300,000 population, only 15,000 paid income taxes (the government preferring to depend instead on excise revenues), and of these 12,500 were military and civil servants upon whom the burden was nominal. The mere process of discovering such facts, even if nothing was to be done about them, has been an uncomfortable process for both parties.

Traditional administrative patterns are also disturbed by accidental contracts between Americans and Asians. Personnel, accounting, auditing, and organizational arrangements of the aid mission often differ markedly from the concepts of administration in the host governments. Even though no direct changes in the public administration may be introduced as a requirement of foreign aid, the observation of American practices, together with extensive participation by Asians, constitutes an indirect pressure for change (regardless of whether the American techniques are admired *per se* or not).

The very presence of the foreign technicians and administrators is a potential irritant in the domestic politics of aid. However withdrawn from politics they may be personally, their presence cannot be politically neutral. The model of the humble, obscure technician working in the field beside the peasants of the underdeveloped world collapses out of a series of necessities which the authors of *The Ugly American* ignored.[25] As missionaries through the ages have found, the host government tends to resent having foreign technicians work with its citizens outside its surveillance, especially when they are

---

[25] Many of these are discussed in Joseph Buttinger, "Fact and Fiction on Foreign Aid, A critique of *The Ugly American*," *Dissent*, Vol. VI, No. 3 (1959), pp. 317-367.

protected by special privileges. Some Southeast Asian governments closely control the movements of American technicians, requiring special permission for field visits and prohibiting direct approaches to local officials. In Viet Nam the field offices of the United States Operations Mission were actually closed in 1958 at the request of the government, after several years of close cooperation with provincial staff members. Domestic political considerations, together with suspicions stimulated by broadcasts from the Communist north, made it too uncomfortable for the Vietnamese government to accept the indefinite presence of permanent local branch offices of USOM staffed by American technicians and observers.

On the whole, the administrative relationships arising out of foreign aid tend to reinforce existing trends. The administrative changes that occur in the host government as a result of foreign aid represent an important reform potential, however. Both example and precept may under favorable conditions serve as a means of introducing technical and ideological improvements in the administrative machinery of a government undergoing modernization with American help.

IV. AMERICAN POLITICS IN THE FOREIGN AID PROGRAM

The foreign aid program has engendered domestic hostilities and support of a nature rarely encountered in the conduct of peacetime foreign relations in the United States. A mixture of isolationist indifference to developments overseas and concern over the state of the national budget has contributed strongly to one view, and the strong sense of a purposeful American leadership and a concern for the strategic implications of the Communist power, to the other. The mixture of an altruistic fervor with pragmatic doubts has obscured the character of the basic American objectives and heightened the sensitiveness of the aid program to public opinion and political pressures.

These contrary views are faithfully reflected in fluctuating Congressional attitudes toward foreign aid generally and toward specific overseas programs especially. The executive branch has likewise hesitated to formulate objectives and programs consistently and firmly. This apparent uncertainty is revealed in the annual character of the Mutual Security Act appropriations, which are not only subject to a one-year budgetary life, but also require legislative renewal for the program itself, as well, at twelve-month intervals.[26]   The extensive hearings leading to both budgetary decisions and legislative authorizations impose serious burdens upon the ICA representatives. Mr. Paul Hoffman once stated that his Congressional obligations required him to spend 70 per cent of his time testifying and preparing testimony.   The ordeal of Congressional hearings in Washington has its parallel in the field in the form of a steady stream of Congressional investigations and visits.   The two-day visit of Congressman Passman's group to Viet Nam in September 1958, for example, required a total of 328 man-days in preparation on the part of the U. S. Operations Mission.   Several mission directors in Asia have estimated informally to the author that half of their time is devoted to preparations for hearings and program presentations.

The American press has freely roamed over the aid program, touching lightly upon sovereign sensitivities and criticizing "waste" as if the achievement of aid objectives could be measured in mathematical terms.   Six articles by a Scripps-Howard reporter forced the recall of the three principal U. S. representatives in Viet Nam to appear before two Congressional hearings, followed by two investigations in Saigon and irreparable damage to the prestige of the United States in Southeast Asia.   Most of the charges presented in the reports were described as factually in error by the Ambassador and the ICA mission chief.   In the hearings, however, it was assumed that this was merely one man's word against another's, and the subsequent treatment of American officials in Saigon proceeded on the same assumption.   The vulnerability of foreign aid was nowhere better illustrated than in this series of episodes, which would have been unpleasant enough on the domestic scene but approached catastrophic proportions as applied to foreign aid.[27]

[26] See H. Field Haviland, Jr., "Foreign Aid and the Policy Process: 1957," *American Political Science Review*, Vol. LII, No. 3 (1958), pp. 689-724.

[27] The articles by Alfred Colegrove appeared in the Scripps-Howard newspapers between July 20 and 25, 1959.   These papers, some seventeen in number, have a total circulation of about two and a half million.   See, for example, the New York *World Telegram and Sun* and the Washington *Daily News* of July 20-25, 1959.   The congressional hearings occurred on July 30 and 31, 1959, before the Senate Foreign Relations Committee and on July 27, August 3, 11, and 14, 1959, before the House Foreign Affairs Committee.   Pertinent committee hearings are as

The politics of foreign aid in America is also influenced by interest groups within and without the government. The Department of Agriculture and the farm blocs; the Office of Small Business and the Small Businessmen's Association; the merchant marine and American shipping interests; church groups; and private companies interested in specific projects or countries: all exert pressures of varying intensity upon Congress and the aid agencies. American aid policies have begun to shift from grants to loans and to a lesser degree from country to region and from governmental aid to assistance in the private sector. Most of these trends are responses to external pressures, and all are beginning to influence the relationships among agencies concerned with the aid program.

American allies and the recipients of aid also exert some political influence on the design and purposes of the aid program. Among the Western allies, the division of responsibility for offering assistance has sometimes proved a sensitive subject, especially where former colonies were involved, or where national prestige might be affected. Thus American funds have sometimes supported technical assistance from French, Dutch, or Spanish military personnel and technicians against the judgment of some American advisors, and funds used for the purchase of commodities for American projects have, until recently, been spent on a competitive, worldwide basis among all the Western powers. The administration's decision to tie such funds to American sales was not made without uncomfortable side glances at the responses of our allies.

At the same time, the governments playing host to aid programs have not ignored the potentiality of public relations as an instrument of their own ambitions in the United States. The American Friends of Viet Nam and the Committee of One Million demonstrate how effective private organizations may be in focusing public attention on important issues of national policy. Commercial public relations

follows: United States Senate, Committee on Foreign Relations, *Hearings before Sub-committee on State Department Organization and Public Affairs, Situation in Vietnam* (Washington, 1959) and House of Representatives, Committee on Foreign Affairs, *Hearings before the Sub-committee on the Far East and the Pacific, Current Situation in the Far East* (Washington, 1959). The investigations in Saigon by the representatives of these two subcommittees took place in November and December 1959. Senators Albert Gore, Gale W. McGee, and Bourke B. Hickenlooper, and Representatives John L. Pilcher and Walter H. Judd represented the respective committees.

firms on contract to mutual security governments and government information services and cultural missions, are also important sources of
information and recommendations for members of Congress and
others interested in country programs. All of these agencies perform
in varying degrees services commonly identified with domestic lob-
bies.

The political context in which the American agencies of foreign
aid have struggled for survival has provided one of the chief limitations upon its long-range effectiveness as a major national instrument.
The defensive posture of American aid agencies, their procedure
rigidities, their concern over immediate objectives, and their uncertainty over their own future, are products of American rather than
overseas politics.

V. Some Policy Conclusions

It is still premature to appraise the political effects of foreign
aid on the underdeveloped countries of Asia. The above analysis,
concentrating on political processes, can nevertheless lead to certain
conclusions that may prove useful both in developing further studies
of foreign aid and in evaluating American foreign aid policies.

The political complexity of foreign aid far surpasses the extent
of direct American interests. Given the interplay of political processes in the United States and the host governments, the regional
relationships, Communist bloc activities, and the administrative effects of foreign aid, American purposes are easily obscured. Only a
strong, clearly formulated sense of American purpose can be expected
to have a major impact in such complex circumstances.

An adequate foreign aid philosophy cannot be constructed out of
a compromise satisfactory to all conflicting interests. The attempt to
conciliate inconsistent approaches has led to a gradual seepage of
American purpose and prestige in every political dimension in spite
of continued and even increased technical and economic efforts. A
dynamic, vigorous reassertion of leadership might reverse the losses
suffered through political inadvertence and administrative deteriora-
tion. Because Congress must reflect such a wide variety of domestic
interests, and for practical reasons of statecraft, it is clear that this

direction could come only from the executive branch. Sabotage of
the program, on the other hand, is easily accomplished, whether at
the hands of the press, Congressional committees, or domestic interest groups. Minimizing attacks from these sources would require
strong, even unassailable support of the philosophy and the practices
of foreign aid, deriving from the President himself. Attacks on
foreign aid reflecting ignorance of its intrinsic character and limitation serve no useful purpose. The many attempts to measure it in
accounting terms, or according to standards of engineering efficiency,
or as a lever to be used in forcing other governments to our will,
have yielded results so irrelevant to its purposes and to political
practicality that they actually jeopardize its continued existence.

It is not enough, of course, to call for strong leadership, although without it foreign policy is a helpless political prisoner.
There are specific things to avoid, and others to profess, in any future
direction of American policy. One important requirement, affecting
both policy statements and administrative organization, would be
to adjust American objectives to accommodate the political necessities
of foreign aid overseas. The fact that foreign aid tends to reinforce
existing tendencies rather than initiate them suggests that American
policy should avoid too rigid a commitment to American techniques
that may be unacceptable or irrelevant to local traditions. Only basic
principles must be firmly maintained, and they must first be identified
and stated. Temporary accommodations are easily found but even
more easily ignored once they have served their purpose. Neither
the threat of fund stoppages nor withholding technical advice is
likely to force permanent changes of behavior, unless a mutually acceptable purpose is involved. Wisely applied pressures can achieve
irreversible legislative and organizational changes, provided American policy is firmly committed to them.

Executive leadership can also do much to avert an excessively
rigid application of American standards of efficiency to projects jointly
undertaken with the government of an underdeveloped country.
Public criticisms so couched offend the most sensitive nerves in the
Asian body politic. Investigations of waste or corruption carried out
in ways that insult or discredit Asian technicians tend to aggravate
rather than to correct the objectionable condition, at the same time
developing a future resistance against participating in American-spon-

sored projects. Headlines in the American press gained at the expense of a friendly government are a useless and costly charge against American prestige and standing.

Some critics of the American performance have suggested avoiding the political discomforts to which ICA is subject by assigning full responsibility for foreign aid policy and administration to the UN or other international agencies. And it is undoubtedly true that there are both functional and geographic areas in which the UN can operate more effectively than the United States, where American ideas and techniques are suspect, or where more suitable approaches are available from other national traditions. But the purposes of the United Nations are not in all respects identical to those of the United States. The political requirements of foreign aid, including military and strategic considerations and the need for using combinations of economic and technical assistance to achieve the optimum alternatives to the Communist way of development, suggest that a continued direct American involvement is unavoidable.

Given the likelihood—and the desirability—of a long-term American commitment to foreign aid, the effects of the short-term preoccupations of legislative and executive review can be minimized. The favorite argument that long-term planning is impossible because of the annual appropriations cycle evades the issue. Program designs already include projects of five to ten years' duration and longer. Once under way, these represent the practical commitment of a series of annual programs, relatively secure against the specter of year-to-year termination. What has been lacking to date has been equivalent planning for achieving a maximum political impact capable of outweighing short-term military and strategic requirements.[28] Additional resources devoted to foreign aid can be assigned to give economic successes the greatest and most favorable

[28] The possibility of using foreign aid as a conscious means of encouraging groups favorable to democratic growth has still not been satisfactorily explored. Senator Allen Ellender's misgivings about supporting dictatorships (*Review of U. S. Foreign Policy and Operations*, Senate Document 78, 1957, esp. pp. 85-86, 140-141) can be quieted not by abandoning such countries to communism but by vigorous attention to using American resources to favor contrary developments. J. Amuzegar concludes that an "independent, non-partisan agency responsible to Congress" would enable foreign aid to escape the consequences of tactical preoccupation ("Point Four: Performance and Prospect," *Political Science Quarterly*, Vol. XIII, No. 4 [1958], pp. 530-546), but it seems more likely that strong policy direction could come from the executive than from the rather indecisive Congressional apparatus.

political impact once this is considered relevant to American purposes. Massive programs designed for countries whose technological resources and national will are at the turning point in economic development, where industrialization has reached the point of "take-off," might constitute an important measure. The "miracle of the Marshall Plan" could thus be selectively reproduced in Asia, where such a demonstration could be a decisive symbol, if this were given the required weight as an American objective.

A corollary to massive additions to the most likely foreign aid programs is a stronger position on termination and withdrawal from projects not serving such political and economic objectives. The continuation of any project could be made a voluntary action for both parties, undertaken out of considerations of their own national interests. Continuance of a program in itself politically undesirable could be justified as an exchange that would constitute a freely undertaken obligation from which withdrawal would become possible if considerations of national benefit were no longer served. Resentments against commitments of the past could be avoided if unproductive aid activities were subjected to critical review based on known certainties of purpose and direction and a minimum preoccupation with tactical considerations.

Participation by the host government in basic planning and evaluation of projects should be maximized at all levels. Where several countries in a region are working independently in support of similar or parallel projects, regional conferences and critiques may prove a useful device in developing and asserting American policy. It would also help satisfy the desires of host governments to participate formally in constructive criticisms of proposed American aid programs. Public discussion of developmental activities within the host country could also prove a useful means of forestalling errors in judgment on both sides.

Even when foreign aid is not involved, economic and technological development itself is in part a political process.[29] The enrichment of farmers changes their political standing; the rise of new commercial and industrial classes changes the social complexion and

---

[29] The author has explored some of these aspects in " 'Gilded Missiles': Reflections on the Politics of Foreign Aid," *Far Eastern Survey*, XXVII (1959), 81-89.

the political life of a developing nation; improving public health services prolongs life and creates social problems of political significance to a society not previously inclined to accept responsibility for less productive members; creating a national army produces new educated and privileged classes possessed of great material resources and a high degree of internal cohesion. It is difficult to find any area of technical assistance that is completely free of some political implications, from the taking of a census that may be used to determine when—and whether—to hold plebiscites and elections, to the establishment of accounting procedures that will enhance the power and standing of local government officials.

The mechanisms of foreign aid are undergoing changes as radical as the program itself. International "competition" for the privilege of giving has already set in, leading to forms of specialization that offer underdeveloped countries a well-stocked bazaar at which to choose. Possibly the current "Buy American" approach might lead to similar approaches in other Western countries, and still better "packages" of foreign aid might be developed. Enrichment of the program is also occurring by means of international co-operation through the United Nations, regional agencies, and *ad hoc* triangular and other devices. The sum total of these instruments presents a great variety of resources for offering aid in its most attractive form under different political and economic conditions. Such developments may also afford the U. S. government an opportunity to concentrate its efforts where the impact can be economically and politically the greatest. But they will also point to the necessity for co-ordinating the activities of the donor nations.

The very existence of these alternative sources of foreign aid increases the importance of examining the role to be played by the U. S. government in developing its own program and integrating it with those of others. As economic programs (especially those of a revenue-producing character) are financed by the World Bank, the Development Loan Fund, and private sources, political and strategic considerations may well become an increasingly important aspect of U. S. aid. American funds can accomplish massive results of a permanent nature that will give our way of life a more impressive demonstration than has heretofore been possible.

If such tendencies can be discerned in developing American aid policy, they will also be reflected in the field operations of overseas aid missions. Among other things, American technicians can serve increasingly as consultants to the host government in designing and drafting projects calculated to attract loan and grant financing from other sources.

Adequate consideration of the politics of aid can supply the basis for much greater mutuality and confidence than has been possible in the past. International understanding of the processes of development and the optimum role of aid as a political as well as economic factor can lead to something approaching an international consensus, a condition which is achieved not by processes of giving and receiving but by discovering a community of purpose and then developing means of enlarging it.

9

Social Change in French Canada

Mason Wade

The purpose of this essay is to give a pragmatic account of social change in French Canada, from which certain ideological and theoretical conclusions may be drawn which will have a broader bearing. The dangers of the opposite approach, which has frequently been used on this topic, are perhaps best illustrated by Mr. Hugh Trevor-Roper's review in *The New Statesman* of my book, *The French Canadians, 1760-1945*. Flushed with Toynbee's view of colonial peoples and heated by the fires of the Enlightenment, Mr. Trevor-Roper opened his essay with these observations:

In history, as in Zoology, there is a "residuary fauna"—detached peoples isolated from their kind and arrested in an earlier stage of development like the Carthaginian elephant or the Tunisian crocodile. Who can think of the Boers as heirs to the liberal traditions of Erasmus and Grotius, the mercantile genius of Amsterdam? Of course, they are not. They are the heirs of inland Calvinist peasants of the seventeenth century, detached from the Holland we know, severed from its culture, and fossilized in a later English invasion. They have become provincial, fanatical, retarded. Similarly, who can regard the French Canadians as French members of *la nation civilisatrice,* the country of reason and the ideas of 1789? They have become a residuary people, multiplying defensively in their native reserve while the English settlers have expanded around them: a timid, defensive, prickly community, jealously preserving not the liberal French ideas that we know, but provincial and obscurantist ideas of the peasantry and *petite noblesse* of the *Ancien Regime*.[1]

Mr. Trevor-Roper went on to denounce the French Canadians as "Frenchmen without the French Revolution," whose only phi-

[1] *The New Statesman and Nation*, March 26, 1955, pp. 443-444.

losophy seemed to be hatred of that revolution. He found sympathy among them for their mother country only "in the later, clerical days of Napoleon III, when the peasant journalist Louis Veuillot was uttering his detestable obscurantism, and in the reign of Marshal Pétain." Mr. Trevor-Roper gave the British credit for doing everything that had been done in Canada since the Conquest, while the French Canadians sat still.

Not surprisingly, Mr. Trevor-Roper drew the fire of the editor of *Le Devoir*, the leading French-Canadian nationalist newspaper, who, after pointing out an "impressive number of manifest errors and ridiculous prejudices," concluded:

Mr. Trevor-Roper's criticisms fairly represent, I think, the arrogance with which the metropolitan English regard subjugated peoples. He is of a superior race; he is the conqueror. The conquered, white, yellow, or black, European, American, or Asiatic, are all, more or less, residuary fauna, including, I suppose, the Indians with their four thousand year old culture.

It is not easy for a people used to dominate to put themselves in the place of the conquered, as it is not easy for the conquered to put themselves in the shoes of the conqueror. Between the two there exists a fundamental incomprehension. The dialogue cannot be resumed without the emancipation of the slave and the rehabilitation of his dignity as a man.

We would be wrong to be indignant about the remarks of Mr. Trevor-Roper, but we should draw a lesson from them. This lesson is that conquered people should not count on the sympathy of their masters to ensure their emancipation. Liberation must come from their own guts.[2]

But Mr. Trevor-Roper must have been surprised to find the Montreal *Star*, a leading English-Canadian newspaper, reprinting *Le Devoir's* editorial and commenting on it in a leader which commended *Le Devoir's* attack on "Mr. Trevor-Roper's stupid aspersions on the culture of Quebec." The *Star* went on to say:

If he dismisses French Canadians in this fashion, he dismisses English Canadians similarly, for English Canadians themselves are the product of a dual culture. The French Canadian reacts upon the English Canadian, just as the latter reacts upon the French. We are—all of us, no matter what our origin or our speech—joint products of a common

[2] *Le Devoir* (Montreal), May 11, 1955, p. 4.

country.   Our politics, our economics, our civilization are all profoundly affected by the fact of our bi-racial, bi-cultural foundations.[3]

Mr. Trevor-Roper found himself under this editorial crossfire because he was unable to rid himself of the preconceived ideas he had about French Canada.   Since a French-Canadian myth is widespread in the English-speaking world, it might be well to compare the stereotype with the reality.   Those who do not know French Canada at first hand are apt to think of a quaint, picturesque, predominantly rural region which is an island of seventeenth-century France in twentieth-century North America.   The French Canadians are thought of as amiable, but backward and priest-ridden folk, concerned with nothing beyond the sound of their church bells, "a people with no history and no literature," deprived of "the enjoyment and civilizing influence of the arts," in Lord Durham's facile phrases.   The noble lord could hardly conceive of "a nationality more destitute of all that can invigorate and elevate a people, than that which is exhibited by the descendants of the French in Lower Canada, owing to their retaining their peculiar language and manners."   It was to relieve them of this "hopeless inferiority" that he proposed in 1839 to anglicize them, to give to Lower Canada the national character "of the British Empire; that of the majority of the population of British America; that of the great race which must, in the lapse of no great period of time, be predominant over the whole North American Continent."[4]   The unanticipated effect of Durham's well-intentioned recommendation of national extinction was to crystallize the French-Canadian sense of nationality and to provide the impulse for a great intellectual awakening which is still continuing, long after the French Canadians successfully used Durham's other recommendation of responsible government to insure their political survival.

So much for the myth.   What is the reality?   It is important to remember that French Canada is really a variant of the North American pattern, not something completely different.   New France was never a feudal society, any more than New England was a manorial one.   The old social institutions of France developed along new lines in the colony where the environment was so different,

[3] Montreal *Star*, May 12, 1955, p. 12.
[4] *The Report of the Earl of Durham* (London, 1905), pp. 212-218.

just as those of England did in the American colonies. The *seigneurs* of New France were by no means all nobles; by the beginning of the eighteenth century *habitants* held a third of the *seigneuries*, and many others belonged to ecclesiastical bodies, officials, and merchants. In fact the ecclesiastical corporations were the most successful *seigneurs*, for they carried on the work of settlement without interruption by expeditions against the Indians or English, and they had the collective financial and intellectual resources to meet the problems of pioneering. No *seigneur* could live on his rents; most of them earned their living by military service or fur trading, while some tilled the soil beside their tenants. The French-Canadian *habitant* was as different from the French peasant as the New England farmer from the English serf; Lahontan noted that "None must say *habitant*, for the title of peasant is no better received here than in Spain, whether because they pay neither *sel ni taille* and have the liberty to hunt and fish, or because their easy life puts them on a level with the nobles."[5] The *habitant* was not tied to the soil, and he was constantly running off to the *pays d'en haut* or to the towns, to the distress of the officials of the colonies. By 1754 no less than 4,000 men out of a total population of 55,000 were engaged in the main industry of New France, the fur trade; and a quarter of the French Canadians lived in Quebec, Trois-Rivières, and Montreal. The administrators of New France sought to limit the number of fur traders in the interior; the only result was to cause more *coureurs de bois* to desert to the English. By ordinance after ordinance the officials strove to stem the movement of the population from the country to the towns, without success. The society of New France was an open, not a fixed one; the individual had great mobility, and the way was open up the social ladder to those who had the will and the energy to climb it, like the humble Gascon, Antoine Laumet, who came to call himself Antoine de Lamothe, Sieur de Cadillac, or Iberville, the son of the Montreal armorer, who became the greatest military leader on land and sea that New France produced. The extent of the difference which had developed between Frenchman and Canadian is revealed in Bougainville's comment in the 1750's: "It seems we are of a different nation, even an enemy one."[6]

[5] R. G. Thwaites, ed., *New Voyages to North America by the Baron de Lahontan,* (Chicago, 1905), I, 34-35.

[6] Cited by L. Groulx, *La Naissance d'une race* (Montréal, 1919), pp. 239-240.

New France was much more like New England than Old France. The *curé* was no more or no less important than the Puritan minister, who when asked if he served in a certain town, replied: "I am, sir, the person who rules here."[7] What Frontenac wrote to Colbert in 1677, "Nearly all the disorders existing in New France have their origin in the ambition of the ecclesiastics, who wish to add to their spiritual authority an absolute power over temporal matters,"[8] might have been written by a royal governor of Massachusetts. The militia captain of New France had his exact counterpart in New England. The Quebec parish, like the New England town, was an administrative, educational, political, and ecclesiastical unit. New France became an urban and commercial society, just as New England did. But the American sociologists who have studied Quebec in recent years postulate the tradition of a folk society, isolated and without a money economy, which has undergone no change since the seventeenth century. They would hardly say the same of New England, though in both colonies "It was a commercial frontier that was being pushed forward, and an urban culture that was being spread."[9] By the time of the British Conquest the French Canadian had become as distinct from the Frenchman of France as the New Englander had from the Englishman. Both had become North Americans, with much in common despite their differences of faith, language, and culture.

So much for the myth and the reality of New France. What is French Canada today? Quebec, the heart of French Canada and the home of three and a half million of the four and a half million French Canadians, is a highly industrialized and urbanized region closely connected with the increasingly integrated Canadian and American economies. The Montreal metropolitan area alone includes nearly half the population of the province, and there are

[7] Agnes Repplier, *Eight Decades* (Boston, 1937), p. 75.
[8] P. Margry, ed., *Découvertes et établissements des Français* (Paris, 1876), I, 302.
[9] See Philip Garigue, "St. Justin: A Case-Study in Rural French-Canadian Social Organization," in *The Canadian Journal of Economics and Political Science*, XXII No. 3 (1956), 301-318, which takes issue with the views of Horace Miner, *St. Denis, a French-Canadian Parish* (Chicago, 1939) and E. C. Hughes, *French Canada in Transition* (Chicago, 1943), as well as with those of Léon Gérin, the founder of French-Canadian sociology, who first formulated in 1898 the hypotheses upon which much later French-Canadian sociological writing has been based. Cf. L. Gérin, *Le Type économique et social des Canadiens* (Montréal, 1937).

fifteen other urban centers whose population swells the total urban population to over three of Quebec's four and a half million people. Three quarters of a million people are now employed in manufacturing in Quebec, three and a half times as many as in 1900; while less than 200,000 are engaged in agriculture, actually a slightly smaller total than at the opening of the century. The face of Quebec has changed radically, as Jean-Charles Falardeau, the Laval University sociologist, pointed out in a fictitious epilogue to *Maria Chapdelaine*, that impassioned if misleading elegy of the rural traditions of French Canada. Falardeau observed:

The daughter of Maria Chapdelaine, who was a munitions worker at Valcartier during the War, now lives with her own family of five children in the Rosemont ward of Montreal. Maria's married brothers are employees of the Aluminum Company at Arvida and Shipshaw, after having been workers at the Jonquière pulp plant.[10]

In short, Jean-Baptiste has gone to town. The industrial worker, not the *habitant*, is the typical *Québecois* today.

While Canada as a whole has also undergone a rapid change since the beginning of the century, in Quebec the change has been particularly rapid and revolutionary, for not only has Quebec's growth since 1939 been ten times as great as during the whole preceding century, but it has also been far higher than that of Canada during the same period. And this rapid change has taken place in what was once the most traditional, conservative, and homogeneous society in North America. French Canada's long preoccupation with cultural survival, and with the recognition of its special rights, has made this process of rapid industrialization a somewhat stormy one. Everett C. Hughes' study of this process, *French Canada in Transition*, was based upon the hypothesis that Quebec was being drawn into a new way of life by the expansion of industry, that the old peasant society of the isolated, well-integrated rural parish was being transformed into a modern, urban, industrial society without a similar basic social organization. Philip Garigue has pointed out that Hughes' study was made during the depression of the 1930's and that much of his analysis relates to a situation of economic crisis, that he was dealing with "not a conflict between

[10] J.-C. Falardeau, ed., *Essays on Contemporary Quebec* (Quebec, 1953), pp. 110-111.

two incompatible cultures, but a conflict between two ethnic groups whose historical relationship had worsened because of the economic crisis."[11]

Since the myth of a predominantly rural French Canada dies hard, it might be well to review some of the conclusions of a group of French-Canadian, English-Canadian, and American scholars who examined the social repercussions of industrialization in Quebec in a symposium held as part of Laval University's centenary in June 1952.[12] One of the novel findings, though once enunciated it seemed evident enough, was that the economic history of Quebec was closely associated with that of the rest of North America, and particularly with that of New England, from the very beginning of the industrial revolution on this continent.

The process began with the British conquest, when the Albany and New England fur traders took over the French fur trade. They founded or expanded existing small industries to supply such staple tradegoods as the *ceinture flèchée* or Assumption sash, iron utensils and tools, and tobacco. They made Quebec, which had rarely been able to supply its own food needs during the French regime, an exporter of wheat. In the early nineteenth century Quebec City, like other North American ports, participated in the foreign trade in grain and timber stimulated by the Napoleonic Wars. Subsequently consumer's goods industries developed in this obvious outlet for inland natural resources. In the new industrial age, with the shift from wood to coal and iron as the primary factors of industrial development, and with the railroads replacing the waterways, there was a general displacement of the center of economic gravity. The old seaboard centers largely lost their dominance to newer inland centers. Quebec first lost ground to Montreal, and then both did to southern Ontario, so strategically located for both water and rail traffic to the new western hinterland, and so close to the Appalachian coal fields and the steel mills of Pittsburgh and Cleveland. Quebec, like New England, adapted itself to the new era by developing shoe, textile, and lumber industries, which took advantage of a plentiful supply of cheap skilled labor and a protective tariff. The shoe industry was launched in Montreal in 1847 and became dom-

[11] Garigue, *op. cit.*, p. 317.
[12] J.-C. Falardeau, ed., *op. cit.*

inant in the province by the early 1880's. The textile industry was launched in the 1870's and early 1880's, and by 1909 employed more than 9,000 workers, replacing the shoe industry in the leading role.

However, at the close of the nineteenth century, Quebec's economy still remained predominantly agricultural, with farming contributing 65 per cent of the total production of $150 millions, forest industries 25 per cent, and manufacturing only 4 per cent. This was not the result, as Mr. Trevor-Roper would have us believe, of a general cultural backwardness on the part of the French Canadians; but rather was the natural result of the fact that Quebec had no coal and little iron—the bog iron deposits near Three Rivers, whose exploitation had been begun by the Intendant Talon in the 1670's, were exhausted; and while the occurrence of iron in Ungava had been noted by A. P. Low in 1885, little attention was paid to it until the 1940's. Quebec was also far from the Cape Breton and Appalachian coal fields. The province's special problem was a surplus of population, which led to ill-advised agricultural expansion beyond the limited amount of good farming land (only 5 per cent of the total area), and to a very large emigration to New England, where Quebec farmers' sons soon proved themselves well equipped for skilled factory labor, as they replaced a native labor force which had moved to the Middle West in search of greater economic opportunity after the Civil War.

Soon after the turn of the century Quebec began to follow a different course of development from that of New England, though one still closely associated with the North American economy. Quebec's economic growth henceforward complemented rather than imitated the American pattern. Already the United States was beginning to suffer from an increasing depletion of its own natural resources, and Quebec timber, pulpwood, copper, and asbestos began to exercise an ever-growing attraction for American industries based upon these raw materials. Quebec's own industrialization really began on a large scale when hydroelectric power became cheaper than coal for industrial purposes. The new staple of the air age, aluminum, which replaced to some extent the steel of the railroad age, found great reserves of waterpower, and hence the unlimited cheap electricity the industry requires, in Quebec; so that industrially "backward" Quebec became the site of the largest aluminum plant in the world, as well as of industries dependent upon aluminum and other non-ferrous metals. The Laurentian Shield, which includes about 80 per cent of Quebec's territory, was discovered to be not a useless wilderness but a treasure house of riches, in the new age of hydroelectric power, non-ferrous metals, and insatiable demands for pulp and paper.

At first the industrial development was slow, and unnoticed by most French Canadians, although as early as 1901 Errol Bouchette was perceptive enough to change Ludger Duvernay's nationalist cry of the 1840's, "Let us secure the land," to "Let us secure industry." Both were prophets crying in the wilderness, and their summonses were not heeded by any significant number of French Canadians until years later, when control of Quebec's economy had been grasped by more perceptive Englishmen, English Canadians, and Americans who had access to the large amounts of capital not available to French Canadians. Popular awakening to what was happening in Quebec only came in the 1920's, when the new raw material and power-oriented industries, in the happy phrase of two Laval economists, Maurice Lamontagne and Albert Faucher, "were married to the polygamous hydroelectric concern."[13] It was then that political agitation against "foreign" exploitation of Quebec's natural resources began. It was to become an integral part of the nationalist litany. Halted by the crash of 1929 and the great depression of the 1930's, the rapid industrialization of Quebec thus launched later saw a tremendous wartime and postwar expansion which has not yet been checked. One major reason why there was no postwar recession in Canada was the fact, noted in the *Paley Report*,[14] that the American economy had virtually exhausted its own natural resources, and was becoming increasingly dependent upon foreign sources for the raw materials vital to many of its industries. The closest, most convenient, and most stable source of such raw materials now in short supply in the United States is Quebec. The result has been the exploitation of the great Ungava iron field and Chibougamou and Gaspé copper deposits by predominantly American interests.

These economic developments could not fail to have political

---

[13] Falardeau, *op. cit.*, p. 32.

[14] The President's Materials Policy Commission, *Resources for Freedom* (Washington, D. C.; United States Government Printing Office, 1952), 5 vols. See especially Vol. I.

repercussions in a province so politically minded as Quebec, particularly when economic power is largely in the hands of those culturally
alien to a great majority of the population. In addition to the usual
drawbacks of absentee ownership and entrepreneurship, Quebec has
special problems arising from cultural differences between management and labor, and indeed between Quebec labor and the international unions operating in Quebec.[15] At the beginning of the industrial revolution in Quebec these problems were largely ignored
and considered to be non-existent. Some of the foreign companies
operating in Quebec proceeded on the principle of as much as possible for master-race management and as little as possible for subject-
people labor. The old English lumber companies regarded the
French Canadians as hewers of wood and drawers of water; none
could rise higher than foreman, and in many cases even such minor
posts of command were reserved for members of the master race.
Their ideas were not very different from those of New France's administrators, who were assured by Colbert, when they dreamed of
building a commercial empire in the New World, that the colony
was good only insofar as it was profitable to the mother country.
When American industry moved into Quebec, it tended to follow the
prevalent management pattern, until political and labor unrest during
the Second World War convinced at least one of the largest "foreign"
industries in the province that it would do well to employ as many
French-Canadian managerial and technical personnel as possible, to
avoid nationalization on a provincial basis. A reservoir of ill will towards American ownership was also created by the arrival of runaway
industries, unable to function in the States under New Deal labor
legislation. To be sure, such industries were frequently attracted to
Quebec by provincial government advertisements in the American
financial press, listing among Quebec's advantages "cheap, docile
labor." But the French-Canadian worker did not see these advertisements; he merely saw their fruit.

   Why did Quebec so long remain an underdeveloped country, and
why was it left for outsiders to launch the development? As Dr.
O. J. Firestone, economic advisor to the Minister of Trade and Com-

---

[15] See S. Jamieson, *Industrial Relations in Canada* (Ithaca, 1957) and Samuel
H. Barnes, "The Evolution of Christian Trade Unionism in Ouebec," *Industrial &
Labor Relations Review*, Vol. XII No. 4 (1959), pp. 568-581.

merce, has suggested, the Intendant Talon's reports of nearly three centuries ago are strikingly contemporary in their recognition of Quebec's resources and the great possibilities open to the enterprising and the imaginative.[16] But the opportunities that Talon saw were long neglected, partly because of mercantilist doctrine, partly because of inadequate local financial resources, and partly because of insufficient local initiative. It has been said that prudence is regarded as the highest virtue of all by the French Canadians, and it is certainly not a virtue unhonored by English Canadians. Despite Quebec's historical tendency to vote Liberal in federal elections, it is fundamentally a very conservative province. Up to very recently there has been a shortage of Canadian risk capital, until the risk was demonstrated to be a sure thing. English or American or European investors have enjoyed the fruits of their daring in Canada, while Canadians have preferred to place their investments in the United States rather than in their own country.

There was also a special cultural factor involved. In 1902 Msgr. L.-A. Paquet, the most popular French-Canadian orator of his day, declared at a St. Jean-Baptiste Day celebration: "Our mission is less to manipulate capital than to change ideas; it consists less in lighting the fires of factories than in maintaining and making shine afar the luminous fire of religion and thought."[17] Here is a clear expression of the old French doctrine of *Gesta Dei per Francos,* of *la nation civilisatrice,* of the Counter-Reformation's religious zeal which played its part in the exploration of this continent by the early French explorers and which still stimulates a world-wide French-Canadian missionary movement. Msgr. Paquet's doctrine prevailed unquestioned among the French-Canadian elite of clerics and professional men until recent years, though more and more it tended to become a somewhat sour rationalization as non-French Canadians harvested the industrial crops which French Canadians had not sown.

Now that the integration of Quebec into the North American economic system has gone beyond the point of return, whether or not Quebec likes it—and on balance the majority of French Canadians do like their gradual attainment of the high standard of living which has long prevailed in English-speaking North America—new

[16] In Falardeau, *op. cit.,* p. 38.
[17] An edition of this sermon was published for use in the classical colleges under the title of *Bréviaire du patriote canadien-français* (Montréal, 1925).

French-Canadian attitudes towards industrialization are developing. There are still thunderings from high places against "Anglo-Saxon" materialism and the evils of industrialism and urbanism, but there is a growing recognition that material progress is not to be despised. It is even being realized that the French of France have always been somewhat material-minded, as well as the torch-bearers of Latin and Catholic civilization, the idealized role traditionally assigned to them in Quebec and claimed as an inheritance by the French Canadians.[18] There is also increasing recognition of the fact that industrialization and urbanization are not part of an "Anglo-Saxon" plot against the French-Canadian way of life, as some nationalists were inclined to think during the 1930's, but rather a part of a worldwide process to which no national flag is attached, though the working language is more apt than not to be English. There is even some realization of the fact that the French Canadians are more North American than French, as was witnessed by the much greater success of Chrysler engineers than Schneider-Creusot ones in running an arms factory employing French-Canadian labor at Sorel during the Second World War.

The attitude of the French-Canadian elite long made it difficult to adapt the educational system of French Canada to the needs of the new industrial age. That system was very different from the one prevailing in English-speaking North America. By American standards, it was undemocratic, since it did not try to educate everyone but rather to educate a few to a very high standard. Primary education was open to all, but not compulsory up to the age of fourteen until 1943. Since many boys left school early to work on their fathers' farms, French-Canadian women were apt to be better educated than the men. Secondary education was long limited to the classical colleges, whose eight-year course was strong on Latin, Greek, rhetoric, and philosophy, but weak in science. Economics, sociology, and political science were not taught. The humanistic classical college curriculum was intended to produce priests, doctors, and lawyers; it was an education better designed, as one French Canadian remarked, for life in the Kingdom of Heaven than life in the Province

[18] The cover of a nationalist work, D. O'Leary, *Séparatisme, doctrine constructive* (Montréal, 1937), shows an arrow passing from Athens by way of Rome and Paris to the St. Lawrence.

of Quebec. It was also expensive and beyond the means of many, since the classical colleges are private institutions, and without completion of the full eight-year course the road to the universities was barred, since French-Canadian universities are graduate institutions. Only about 2 per cent of the eligible students completed the classical course and thus could look forward to professional careers. The result was that French-Canadian society consisted of a small, highly educated elite of great culture, and a large mass who had only the bare rudiments of education.

When it became clear that the French Canadians were being left behind in business and industry, where the prizes went to men trained in economics, engineering, and the physical sciences, the province sent some of its brightest young men to Europe on scholarships, so that they might remain French in culture while acquiring the techniques of the new industrial age. A group of deeply patriotic men sought to modify the traditional educational system to meet the new conditions. Henry Laureys and Edouard Montpetit launched training in economics at the new provincial School of Higher Commercial Studies in 1907, and later in the social sciences at the University of Montreal, which became independent of Laval in 1920. Dr. Augustin Frigon tried to swing the Ecole Polytechnique (established in 1874) from the exclusive training of civil engineers to a broader engineering program, but encountered the resistance of the class-proud elite to any occupation which involved rolling up one's sleeves and getting one's hands dirty. This reluctance was born of the strength of the professional tradition, and was not unrelated to the traditional English-Canadian taunt that the French Canadians were a nation of hewers of wood and drawers of water. Brother Marie-Victorin, the founder of Montreal's Botanical Garden, set about his great work of making French-Canadian youth science-minded. He stressed the importance of observation and experimentation as opposed to the tradition of dogmatic teaching in non-dogmatic fields. All these efforts in the technical and scientific fields encountered grave difficulties from the fact that teaching tools and practices had to be adapted to North American conditions from French models, translated from the English, or created to meet the special needs of the French Canadians.

Faculties of science, modeled in the case of Montreal on that of the Sorbonne and in the case of Laval on those of English-Canadian universities, were established in the early 1920's. Gradually more science was introduced into the classical college curriculum, while primary superior schools, designed for those unable to attend the colleges and equivalent to the English-speaking high schools, were established in Montreal and Quebec, whence they spread to most of the cities in the province. Their graduates could enter the science and engineering faculties, though until recently it was difficult for them to enter the liberal professions. The provincial government fostered the development of a wide range of trade, technical, and commercial schools throughout the province, and supported the agricultural, forestry, and fisheries schools affiliated with Laval and Montreal. The advance of scientific and technical education, aided by federal research funds and scholarships, has continued, while in recent years the classical college curriculum has been liberalized and the whole system has been made more democratic. The first graduates of Laval's Faculty of Social Science have taken a leading role in this educational revolution. French Canada remains true to its humanistic educational tradition, and takes pleasure in the fact that leading American technical institutes, such as M.I.T., are now stressing the importance of the inclusion of such studies in a technical education. But French Canada is now producing scientists, engineers, highly skilled technicians, accountants, and economists whose training fits them to participate in the development of the natural resources of the province. They are much in demand among the more intelligently managed "foreign" companies operating in Quebec who realize that the old order of master-race management and subject-people labor has gone forever.

Quebec labor is no longer the disunited mass of docile, patient workers that it once was. More than a third of the 750,000 industrial workers in the province are members of unions, and the once disunited Quebec labor movement, torn by rivalries between AFL, CIO, and Catholic syndicate members, very largely made common cause against the anti-labor Union nationale government of Premier Maurice Duplessis. The Catholic syndicates, formerly regarded by anti-union employers as a lesser evil than the strongly entrenched in-

ternational unions, made it clear in the Asbestos strike in 1949[19] and
the Murdochville strike of 1957 that they intend to be just as tough
as other unions in their insistence upon higher wages and better
working conditions. All labor unions are united in the demand
that wages in Quebec be raised to the level prevailing in Ontario and
the rest of English-speaking North America. The amalgamation of
the AFL and CIO unions into the Canadian Labor Congress, and the
decision in principle of the Catholic syndicates to join the Congress,
indicate the extent of the new unity of the labor movement. Differences in philosophy remain between the syndicates and the rest of
the labor movement, but these differences are not to stand in the way
of common action against industries which are largely national or
international, and cannot be dealt with effectively on a purely provincial or local basis.

No evolution has been more marked than that of the social
thought of the Catholic bishops of the province. The international
unions had been consistently opposed by clerical leaders in Quebec
since the rise in the 1880's of the Knights of Labor, who were condemned by Cardinal Taschereau of Quebec though finally approved
by the American hierarchy. The Church threw its support behind
French and Catholic syndicates, which were first founded in the Quebec shoe industry in 1901. The Confederation des travailleurs cath-
oliques du Canada was founded in 1921. Favored by the provincial
labor authorities as well as by the Church, by 1949 it had some
80,000 members, representing a third of union membership in the
province. In the 1930's, when the French Canadians turned against
a capitalism which had served them badly, there was much enthusiasm for corporatism on the Portuguese model; but despite the
popularity of corporatist theories with the elite, they never had
much impact on the French-Canadian working class. The international unions continued to gain members at a more rapid rate than
the Catholic syndicates, which were held not to have the workers'
interests at heart, since they were under clerical direction, and were
thought to be in many instances little better than company unions
encouraged by the employers to prevent the internationals from
moving in. In their pastoral letters and in the annual *Semaines
sociales* devoted to Quebec's social problems, clerical leaders con-

[19] See P. E. Trudeau, ed., *La Grève de l'amiante* (Montréal, 1956).

tinued to hymn a return to the land as the sovereign cure for social ills. But in 1949, in a sharp break with their past tradition of acting only as mediators in strikes, the bishops approved a collection at the churchdoor for the Asbestos strikers. Commenting on this announcement, Archbishop Charbonneau of Montreal made this public statement:

> We wish social peace, but we do not wish the crushing of the working class. We attach ourselves to man rather than capital. This is why the clergy has decided to intervene. It wishes that justice and charity be respected, and it desires that more attention cease to be paid to financial interests than to the human element.[20]

The strike was finally settled through the efforts of Archbishop Roy of Quebec. Subsequently, early in 1950, the Quebec hierarchy issued a collective pastoral letter on the social doctrine of the Church which faced the fact that Quebec had become an industrial province and laid down the doctrinal principles which applied to both employees and employers. This document was a notable landmark of social thought which attracted worldwide attention.[21]

This important statement by the Quebec bishops is but one bit of the large amount of evidence which makes it clear that French-Canadian nationalism has had since 1945 a new socio-economic orientation which is far more realistic and pragmatic than the old, rather sterile political nationalism of Henri Bourassa before the First World War, the still more sterile provincialist racism of Abbé Lionel Groulx in the 1920's, and the politico-economic separatism of the depressed 1930's. Only a tiny minority of French Canadians are now at all concerned with the old nationalist dream of a separate French-Canadian state, a dream shattered by the facts of geography and economics, which are now far better taught in Quebec institutions of learning than ever before. Separatism has been doomed by the achievement of a better political relationship with the federal government—largely under the prime ministerships of Mr. Mackenzie King and Mr. St. Laurent. In this relationship the traditional federal

[20] *Le Devoir*, May 2, 1949, p. 1.

[21] The bishops' change of attitude is indicated by the statement: "If urban industrial life, as it has developed in the past, proved less healthy and less heedful of human values than rural life, it must not be believed that it is necessarily destructive to souls . . . The industrial environment can be sanctifying." *Le Problème ouvrier en regard de la doctrine sociale de l'Eglise*, (Québec, 1950), p. 32.

provincial wars of Ottawa and Quebec have become minor skirmishes, rather than the devastating conflicts which in the past threatened the very existence of Canada. With the spread of a better understanding of economics, and with Quebec enjoying a lion's share of postwar Canadian prosperity, the life has gone out of the old politico-economic nationalism which painted a picture of endless conflict between English and French in Canada, and postulated that French Canada's inferior economic position was due to racial discrimination and the abuse of economic power by the ruthless English-speaking overlords of what should be a French-Canadian economy. The French Canadians, being Gallic realists at heart and far more realistic than their own elite, have realized that their economic lot is bound up with that of the English Canadians and the Americans. The great problem for intelligent French Canadians today is how to insure the survival of French-Canadian culture when alien influences reach into every corner of the province; how to meet the new order, rather than merely to resist it. This is a very real problem for a cultural minority of some five millions whose once largely isolated world is increasingly being interpenetrated by that of 180 million English-speaking North Americans, who also control a large share of Quebec's economy.

Le Devoir, once the favorite journal of the nationalist professional elite, has now become devoted to the French-Canadian worker's cause. It no longer indulges in exercises in mathematical nationalism, proving that French Canada has at Ottawa two and three-quarters fewer deputy ministers and ten less army officers above the rank of colonel than it should have in proportion to population. It is much more concerned with the basic social problems of Montreal and the province—higher wages, better working conditions, more reasonable housing. The younger generation of the elite is taking a leading role in the labor movement, after studying economics and labor relations abroad. Many of its members are also serving the federal government, not as mere back benchers in a well-disciplined Quebec bloc, but as top-rank civil servants in Ottawa and abroad. As a result of the tremendous growth of English-Canadian nationalism during the Second World War and in the postwar period, French and English nationalism are blending into a common Canadian nationalism. The French Canadians have learned that the first loyalty of most English Canadians is not to Britain but to Canada, while the English Canadians have learned that their compatriots are not Frenchmen but Canadians. A common pride, born of Canada's wartime record and postwar role in international affairs, has tended to make the relations between French and English Canadians better than they ever have been before.

One major factor in this development was the recognition in 1951 of Canadian biculturalism in the *Report of the Royal Commission on National Development in the Arts, Letters, and Sciences*— better known as the *Massey Report*, after its chairman, Vincent Massey, later the first Canadian Governor General. The sympathetic respect shown by the Commission for French-Canadian culture and the emphasis placed on developing a dual Canadian culture caused the *Report* to be well received in Quebec, despite the political fireworks set off by its recommendations of federal aid for education, a field constitutionally reserved to the provinces and one zealously guarded by Quebec to insure cultural survival. Since the Second World War more and more English Canadians have realized that culturally Canada must be both French and English if it is not to become American, and there have been an increasing number of points of contact between the two cultures which for so long have been separate. In 1876 Pierre Chauveau, former superintendent of public instruction and first premier of Quebec after Confederation, likened Canada to the famous double staircase of the Chateau de Chambord, so constructed that two persons could ascend it without meeting and without even seeing each other except at intervals: "English and French, we climb by a double flight of stairs toward the destinies reserved for us on this continent, without knowing each other, without meeting each other, and without even seeing each other, except on the landing of politics. In social and literary terms we are far more foreign to each other than the English and French of Europe."[22] The situation today is very different. As the *Fowler Report*, noting requests from Ontario and Winnipeg for the extension of French network programs to largely English-speaking areas, observed: "Canada has travelled a long way over the course of one generation—and at a particularly rapid pace since the Second World

[22] P.-J.-O. Chauveau, *L'Instruction publique au Canada* (Québec, 1876), p. 335.

War—on the road that leads to the complete English-French reciprocal tolerance and mutual understanding in all parts of the country that now characterize the ancient settlements where English and French have been rubbing shoulders for generations."[23]

Through the Canadian Broadcasting Corporation and the National Film Board the federal government has encouraged Canadian cultural dualism, while seeking to bring Canada's two cultures into closer relation, so that Canadians may be more aware of what they have in common than of their differences. The work of these federal organizations was endorsed by the Massey Commission, and its recommendation that they receive further government assistance was implemented. The Canada Council, established in 1957 in accordance with the Massey Commission's recommendations with resources of $100 million, has the same philosophy in its task of encouraging the arts, humanities, and social sciences. Under these favorable conditions French-Canadian cultural achievement, which has long been remarkable in view of the small numbers and minority status of the French Canadians and the comparative poverty of French Canada, should be still more notable in the future.

In the postwar years French Canada has been a society in full and rapid evolution. The old isolationism has disappeared, with French Canadians serving in many parts of the world in the armed forces and the civilian services, and with radio and TV reaching into the most remote parts of the province. The French Canadian now thinks of all Canada as his country, not just the Province of Quebec, though he retains a special fondness for his *pays*. Under the influences of industrialization and urbanization the old social order, which was likened by a premier of Quebec to an iceberg, with nine-tenths of its body underwater, has radically changed. The supremacy of the old elite has been challenged by a broader-based group who are not willing to let a ruling class make their decisions for them. There has been a marked development of Catholic anti-clericalism in opposition to the traditional extension of clerical authority into non-ecclesiastical fields. Laymen, not chaplains, now dominate the syndicates. Even in the educational world, long dominated by the Church, laymen are taking an increasingly prominent role, and have made good their contention that a cleric is not en-

[23] *Report, Royal Commission on Broadcasting* (Ottawa, 1957), p. 241.

titled to teach merely by virtue of his cloth, without further academic qualifications. A wise priest has observed: "Today in the Province of Quebec there are only four classes: the clerical clerics, the anti-clerical clerics, the clerical laymen, and the anti-clerical laymen. The second and fourth classes are becoming dominant, and this is no bad thing." In the political world the industrial workers, under the leadership of academically trained intellectuals, are turning against the traditional dominance of the lawyer-politician who acted as a middleman between the French-Canadian masses and the English-speaking economic overlords. The labor movement is becoming a political force, and one which has little patience with the old two-party system, with its hereditary loyalties which were so strong that the marriage of a Liberal with a Conservative was once regarded as a mixed marriage. Many labor leaders are sympathetic with the CCF, the Fabian socialist party which was denounced by the Church in 1934, only to be recognized ten years later as one for which a Catholic could legitimately vote. With the provincial Liberal Party long disorganized and discredited, and the younger generation virtually united against the failing tyranny of the Union nationale government, an increasingly militant labor movement may form a new party, if it fails to make common cause with the CCF, which promises to be the political vehicle of the Canadian Labor Congress.

Emancipation from old shackles is everywhere evident in French Canada today. The largest French-Canadian paper, *La Presse*, has abandoned its traditional political neutrality to campaign vigorously against the Union nationale under the editorship of Jean-Louis Gagnon, who some years ago was regarded as a radical. The most influential review is the highly independent *Cité Libre*, whose editors regard no cow as too sacred to be anatomized. Thanks to the prevalence of traditional English concepts of free speech on the CBC, French Canadians enjoy a liberty of public speech previously unknown in the province. The two old French universities of Quebec are packed with students and it has been necessary to found a third (the University of Sherbrooke) to make room for those seeking higher education. In 1958 the university students showed more courage than their elders in going on strike against M. Duplessis' refusal to allow the Quebec universities to accept the federal grants now given to all Canadian universities. The sums set aside for the

Quebec universities remain available to them whenever they may decide to accept them, and each year the incentive to reject political control will grow. The French universities exchange students and professors with English-speaking universities, and send more and more of their best graduates to Ottawa for federal service. The old racism is virtually extinct, and French Canadians are content to make common cause with their English compatriots in asserting Canada's growing importance and influence in the world.

The true portrait of French Canada today bears not the slightest resemblance to Mr. Trevor-Roper's caricature.

INDEX

Abbasids, 198, 199, 200, 210
Abd-ur-Rabb Nishtar, Sardar, 237
'Abd-u'r-Rāziq, 'Ali, 228 n.
Abegglen, James G., 93, 94
Aberle, Kathleen G., 83 n., 109 n.
Abū Bakr, 186, 187, 188, 189, 210
"Acceleration principle" in development, 69
Acculturation: diagram of, 154; external ideas and structures in, 156-159; process of transmission in, 159-165; process of transformation in, 165-168; new cultural configurations of, 168-170. *See also* Political science
Administrative Science Quarterly, 177
Afghanistan, 221
AFL. *See* American Federation of Labor
Africa: habitual mealtime in and conflict with factory routine, 89-90; theory of cultural dynamics applied to, 127-136; mentioned, 120 n., 142 n., 163 n., 168, 169, 177, 244
Agriculture, Department of, 269
al-Ahkām-u's-sultāniyah, 200
Aḥmad, Shaikh, 215 n.
Ahmed Khan, Syed, influence of on Indian Muslim thought, 224-225; mentioned, 226
Akbar (poet), 227
'Ali, 189, 195
Aligarh, 225, 226
Allen, Carleton Kemp, 157
Almond, Gabriel A., on theory of political development, 177-180; mentioned, 170
Ameer Ali, Syed, 226
American Federation of Labor (AFL), 289, 290

American Friends of Viet Nam, 269
"Anti-Americanism," 264 n.
Anti-clericalism in French Canada, 294-295
Apartheid, 137
Arabia, 213, 215
Arabs: and Islam, 182, 183, 189, 191, 208, 209; rise of nationalism among, 209-211
Aristotle, 42 n., 45, 151, 152 n., 200
Ashanti, 117
Asia Foundation, 161
Asia, underdeveloped countries of and problem of "content of men's minds," 48-49
Asian Conference of the Socialist International (1954), 258 n.
Attlee, Earl Clement, 230
Australia, 121
Ayers, C. E., 55
Ayub Khan, General Muhammad, 235, 242
Azād, Abu'l-Kalām, 226, 229

Bacon, Francis, 31
Baghdad, 210
Bauer, P. T., quoted, 140 n.
Behavioral sciences, elements of, 119-122
Belgian Congo: solution of conflict of concept of time in, 130; mentioned, 114
Bemba (of Northern Rhodesia), 132 n.
Bendix, Reinhard, 83 n., 173
Bhoodan movement, 105
Black, M., quoted, 20 n.
Bombay, University of, 103
Botanical Gardens (Montreal), 288